Beyond Ujamaa
in Tanzania

Beyond Ujamaa
in Tanzania

UNDERDEVELOPMENT
AND AN UNCAPTURED PEASANTRY

GORAN HYDEN
Social Science Research Adviser
to the Ford Foundation in Nairobi

LONDON
HEINEMANN
IBADAN NAIROBI

Heinemann Educational Books Ltd
22 Bedford Square, London WC1B 3HH
P.M.B. 5205, Ibadan · P.O. Box 45314, Nairobi

EDINBURGH   MELBOURNE   AUCKLAND
HONG KONG   SINGAPORE   KUALA LUMPUR   NEW DELHI
KINGSTON   PORT OF SPAIN

ISBN 0 435 96300 7 (cased)
ISBN 0 435 96301 5 (paper)

© Goran Hyden 1980
First published 1980

British Library Cataloguing in Publication Data

Hyden, Goran
    Beyond ujamaa in Tanzania.
    1. Tanzania – Economic conditions
    2. Africa, Sub-Saharan – Economic conditions –
    Case studies   3. Peasantry – Tanzania
    4. Peasantry – Africa, Sub-Saharan – Case studies
    I. Title
    330.9′678   HC557.T3

    ISBN 0–435–96300–7

Filmset in 'Monophoto' Times 10 on 11 pt by
Northumberland Press Ltd, Gateshead, Tyne and Wear
and printed in Great Britain by
Richard Clay (The Chaucer Press) Ltd, Bungay, Suffolk

Contents

Preface

The production of knowledge about Africa is still very much dominated by a Western perspective, 'bourgeois' or Marxist. While a considerable amount of interesting material has been produced, it is hardly exaggerating to say that topics for research, or examples for debate, have often been chosen to strengthen prevailing paradigms. At any rate there is little evidence that we have been able to envisage the contemporary development situation in Africa in terms other and wider than the context of our own culture. The intellectual menu has been prepared outside Africa. Few attempts have been made to venture into new recipes altogether.

This book has been written so as not to be mistaken for the intellectual equivalent of a McDonald's hamburger-steak. If anything, it is the intellectual equivalent of an African *chapati*. In writing it I have looked for a new recipe; for ingredients other than those most readily available in the academic market. I have placed myself in a position where I have been obliged to prepare something of which I have no previous experience. Thus I am aware that the end-product may suffer in taste and composition. Still it is a sincere effort to show that there is more to the social realities in Africa than our standardized choices make us believe. It is on these grounds that I hope the book will be evaluated. It is a genuine attempt to look at Africa on its own terms, not just through the looking-glass of prevailing, standardized models.

In writing it I prepared myself for twelve years by living and working in Africa, and that way came to discover the *chapati*. I cannot recall all those people in rural Tanzania and Kenya who helped me to write it, but their assistance is evident in subsequent pages. Former colleagues at the University of Dar es Salaam to whom I feel a special gratitude include Justin Maeda, Director of the Institute of Development Studies; Samuel Mushi, Head of the Department of Political Science: and his predecessor, Anthony Rweyemamu, now with the United Nations. Former colleagues at the University of Nairobi to whom I feel an intellectual debt are Colin Leys, now at Queens University, Kingston, Ontario, and John Okumu (also a colleague in Dar es Salaam), now Director of the East African Management Institute,

Arusha. The former also offered valuable advice in the final stages of preparing the manuscript. I also wish to mention Jon Moris, with whom I have never had the occasion to work, but from whose insights I have learned in private conversations.

The book was completed while I enjoyed the privilege of a sabbatical leave at the University of California, Berkeley, where I was primarily associated with the Institute of International Studies. I wish to thank the University of Dar es Salaam for supporting my application for such a leave, and the Ford and Rockefeller Foundations for jointly sponsoring it financially. During my stay at Berkeley I benefited from countless conversations with my long-time friend, David Leonard. Many of his colleagues in the Department of Political Science made themselves available for intellectual exchanges from which I learned a lot. I especially wish to mention Carl Rosberg, Robert Price and Ken Jowitt. While at Berkeley I also benefited from the penetrating comments of Leonard Joy and Michael Halderman. Others who at one time or another offered valuable comments on the manuscript include Bruce Johnston of the Food Research Institute, Stanford University, Michael Lofchie, Director of the African Studies Center, University of California, Los Angeles, Cranford Pratt, University of Toronto, Joel Barkan, University of Iowa and my brother, Håkan Hyden, University of Lund.

The final touches of my *chapati* would have been impossible without the efficient secretarial services of the staff at Institute of International Studies. I owe a deep gratitude to Ann Mine, Hinda Kahane, Bojana Ristich, Nadine Zelinski and Bodine Webster, who all were involved in the typing.

This acknowledgement would be incomplete without a special thanks to my wife, Melania, who more than anybody else has made me realize that as academics we do not have to be confined to the hamburger-steak, rare or well-done. While she, like the others mentioned above, bears no responsibility for the end result, she has helped me to internalize the issues which are further explored here.

Goran Hyden
Berkeley, June 1978

Introduction

It is the privilege of Western society to have been the birthplace of both schools of thought that dominate official debates about development and underdevelopment. Marxism, as much as liberalism, is Western in its origin. The socialist mode of production is conceived as the inevitable outgrowth of capitalism. In other words, both accept premises that are associated with modern society, as it has evolved in the last hundred years in the northern hemisphere, and particularly in Europe and North America.

In creating modern, industrial society, we have also set in motion the development of a cultural superstructure, in which the rules of science and technology prevail. Consequently, modern society is a world in which experiment and continuous abstraction seem to dominate. Modern man has substituted inorganic for organic material, and inorganic energy for organic power. As Zijderveld notes, modernization or development is essentially the spread out over the world of a *nature artificielle*.[1]

In this inorganic environment, the problems of life are accessible and can be manipulated. It gives man satisfaction as master of his own environment, but at the same time it makes him preoccupied with means rather than ends. He lives in a world marked by machines, instruments, experiments, measurability and functionality. His freedom, power and rationality are determined by the 'system' – our usual way of describing this inorganic environment. In modern society even the manipulators are manipulated.

This predicament does not only affect the scientist who accepts the premises of bourgeois society. It impinges also on the socialist revolutionary. The revolutionary act is a temporary liberation from the immediate demands of modern society, but no socialist society has yet been built without yielding to the same principles that have brought about modernization of bourgeois societies. Once the music of the Revolution has died out, everybody has to go back to work in the treadmills of modern society. There seems to be no escape from this predicament. We have created a historical process in which we are irreversibly caught and over which we have much less influence than we believe. As individuals we control a very limited segment of life in modern societies. In collective efforts with others we may extend our influence further but never as far as to challenge the premises of modern society. We have created a set of structures for ourselves which are so complex that we often feel lost when forced to operate within them. Our greater intellectual capacity, as Kenneth Burke noted long ago, has increased not only the range of solutions but also our problems.[2] The system feels no restraint in its demands on us. We get absorbed by its own requirements to such an extent that we cease to experience ourselves as constituents of a surrounding world. We no longer 'live society'; we face it as a challenge.

Being carriers of modern consciousness, we are good at thinking and speaking in terms of highly abstract models and formalistic categories, to experiment and to emphasize calculable effects. At the same time, however, there are many aspects of living that we are unable to experience. Yet, in other societies which have not yet succumbed to modernization, these constitute the essence of life. In comparison with these societies, we have lost the sense of the ultimate meaning of life. We have ceased to appreciate a life in which we are able to participate as total individuals in face-to-face relationships. In the eyes of people of pre-modern societies we are socially handicapped. We are not sensitive and responsive to the same full range of human values as they are.

There grow among us movements to restore lost values, but they remain as artificial and inorganic as modern society itself. Such movements that usually develop on the extreme right or extreme left of the ideological spectrum genuinely seek compensation for the loss of totality in everyday life. They reject the social alienation of modern society and search for a pseudo-totality that restores a coherent framework of meaning. What advocates of these movements fail to realize and accept is the inevitable fact that their efforts to reconstitute true meaning in life offer only a partial truth-perspective. The inorganic environment of modern society is deceptive. It gives man a false sense of mastery. Global or universal ideologies and theories are nothing but the generalization of a given historical experience. They can only be spread by propaganda, something that forces man to express himself in slogans. Intellectual totalitarianism is the natural product of this situation. Subtle conceptual distinctions and nuances are ruled out. Emotional satisfaction is derived from total involvement in the propagation of a set of abstractions, even if the end result is the suffering of other human beings. Modern man is a captive of his own paradigm. He is prepared to die for it and, if necessary, also battle to defend it. It is in the name of partial truth-perspectives that modern man becomes a hero or a martyr.

Pseudo-solutions, however, are not only extremist. They occur among us all the time. Take the large-scale corporation in which increasingly sophisticated management tools are applied to restore the capacity of the employees to interact more effectively with each other. Modern organizations take their toll in terms of human destruction, and the measures that consultants have developed to cope with this problem may all be aimed at restoring human values, but without really questioning the principles and demands of modern organization. The logic of the system absorbs us all. Its imperatives are reflected in our thoughts and actions.

Nowhere are our illusions better illustrated than in the task of changing modern society. Our 'alternatives' are nothing but variations of a theme. This is true even of such major shifts as the creation of a socialist society. Of all the explanations of change historical materialism is the most intriguing, because in the notion of a historical synthesis is implied both an affirmation of the existing order and a denial of it. Continuity is represented by the growth of our inorganic environment, notably through such measures as industrialization. This expansion inevitably rules out alternatives other than those which protect or promote the philosophical underpinnings of modern society. Neither in capitalist nor in socialist society is there room for alternatives other than those in which man is destined to be primarily a role-player.

What we often forget are the limits of our inorganic environment. We have got used to the idea that science, technology and rationalized economy are able to produce enough for everybody. Successful growth is much more important to industrial societies than it is to pre-industrial ones. Without it, modern society, whether capitalist or socialist, is highly vulnerable. The demands of modern society are difficult to escape. Now that our Faustian illusions of infinity appear to be increasingly challenged, we have a lot to learn from those people who live in pre-modern societies. At the same time, however, we must admit that as captives of the systems we have created for ourselves we are not well placed to appreciate values and rationalities other than those which are modern. Nor should we take for granted that our rationality – the narrow concern with optimal use of means to achieve given ends – gains acceptance as we extend our modernizing instruments to these societies. Rather, as one observer concludes in a study of the impact of capitalism on a South American peasantry, reason continues to be pre-modern, that is, the embodiment of the conditions of human existence.[3]

To view Third World countries as mere extensions or satellites of modern societies is unsatisfactory. Leaders of these countries may be committed to one or other modern ideology. Their development orientation may be capitalist or socialist. Their economies, on the other hand, are still largely pre-modern. They have to operate on a material base which does not easily lend itself to capitalist or socialist policy solutions.

The problems of underdevelopment do not stem from an excessive penetration by world capitalism. Rather they stem from the inability of capitalism to produce the same dynamic transformation of the material base as it once did in Europe and America. Capitalism fails to break down the pre-capitalist barriers that still exist in Third World countries. In fact, in many cases, it prolongs their life. Capitalism has whetted the appetite for development but it has not been able to pave the way for its own expansion. This cannot be blamed on capitalism, rather on the strength of the pre-modern structures of Third World societies. In short, underdevelopment is not just a product of capitalism. The problem of overcoming underdevelopment is far more complex than that.

Development is an ambiguous process, in which the risks of loss are as great as the prospects of gain. This ambiguity may be particularly common among those who have been only marginally affected by the forces of development and who have retained a reasonable degree of social and economic autonomy, for example, the many smallholder peasants in Africa. In their case, development is not only a matter of improvement of material conditions. It is also a question of losses in respect of other values and, above all, it is a matter of trading social autonomy for increased dependence on other social classes. Modern society with its inorganic substance – or development as it has been historically defined – is not necessarily an attraction. Development in that context is not a temptation to people but a sacrifice.

A peasant community may be involved in commodity production – based on the capitalist criteria of exchange value – but this need not be its total culture. Even if it is affected by the wider capitalist world economy, the village community is not just a replica of the larger society and the global economy. Pre-capitalist (or pre-socialist) social formations survive because the economic structures that give them life are still at work. Third World societies, therefore, do not lend themselves to an adequate interpretation by analytical models based on the premise of the predominance of capital or any other modernizing agent. Such analytical attempts reflect what Polanyi calls 'our obsolete market mentality'[4] or constitute, as Taussig points out, misguided exercises in an ingenuous ethnocentrism.[5] This 'centrum perspective' on development tends to reduce to secondary importance all those structures that have their origin in the periphery. That modes of production differ in their articulation in the Third World countries has only recently become a subject of research. How these forms of articulation affect the development potential has not yet been fully explored.

The origin of this book

This ethnocentric bias in the production of knowledge is particulalry apparent in Africa, where Western scholars still dominate what is being written in the academic domain. To overcome this bias is no easy thing. It requires a prolonged exposure to pre-capitalist social formations and a willingness to transcend the boundaries of our metropolitan and professional outlook. Both practical and professional factors operate against this, particularly in the case of the expatriate researcher, usually only an instant visitor to the pre-capitalist world.

My own exposure to that world has stretched over a period of twelve years. It has taken place through both professional work and family life. What I have tried to gain from this experience is not only a better understanding of the values that guide peasant behaviour. Although I have come to appreciate their importance, my research task has gone beyond that point. It has been to search for the structural determinants of peasant behaviour in rural Africa. To become part of their *mazingira*, their social and cultural environment, has not been an end in itself. On the contrary, I have tried to sense the parameters of social action in the rural areas. Instead of describing societal structures as deduced from a given model, my purpose has been to identify actual structural articulations. In that respect, this study is an attempt to study peculiarly African phenomena, not Western phenomena using African data.

My command of Swahili has facilitated the conduct of a large number of meaningful and creative conversations with peasants. The terms of these conversations have not been data collection in the strict sense of the word. They have been carried out more as part of a general social experience. I am prepared to credit much of my thinking as reflected here to this type of experience. It has widened my social horizon in a manner that has also caused a revision of my outlook in the professional field. Above all, I have come to realize how many hidden assumptions dictate the conclusions of our 'scientific' studies.

Maybe I would never have appreciated these experiences so much had it not been for their sharp contrast with the intellectual discussions at the University of Dar es Salaam where I worked on a regular basis. After each field visit, I failed to escape the feeling that there was something unreal about our discussions. To be sure, they were lively and stimulating. Many of them would have been a pride to any academic institution in Europe or North America. But that was part of the problem. The parameters of our discussions were set almost exclusively by expatriates to whom modern capitalism and modern socialism were the only known social systems. We were at best able to open the doors to the social realities of Tanzania, but the discussions never led us closer to them. Instead, these discussions often became ends in themselves. It was a struggle to set the rules for our intellectual exercises. It was a matter of who could convince whom, regardless of any test of validity of that viewpoint in the context of the Tanzanian situation. We saw social structures where none exists. We detected enemies where there were none. There was a danger that our expertise, instead of being used to help Tanzania overcome its problems of underdevelopment, was reduced to that of producing social-science fiction. Like Don Quixote we were engaged in an imaginary struggle that kept us going intellectually but turned us into caricatures in the

eyes of non-academic observers. We were about to lose our credibility
as people concerned with the problem of overcoming underdevelopment. We were indeed part of that problem ourselves.

This book is written to prove that a lot more intellectual search is
needed before the problems of underdevelopment in African countries
can be effectively understood and tackled. It is meant as a contribution
to this search by focusing on the peasant mode of production, a factor
that has been almost totally neglected in the political economy literature
on Africa. Rather than writing the peasantry off a priori as submerged,
which is the conventional view of Western writers on the subject, they
are being treated as a social force in their own right. In this book, the
peasantry are discussed in the context of their own mode of production.
Rather than being just adjuncts to the global economy they are treated
as integral parts of social formations that have their roots in the peasant
mode of production and not in the capitalist mode. This opens up new,
important dimensions of the political economy of Africa and it suggests
that the main structural constraints are not necessarily at the international level but at the local level, right in the heart of the peasant
economy of Africa. In fact, the primary development challenge in
Africa is the small peasant, not the large multinational corporation. As
long as African governments cannot tackle the former, they will have to
depend on the latter.

The argument that small is powerful is possible to pursue if the pre-
capitalist formations in Africa are genuinely examined. They usually are
not because, in spite of our insistence on data to support our conclusions, a lot of what we write are simply unproved assumptions. These
assumptions form part of the cultural or political goods that we often
carry subconsciously within our minds. In the case of Western writers,
they overwhelmingly reflect the premises of life in modern society. How
far that is the case may be revealed by reading this book, in which a
deliberate attempt has been made to replace Western assumptions with
the unwritten rules of pre-capitalist society. The purpose is not to
validate the use of a particular set of research methods. It is to
demonstrate how far our writings are determined by the tacit assumptions we hold as a result of a particular life experience. The purpose is
to show the serious limitations inherent in research exercises where the
investigator fails to become part of the social environment that he
examines. In this study the concept of research is stretched to incorporate the phenomenological viewpoint that no data collection is
complete without full recognition of our relationship to the community
we study. *Involvement* in the community we study may be the precondition for a critical understanding of the structures and processes we try
to elucidate through our research.[6]

While this book is in part an exercise in academic self-criticism, it is
essentially about the peasants in Tanzania and how they interact with
the rest of the world. Many articles and books have already been written

on Tanzania and they are a testimony of the relatively open intellectual climate that has prevailed in that country since independence. In spite of the excellence of many of these publications, there is still a long way to go in reaching a better understanding of the policy problems facing the socialist leadership in Tanzania. This study does not hide the fact that the economic achievements of Tanzania's first ten years of socialism have been far below expectation. It does not see this as a failure, nor is the conclusion drawn that Tanzania is turning away from socialism. Instead, the point made here is that Tanzania, during these ten years, has learned more directly what the construction of socialism on pre-socialist foundations implies. To that extent, it offers lessons for many other African countries which in the future might be forced to follow the same path as a result of capitalism's inability to pave the way for its own expansion on the continent.

The organization of the book

The first chapter is an attempt to explain the structural anomaly of rural Africa that allows small to be powerful. It considers the political implications of this structural articulation. The following five chapters apply the thesis of this book to Tanzania. They trace peasant responses to colonial rule and the ways in which peasants have affected the course of events in Tanzania after independence. The last of these five chapters also shows how the pre-capitalist formations flow over into the modern economy and thereby affect its performance. Chapter 7 is an attempt to show that the notion that small is powerful is valid also in the context of other African countries. It concludes that socialism rather than capitalism will be invited to perform the task of modernization in Africa. Chapter 8 discusses the implications of this for socialism. The argument is that because socialism will be called upon to perform tasks which elsewhere have been completed by capitalism, its role will be very different from what conventional conceptions of socialism assume. The final chapter examines the epistemological reasons for our inability to discover the power of small as well as discussing the implications for future social science research in Africa.

References and notes

1. Anton C. Zijderveld, *The Abstract Society: a Cultural Analysis of Our Time* (Harmondsworth: Penguin Books, 1970), p. 77.
2. Kenneth Burke, *Permanence and Change* (Washington DC: New Republic Inc., 1935, p. 13.
3. Michael Taussig, 'The genesis of capitalism amongst a South American peasantry: devil's labor and the baptism of money', *Comparative Studies in Society and History*, vol. 19, no. 2 (April 1977), p. 154.

4. Karl Polanyi, 'Our obsolete market mentality', *Commentary*, vol. 3 (February 1947), pp. 109–17.
5. Taussig, op. cit., p. 154.
6. This point is stressed in H. P. Dreitzel, *Recent Sociology No. 2* (London and New York: Collier-Macmillan, 1970), which discusses the dualism between ontology and epistemology as derived from classical and later positivist ideas of objective theory.

CHAPTER 1

Small is powerful:
the structural anomaly of rural Africa

Economic history is largely the story of how to capture the peasants. Nowhere in the world have other social classes risen to power without making the many small and independent rural producers subordinate to their demands. The road to modern society has been completed at the expense of the peasantry. The many small have been forced to give in and give way to the few large. In the industrialized world, as Barrington Moore shows,[1] the history of the peasantry is already a closed chapter. Although there are remnants of peasant society, for example, in Poland, as a social class the peasantry is virtually extinct in Europe and North America. In Asia and Latin America peasants still form a sizeable percentage of the total population, but their freedom has been effectively curtailed by other social classes. With anything between one-third and a half of the population in these countries being landless or almost landless, peasants are truly 'marginalized' and 'proletarianized'. They are at the mercy of other social classes. The latter determine the conditions under which the peasants must live and work.

It is the argument of this book that Africa is the only continent where the peasants have not yet been captured by other social classes. By being owners of their own means of production, the many smallholder peasants in Africa have enjoyed a degree of independence from other social classes large enough to make them influence the course of events on the continent. Tanzania is a suitable illustration of this point given the decision by President Nyerere's government in 1967 to base its development strategy primarily on the local peasantry. What are the lessons to be learnt from Tanzania's experience? In order to find a meaningful answer to this question it is necessary to examine more closely the unique position of the African peasantry.

The uniqueness of the African peasantry

In a comparative perspective, African countries south of the Sahara (with obvious exception of South Africa and also Zimbabwe-Rhodesia) are unique in that their economies are dominated by rural smallholder producers. They are numerically superior. Their contribution to the gross domestic product (GDP) is generally large, and in the agricultural sector they are predominant. Their exact importance in the economic development of these countries is hard to measure in quantitative terms as much of what they produce and exchange is not registered for official measurement.

Income disparities in rural Africa are not primarily due to ownership of land being in the hands of a few people. Often it is simply a matter of differential skills in using the land. Regional disparities are generally due to variations in resource endowments, notably quality of soil. This is because African agriculture is still pursued with a rudimentary technology. Farms in Africa are small not because other social classes have occupied vast stretches of land, thereby pre-empting peasant ownership of land. They are small because of the limits imposed by the productive forces. In Tanzania, for example, no more than 2·6 per cent of all farms are larger than five hectares and 83 per cent are less than three hectares.[2] There, as in many other parts of Africa, labour rather than land is the critical development variable. With land being no sales commodity, peasant incorporation into the capitalist economy cannot but be marginal.

African agriculture is essentially rain-fed. It does not require the same kind of co-operation among the producers as in the case of irrigated agriculture. The mutual dependence on a key productive resource, such as an irrigation canal, does not exist in Africa. Such functional interdependencies have been at the root of social inequalities in Asian countries, but more recently also instrumental in bringing about far-reaching transformations of the relations of production in those countries. Compared to his Asian counterpart the African peasant is socially more independent. In spite of the small size of his farm, the African peasant has been able to secure his reproduction without significant dependence on others. Africa is not like Bangladesh where a combination of overpopulation and skewed land distribution leave the majority of the peasants to exist on holdings which are far below what they require to meet their own needs.[3]

African peasants are less integrated in the cash economy than peasants elsewhere. Although Africa has its share of capitalist farmers, the majority of the rural producers still eke out an existence without much dependence on inputs from other sectors. Similarly, although they have to sell some of their crops in order to buy necessities, this is still to a much more limited degree than elsewhere. A Latin American peasant, for instance, requires a much greater involvement in the modern economy in order to meet his basic needs.[4]

The uniqueness of the African peasantry can only be fully understood in a historical perspective. As a social class the peasantry in Africa is the creation by the colonizing powers. It is only in the last hundred years that the rural producers in Africa have become incorporated into a wider social economy to which they are expected to make a regular contribution. Thus, the African peasantry is only beginning to play their historical role at a time when peasantries elsewhere in the world are being pushed off the historical stage.

In fact, the African peasantry is still in the making. It is no coincidence that some years ago there was some hesitation to use the concept of peasantry to describe the rural producers in Africa. Allan, for instance, preferred to refer to them as husbandmen, stressing their strong dependence on soil husbandry.[5] Lloyd Fallers was hesitant before he agreed to talk of them as 'proto-peasants' or 'incipient peasants'.[6] Today the debate has moved beyond this point and analysts generally use the term 'peasant' to describe the rural producer in Africa.

Given that the peasantry is generally portrayed as being at the total mercy of other social classes and as having no alternative recourse but revolt against these classes, the original hesitation towards the concept is understandable. Our conception of the peasantry has been shaped by writings from other parts of the world, in recent years mainly from Asia and Latin America.[7] This image of the peasantry as an overpowered class has in recent analysis of rural Africa been too indiscriminately applied. While it is true that peasants in most parts of the world have been forced to trade their dependence on nature for a dependence on other social classes and that this process is taking place in Africa today, it is wrong to assume, as many analysts do, that it is already complete. In Africa the process is only at its incipient stage.

The conventional definition of peasants contains reference to both their autonomy and their dependence. What makes the peasants different from other social classes is their position as producers with direct access to land, production with the help of family members largely for their own consumption but at the same time integration into a larger social economy to which they are forced to make a contribution in one form or another, notably tax or rent.[8] As Saul and Woods point out, the peasant stands somewhere between the 'primitive agriculturalist' and the 'capitalist farmer'.[9] With the former they share the notion of right to land and the reliance on family labour for ultimate security and subsistence. Capitalist farmers, by contrast, have other livelihoods available. Like the latter, peasants are integrated into a complex and differentiated society, in which demands can be placed upon them. It is the peasant's exposure to regular extraction of a surplus of his production that, as Wolf notes,[10] distinguishes him from the primitive agriculturalist.

Effective surplus extraction from the peasantry is a phenomenon that in every society has taken centuries to occur. The instruments to subordinate the peasantry have taken time to create. During all these years the peasants have been able to enjoy a definite measure of autonomy. Africa is today virtually the only place where peasants still have such an autonomy. Ninety years of colonization have not

NB
⟶

eradicated it. In fact, the rural producers in most parts of Africa are still in the process of becoming peasants: they are transcending the boundary between primitive cultivator and peasant. There are, of course, those who are turning into capitalist farmers or, as a result of the same process, into labourers. Still, the number involved is very small. The principal feature of rural Africa is therefore, as Ken Post calls it,[11] 'peasantization', the process of becoming a peasant, and not as many other analysts imply, the proletarianization of the rural producers.[12] Peasant production has a logic of its own. It cannot be adequately understood only as a social phenomenon submerged by capitalism.

The peasant mode of production

There are good reasons to speak of a peasant mode of production in Africa. Given the many variations that exist between rural production systems in Africa, there are those who prefer to talk of peasant modes of production. There are also those who would wish to make a distinction between sedentary and nomadic systems. Such distinctions, however, seem unnecessary. First of all, a mode of production is an abstraction identifying the basic logic and structures of given social formations. It is never articulated in a single and pure form. In the same way as the capitalist mode gives rise to different types of societies, so does the peasant mode. Furthermore, it must be noted that most social formations reflect more than one mode of production. In Africa, for instance, societies are products of both the capitalist and the peasant modes. Most writers on Africa have assumed that the former is unequivocally predominant. In fact, no analysis has been made in which the peasant mode is a central focus. Before proceeding to an analysis of how the peasant mode interacts with capitalism and what forms of social and political action ensue, it is necessary to identify its basic features.

Any mode of production is more than a matter of production. It has its own way of organizing reproduction of both material and social conditions, circulation of goods and services, and consumption. The concept refers to the economic organization of society in its widest sense. Still, 'mode of production' is used for epistemological reasons: it is part of an analytical school in which material production is assumed to dictate other activities in society. How men relate to the means of production, land and factories, is also the major criterion used to distinguish between different modes of production. The conceptual scheme of political economy reflects the features of societies in which complex economic structures prevail and people have already become irreversibly locked into antagonistic relations with each other. As we will see further below, it is one of the reasons why, in the analysis of African conditions, the Marxist paradigm needs to be transcended in

NB - how far is this true of kenya? and especially of central province? Is the process of peasantization, i-e transition from primitive farming to peasantry not yet completed?

some important respects. The peasant mode gives rise to forms of social and political action which are not easily handled within the conventional framework of Marxist analysis. Below follows the presentation of the social logic of the peasant mode.

THE DOMESTIC ORIENTATION

The peasant mode of production is characterized by a rudimentary division of labour. Each unit of production is still small. Without any real product specialization there is very little exchange between the various units of production. Although these units, that is, the peasant households, are not usually self-sufficient, management decisions are taken in the light of domestic needs and capabilities. There is no functional interdependence bringing them into reciprocal relations with each other and leading to the development of the means of production. Each unit is independent of the other and the economic structure is cellular. To the extent that there is co-operation among producers in these economies it is not structurally enforced but purely a superstructural articulation rooted in the belief that everybody has a right to subsistence. Consequently, co-operation among peasants is temporary, for example, at the time of an emergency, rather than regular and formalized.

There is also a definite limit to how much time and effort peasants can spend on co-operation with others. Ensuring the reproduction of their own household is almost a full-time occupation. Meeting the needs of the household members is the primary concern of the peasant and also a determining factor, as Chayanov argued long ago,[13] of the amount of labour that the working members of the household are prepared to put in. One of the few studies of African agriculture in which some of Chayanov's theses are tested also confirms the strong positive correlation between family size and land under cultivation.[14] Given their rudimentary technology and the lack of variety of product among the households, producing the basic necessities is a cumbersome task. The peasant invests so much time and effort in it that he is naturally reluctant to take chances. In fact, production is so important to him that it may well be the primary reason why he is unwilling to adopt innovations, even if they hold out the promise of financial gains.

Producing the basic necessities is not the same as subsistence production, although the latter in most of Africa is a large proportion of it. One observer estimated a decade ago that peasants in Africa devote approximately 60 to 70 per cent of their labour time to subsistence farming.[15] Although this figure no doubt varies depending on which crops are cultivated, it probably carries validity also today. There are very few studies of household budgets in rural Africa and it is difficult, therefore, to generalize about how much money is spent on food, clothes and other basic necessities. One study, however, shows that the incorporation of the peasant into the capitalist economy essentially has the effect of making him purchase some of the items which were formerly produced within the household.[16] This suggests that it is as consumer rather than producer that the peasant, of his own volition, approaches the market.

Meeting minimal human needs in a reliable manner forms the central criterion which knits together the peasants' choices of seeds, techniques, timing, rotation, etc. The size and composition of the family as it goes through its biological development cycle largely determine what constitute minimal needs at any given time. These needs do not only include the maintenance of the means of subsistence of the present generation, but generally include the provision of the means of subsistence for the next generation in the form of, for example, land or modern education. A recent study of peasant farming in north-western Tanzania confirms this to be its predominant characteristic.[17] There is a long-term planning perspective within the peasant household, but it relates less to productive than to socially reproductive needs. Expressed differently, one can say that the needs of man rather than those associated with the development of the means of production take precedence. In his study of the Russian peasants Chayanov argued in a similar fashion: they operate according to the law of subsistence rather than the law of value.[18] This law of subsistence still permeates much of rural Africa and this means that the threat of *individual* starvation is virtually absent. In that sense, as Polanyi has pointed out,[19] these societies are more human than those where the law of value prevails, but they are at the same time less efficient. The cost of reproduction is high and it leaves the peasant with limited interest in adopting practices that may raise agricultural productivity. Agricultural modernization is a threat to the domestic orientation of the peasant household.

RESOURCE-BASED AGRICULTURE

Farming in tropical Africa is still overwhelmingly dependent on the natural resource endowment and on human labour and simple hand tools, augmented to some extent by animal draft power and, still less, engine-powered equipment. The systems of shifting cultivation and bush fallowing evolved by African peasants represent striking examples of resource-based agriculture. Such systems give proof of an effective adaptation to the economic and physical environment, including the abundance of unused land. Except for the cost of clearing the bush or forest, land is a free good. Fertility has been maintained by rotation of fields rather than by crop rotation or by application of organic or chemical fertilizers. As one observer has noted, the systems of bush fallowing are often a complex and skilful adaptation to the natural conditions and are typically a transition phase between shifting cultivation and permanent cropping.[20]

It would be wrong to assume, however, that peasants when growing permanent crops are less dependent on nature. Even this kind of farming in Africa depends on adaptation to existing natural endowments. In most of Africa peasants have achieved such an adaptation, often through effective intercropping systems. Intercropping, like shifting cultivation, has generally been considered a backward form of agriculture, but a recent symposium on intercropping in semi-arid areas of Africa concluded that it has a development potential which has not been fully explored.[21]

Peasant agriculture is always a difficult and complex activity. It is increasingly being realized that such agriculture, when practised in the tropical areas, is much more hazardous and time-consuming than in more temperate climates. The most adverse effects of the tropical climate on agriculture are caused by the poor quality of soil, irregular quantities and frequencies of rainfall and the multitude of pests and diseases.[22] Control over these factors is usually beyond the reach of the ordinary peasant. Still, it would be wrong to underestimate peasant knowledge of the environment in which he produces. Being in an organic environment he is better placed than the scientist to provide the right know-how. The scientist has solutions to problems of production that have been developed in an inorganic environment. He himself is a product of the *nature artificielle* and follows the dictates of a world very different from the natural one in which the peasant operates. These two worlds, as one observer notes,[23] obey different imperatives, different directives and different laws which have nothing in common.

Knowledge in the organic environment is by definition pragmatic. What the peasant needs to know about plants he cultivates, the weeds that interfere with their cultivation, the soil and how it can be preserved and enriched, the weather and the various implements needed for cultivation, does not require a scientific approach. The test of peasant know-how is its practical application. A peasant certainly operates with a considerable variety of information in order to perform his occupation satisfactorily. In order to be successful he must be able to combine this information in a manner relevant to the conditions determining his occupation. In this exercise he is guided by past experience. His most important counsellors are from the previous generation.

The success of a particular action is regarded as a sign that the peasant knew all that was necessary for him to know in order to achieve success and that he made use of that knowledge at the right time in the course of his action. Failure, on the other hand, means that he either lacked some of the knowledge or he did not apply it as he ought to have done. In this situation there is no question of incorporating any separate scientific truth within this set of knowledge. As Znaniecki points out, this type of knowledge is not theoretically systematized separate from the personality of the peasant but practically organized by him for the active performance of his function.[24]

In his organic environment, the peasant does not operate with abstract categories or universal knowledge. He works within a non-universal sphere of knowledge. The limit of advance in such situations is fixed by the personal knowledge of the particular peasant (or peasants) who are regarded as the most knowledgeable in the local community. What matters here is superior skill, not scientific knowledge. The person best placed to perform innovations in peasant economies, therefore, is not the technocrat but the skilful peasant who knows how to make best use of the various components of the existing resource-endowment. The peasant farmer has no reason to be interested in the extension agent as long as his agriculture is carried out in an organic environment. The social logic of the peasant mode of production pre-empts any serious interest in practices developed within the context of modern modes of production.

THE SUPERIMPOSED STATE

The interesting paradox in the peasant mode of production is that for its own reproduction it does not presuppose exploitation or the existence of social classes, yet only when parts of the rural production are appropriated by other social classes are the producers 'peasants', as opposed to 'primitive agriculturalists'. As Hindess and Hirst note in their study of pre-capitalist formations, in this case the state has no necessity: 'it appears suspended over society as a given without conditions of existence in society.'[25] The state is not linked to the system of production in the same way as it is in other modes. The basic units of production are not only socially independent of each other but also of the state. It plays no necessary role in production. Appropriations by other classes through such instruments as taxation are simple deductions from an already produced stock of values. The peasants do not need the state for their own reproduction. They would prefer to be without its interventions. On the other hand, it is impossible to conceive of other social classes reproducing themselves without access to state power. History has demonstrated that the development of modern society is inconceivable without the subordination of the peasantry. As long as this process is unfinished, the ruling classes, those who control the state, are bound to be dependent on the peasants. The peasants cannot conceivably be in the forefront on the route to a modern society, as such a development is bound to be at their expense. Therefore, it is only logical that the peasants resist state policies as well as a total absorption by the market economy. Such is the logic of the peasant mode of production.

The peasant mode dictates a practice whereby everybody is ensured a share in the total labour product so as not to fall victim to starvation. Where the peasant mode prevails, there is a fundamental egalitarianism which claims that all should be granted a place, a living. This is a subject that has fascinated many social scientists, writing in the 'peasant society' tradition, most recently James Scott who stresses that this orientation does not necessarily presuppose economic equality.[26] In that sense, this form of peasant egalitarianism is conservative rather than revolutionary. Peasants are interested in equality within the parameters of an organic environment but have little understanding of the type of equality that is artificially created by man in his inorganic environment.

In the peasant mode the family is the basic work unit and commerce is undertaken in the context of familial principles of organization and orientation. The individual remains subordinate to the corporate household. Similarly, wealth remains subordinate to status. In this situation social classes do not appear in a pure form. Class relations tend to be encapsuled in other types of social relations, for example, patron–client networks. As Terray notes, in the capitalist mode of production classes are realized directly, while in pre-capitalist modes they are realized in an element whose nature remains to be defined.[27] In the former, the economic base is both determinant and dominant. In the latter, by contrast, it is only determinant. Thus, social formations are bound to take a different shape. A principal objective of this study is to identify what kind of social structure evolves in a society where the peasant mode still prevails.

One major political consequence of the dominance of the peasant household economically, and the familial mode socially and culturally, is indifference, sometimes active resistance, to operating in a framework of impersonal rules.[28] State action, which forces peasants to encounter such rules, runs counter to the logic of peasant production. The latter, by contrast, calls for an existence rationality that negates the role of the state, that turns the peasant mind away from dependence on outside advice and instead gives priority to know-how derived from the local farm–family situation.

Historically the peasant mode of production has generally been overpowered by more effective modes. New social classes have risen to power and captured the peasants for their own ends. This will no doubt happen also in Africa. Experience has shown, however, that this is a slow and difficult process as long as peasants have access to land on which they can practise their extensive agriculture. As long as peasants find the means to secure their own reproduction they will resist conquest by other social classes. The colonial history of Africa is full of examples to illustrate this.

Because, however, peasants are highly dependent on their natural environment, drastic changes in the latter may accelerate the demise of the peasant mode of production. In these situations local know-how becomes obsolete. The peasants have no choice but to be more outward-oriented. In parts of Africa this is already happening. For instance, vast development projects have been planned for the Sahelian zone in West Africa to take advantage of the weakness of the peasants, caused by the persistent drought, and turn them into more productive producers. The main point here is that whether these projects succeed or not, the conditions of the peasantry will deteriorate. Even if their material conditions were to improve they will lose their economic independence, and thus their strongest guarantee of some measure of political freedom.

The economy of affection

Each mode of production gives rise to its own type of economy. Capitalism leads to the predominance of a market economy which in turn produces a system of class stratification based on the conflict between capital and labour. The peasant mode gives rise to an economy in which the affective ties based on common descent, common residence, etc., prevail. We refer to it here as an 'economy of affection'.[29] In the absence of contradictions that characterize social action in capitalist and socialist modes of production, familial and other communal ties provide the basis for organized activity. Communal action prevails and conflicts naturally tend to arise between communities rather than between other forms of social organization.

Peasants are not likely to engage in class action unless their chances of reproducing their own mode of production are in danger. As long as the peasant mode is kept alive, other forms of social action will prevail. This is the case even in situations where the peasantry may be effectively incorporated into the capitalist or socialist economy. The main reason for this is that the economy of affection is primarily concerned with the problems of reproduction rather than production. Work, or improved productivity, is not an end in itself. While in the modern economies – both capitalist and socialist – the leading motto is 'live in order to work', in the economy of affection it is 'work in order to live'. As Meillassoux also found in his study of the Gouro in the Ivory Coast, stratification in society tends to be based on control of the means of reproduction.[30] The latter is the dominant factor determining the social structure of peasant society. Obviously, as the peasants get more and more incorporated into a modern economy other factors will grow in importance. As long as the vast majority of the rural producers remain independent smallholder peasants, however, the social structure will reflect men's relations to the means of reproduction. These structural articulations, moreover, will often prevail over demands associated with the development of the means of production.

As Sara Berry notes, the literature abounds with the tales of poor peasants who, for example, purchase subsidized inputs from government and then re-sell them to wealthier neighbours, using the cash for bride-wealth, school fees, funeral expenses, bribes or – even more to the consternation particularly of international donor agencies – tithes, alms and sacrifices.[31] The point is not that these peasants are wasteful or irrational, but that investment in maintaining their position in kinship, community, or religious networks may pay off in the long run by expanding their potential claims on assets and, therefore, their risk-bearing capacity. In the economy of affection, economic action is not motivated by individual profit alone, but is embedded in a range of social considerations that allow for redistribution of opportunities and benefits in a manner which is impossible where modern capitalism or socialism prevails and formalized state action dominates the process of redistribution. Based on the social logic of the peasant mode, the economy of affection negates many of the power relationships that characterize the modern economies. For instance, in rural Africa, dispersion of favours or services, not related to reproductive needs of the local communities, leave the recipients with a hold on the patron. The expensive patronage practices of African election candidates is only one example of how clients may control patrons. In the economy of affection an element of reciprocity exists that is structurally induced. In making this point there is no need to romanticize, like for instance Karl Polanyi, the social richness of pre-capitalist societies. The argument is rather that in Africa, where the peasant mode is still very much alive, there is an economy other than the market economy. Moreover, this economy of affection is being maintained and defended against the intrusions of the market economy. The resistance of the African peasant economies to capitalism in the pre-colonial period, emphasized both by Polanyi[32] and Rey and Dupré,[33] is still a phenomenon not to be ignored. The market economy does not unilaterally cause the destruction of the economy of affection. The latter has the ability to survive and also to affect the mode of operation of the market economy.

Two contending modes of production

There is good reason therefore to start from the assumption that in the contemporary development context in Africa, there are two contending modes of production which influence economic structures as well as social formations. This ought not to be a unique starting-point, as certainly in most Third World societies pre-modern modes of production, side by side with capitalism or socialism, exercise an influence on structural articulations. This is increasingly being acknowledged in the analysis of Asian and Latin American societies. That pre-modern modes of production may be important also in the African development situation still remains to be shown. Maybe because there is no evidence of any well-known pre-capitalist mode, such as feudalism (except in Ethiopia before the 'revolution' after 1975) or the Asiatic mode, there has been a tendency to analyse the situation as if there were no other than the capitalist mode of production. Writers have referred to pre-capitalist formations but have not acknowledged that they operate according to a social logic of their own, that is, they are derived from a mode of production other than capitalism. Most writers on the political economy of Africa have been reluctant to transcend the boundaries of the conventional Marxist paradigm, maybe for fear of becoming associated with other intellectual traditions, notably the one which stresses the unique features of peasant society. As a result, the political economy approach still has a long way to go in coming to grips with the social realities of rural Africa.

Attempts have been made to characterize the economic systems in Africa prior to colonization. Theoretical models of these systems have been developed by French anthropologists working within the Marxist tradition. Coquery-Vidrovitch, for instance, discusses to what extent there was an African mode of production.[34] She is of the opinion that there was such a mode, characterized by a patriarchal agrarian economy with a low internal surplus and the exclusive ascendancy of one group over long-distance trade. She concludes that capitalism eventually overthrew this African mode of production. This view is quite common among political economists: with colonization everything indigenous was destroyed, or at least totally submerged by external forces. It is, however, a misleading if not mistaken assumption, stemming primarily from an exaggerated emphasis on the role of market exchanges. On the whole, Marxist and marginalist economists alike have overemphasized the market as the determinant of African development.

In the case of the latter group this bias is likely to stem from a conviction that policy-makers can get at the peasants by using utilitarian incentives. The Marxist economists, by contrast, follow in the footsteps of Lenin and claim imperialism to be the source of underdevelopment. Lenin's pamphlet on imperialism, written at the turn of the century has been the starting-point of much recent analysis of underdevelopment.[35] Although there are different interpretations of Lenin's argument, one influential school maintains that the contradictions of the capitalist system do not manifest themselves only at the level of the nation but also in the relations between nations. This is the inevitable effect of changes in the capitalist system itself. The argument about the destructive powers of capitalism is particularly strong in the writings of André Gunder Frank.[36] In his view, underdevelopment is the historical product of the relations between the dominant, metropolitan, capitalist societies on the one hand, and the peripheral, satellite states on the other. These relations are an essential part of the structure and evolution of the capitalist system on a world scale. The expansion of capitalism from the metropolitan countries has led to the destruction of earlier viable economic systems of the satellite countries, to their incorporation into the metropolitan dominated worldwide capitalist system, and to their conversion into sources of capital accumulation for the develop-

NB- Dependency theory unsatisfactory as a concept in approximating social reality in the third world - undue emphasis on exchange. No room for pre-capitalist elements

Borsende — Skolen; Frank, Amin, Emmanuel

ment of the metropole. In short, in Frank's view, the metropolitan countries are developed because of the underdevelopment of the satellite countries in the periphery of the world capitalist system. An argument which follows a similar line is presented by Emmanuel in his study of the unequal effects of the imperialist world trade.[37] In recent years Samir Amin has also become increasingly an advocate of this dependency school.[38] It has no or little room for the notion that development in the periphery of the world capitalist system is influenced by another mode of production than capitalism.

The dependency school has in recent years come under criticism mainly because it focuses too one-sidedly on market exchanges and surplus extraction. A mode of production is a more complex theoretical construct and it cannot be reduced to only one or a few of its parts. This is being recognized in the writings of, for example, Bettelheim, who argues that elements of pre-capitalist modes of production are conserved by the forces of capitalism.[39] Banaji suggests that the pre-capitalist modes of production are restructured as their subordination to world capitalism takes place.[40] He maintains that the essence of the problem of underdevelopment is that the colonial peasantries were drawn into the sphere of world commodity circulation on pre-capitalist foundations: servile or feudal relations of production, backward techniques, and low levels of productivity. He is not only interested in how capitalism has altered the forms of surplus extraction in underdeveloped countries. He is equally concerned about how capitalism has affected the means of production. In other words, these writers are not only interested in how *extensively* the underdeveloped economies are *integrated* into the world capitalist system but also how *intensively* capitalism has *penetrated* the system of production in the peripheral countries.

This distinction between integration and penetration is important in order really to assess the impact of capitalism on the African economies. Still it is rarely done. Rey and Dupré are among the few political economists who in their analysis of the African economies have insisted that exchange is only the result of the organization of production, not its cause.[41] Transformation of the means of production is a primary concern in development, especially under capitalism. How far the African peasant economies are incorporated into the world capitalist system is not the most interesting question to ask. This is not to suggest that the market forces are unimportant. It is to stress, however, that these forces can only determine the comfort of the peasant but not his existence. The latter is only affected by transformations of the means of production.

Capitalism in Africa cannot expand without rapid improvements in the agricultural sector. More productive use of the land is essential to capitalist development. It is difficult to see the validity of the argument of some political economists, for example, Lionel Cliffe, that the

Bettelheim & Banaji

NB

NB — One should recognize the obvious fact of the integration of the peripheral economy into the capitalist world market, but it is equally essential to determine level of penetration of the CMP into the PCMP.

transformation of the pre-capitalist formations have stalled because the international capitalist system wants to keep the indigenous societies in Africa as sources of primitive accumulation, not of expanded reproduction.[42] The implication of this argument is that international capitalism has no interest in the development of Africa. Capital, however, does not *by design* seek the impoverishment of Africa. We need to question, as Laclau does,[43] the assumption that the maintenance of pre-capitalist relations of production in the peripheral areas is an inherent condition of the process of accumulation in the metropolitan countries. Capitalism does not really thrive on the 'restructured' pre-capitalist forms of production. It requires their replacement with more efficient forms. Such a replacement, however, has not taken place yet, because the pre-capitalist formations have not yielded to the pressures of capitalism. Thus, in my view, in order to explain underdevelopment in Third World countries we must recognize that there are barriers to the progress of capitalism and explain these barriers. To decry the expansion of capitalism as the source of all evil does not help us much. Such economic romanticism was condemned by Lenin himself, the father of Marxist theories of imperialism, who maintained that failure to recognize the elements of progress in capitalist expansion is reactionary.[44] If we square up to it, as Kay argues, 'we have to face the unpalatable fact that capitalism has created underdevelopment not simply because it has exploited the underdeveloped countries but because it has not exploited them enough.'[45] His point can be taken one step further: capitalist expansion has been impossible because there are barriers to such an expansion in Third World countries.

The ingredients of the explanation of these barriers to capital's expansion lie, as Dore and Weeks suggest,[46] in the sphere of production. The persistence of pre-capitalist relations of production retard productivity growth in the production of wage goods – the means of subsistence. This retardation sooner or later creates a problem to capital, because capitalism can only expand and reproduce itself if it continuously finds ways of cheapening the production of these means of subsistence.

The point which has been obliterated in the debate about underdevelopment in Africa is that the pre-capitalist relations have blocked the effort to cheapen the production of the means of subsistence. This is dramatically illustrated in the field of food production. Although per capita production rose in the 1950s and 1960s, the United Nations Food and Agriculture Organization (FAO) statistics show that the food sector in African countries more recently has failed to keep pace with population growth. It also lags behind the performance of other regions, including Asia and Latin America.[47]

The role of capitalism in Africa needs to be reassessed in the light of figures like these. The incorporation of the pre-capitalist economies of Africa into the world capitalist system did not lead to their demise. The

NB

NB – The barriers inherent in the pre-capitalist MP to capitalist devpt should be sought at the level of production.

TABLE 1.1 Food production per capita in Third World countries, by
region (1961–65 = 100)

Region	1972	1973	1974	1975	1976
Africa	99	92	98	96	97
North/Central America	106	107	107	112	114
South America	101	101	104	103	111
Asia	103	106	105	109	109

effect of capitalism has often been the opposite. It has been recognized
in a few recent studies that the result of capitalist expansion in many
underdeveloped countries is to create barriers to its own expansion.
Lipton, for instance, maintains that capitalism does not destroy or
replace the relics of an already largely destroyed feudalism. On the
contrary, it reinforces this system.[48] Two Swedish anthropologists
come to a similar conclusion in their study of an Indian village
economy: the large landed estate, created under feudal conditions, now
stands in the way of further capitalist development in rural India.[49]
    There is no reason why this argument cannot also be applied to the
pre-capitalist formations in Africa. Capitalism has modified the social
structures of Africa, but the latter are still influenced by the peasant
mode of production which continues to exist in a controversial
relationship with capitalism. They constitute two contending modes of
production. A study of Africa's political economy cannot start from the
assumption that one has submerged the other. Instead the task must be
to explain the structural anomalies that this situation gives rise to.

The limits of state power

In modern society, be it capitalist or socialist, the state is an integral
part of the prevailing production system. The state is called upon to
regulate and manage productive activities as demanded by the use of the
means of production. It engages in a number of activities that complement the work of individuals and private institutions. There may be
ideological controversy over what role the state should play, but such a
controversy is usually resolved in a pragmatic fashion, that is, in terms
of what the prevailing system allows. Where such disputes cannot be
resolved pragmatically, the only other option in modern society is to
fight it; to try to overhaul the state system. Modern man, however,
cannot ignore the state. He enjoys no autonomy from the system.
    The relationship of the state to the smallholder producer in rural
Africa is different. The state does not really enter into the solution of his
existential problems, except in the case of emergency, that is, when the

local peasant community fails to secure its livelihood because of, for instance, a natural disaster. This does not mean that there is no interaction between the state and the peasants. Officials collect taxes from peasants, thereby forcing them to make at least some contribution to the larger social economy. There is a definite limit, however, to how far enforcement of state policies can go in the context of peasant production. Taxation, for instance, whether direct or indirect, is an ineffective instrument of development in peasant societies. While it is true that the colonial powers used taxation to encourage cash crop production, it ceased being an effective policy tool once such production had been established. The colonial rulers had no direct control over production as long as it was carried out within the context of minuscule production units, concerned primarily with their own internal needs.

A favourite policy tool among governments to encourage higher production is attractive producer prices. In development aid circles it is often heralded as the most important instrument to reach the peasants. This policy presupposes that the market is a significant factor influencing peasant behaviour. This seems highly questionable in a situation where peasants are only marginally incorporated into the capitalist economy. Labour constraints within the household often prevent production above a certain level. Thus, even if prices are attractive, there is a real constraint in terms of what the household can produce with its available labour power. This is not to suggest that price incentives are totally ineffective, but there are reasons to believe they are far less important than what is generally considered in policy-making circles. Rudengren, for instance, shows that even in a highly commercialized area, price incentives are mentioned by only 2 per cent of 198 peasant farmers as a reason for cultivating a new crop.[50] Leonard, quoting Ruthenberg, suggests that peasants may respond to price incentives but only if these imply very dramatic rises (100 per cent) over existing prices.[51] Such a high level of profitability may be necessary to induce the peasants to respond. If price increases are more marginal, the prime beneficiaries of such policies tend to be those producers who are already absorbed by the market economy. Apart from large-scale farmers, these are petty-capitalist farmers who have accepted a modern way of farming and thus are much more sensitive to the market mechanisms. They may, or may not, use wage labour with a view to expanded reproduction but the main distinction between these farmers and the ordinary peasants is that the former are generally interested in, and capable of responding to, market forces. They go for higher productivity and greater profitability on the farm. Thus, although they are commodity producers like the ordinary peasants, they do differ in terms of how they secure and expand their reproduction. The long-term effect of this difference tends to be a growing discrepancy in income between the petty-capitalist farmers and the peasant producers.

Political leaders may also try to reorganize agricultural production in such a way as to increase the political subordination of the peasantry. The ruling class can establish state farms or create settlements in which the peasants are more easily accessible to bureaucratic interventions. As Jerzy Tepicht has convincingly shown in his study of collective agricultural production in Poland and other East European societies, the relations of production do not totally change with the introduction of state farms. Remnants of peasant society survive and social relations take on an existence of their own outside the officially prescribed organization.[52] Thus the establishment of modern forms of production does not automatically mean that they will function along the lines the model presupposes. The experience of state farms in Africa suggests that they are particularly difficult to use as surplus-generating institutions in cases where labour-intensive methods are being used. Typically, the main exception from this observation are the prison farms where, in addition to strict supervision, peasant removal from normal pre-capitalist settings may contribute to greater productivity. In Tanzania, for instance, prison farms have always been very successful and often used as demonstration units for neighbouring peasant producers. Given that conditions on the prison farm are so different from the usual peasant environment, rural smallholders, even when farming together on a communal farm, are likely to find it difficult to learn from such a demonstration.

Another way by which governments in Africa have tried to reach the peasants is by creating 'village settlements', new locations of both habitation and production. The idea is that by placing the peasants in totally new surroundings, their local know-how will be invalid and they will consequently be more open to new ideas and methods of production. In addition, through control of the distribution of inputs, government officials hope to direct the peasant producers towards greater productivity. It needs to be stressed, however, that these officials lack real economic power to bolster their authority. The peasants are the owners of the means of production (or at least they control their use more effectively than the officials) and thus they can always seek security in withdrawal. As long as labour rather than land is the real scarce resource, officials will have difficulty in exercising power over the peasants. The peasants, rather than the officials, act from a position of strength. In Africa peasants still hold the key to agricultural development, not the politicians or the administrators, whom the peasants see as contributing neither capital nor expertise, and who personally do not incur the risks involved in production.[53] While it is true, as Frances Hill argues, that in the administrative regimes of contemporary Africa, peasants have few opportunities to use citizen rights to circumvent bureaucratic power,[54] they do have the freedom to stay outside the state system. To use Hirschman's terminology,[55] they have the option to 'exit' out of the system. They can often withdraw from, or ignore, demands placed on them by the officials. This option has not been totally denied them and thus it remains an important factor in the analysis of the political economy of Africa.

In Africa the economic structures do not work in favour of an alliance between workers and peasants as it may in countries where the peasants have already been subordinated to feudal or servile forms of relations. While workers may be interested in a radical transformation of society because they are a class subordinated to the demands of capital, peasants in Africa stand to lose both economic independence and political freedom as development progresses. Lukacs discusses the relationship of the state to pre-capitalist society in the following terms: 'The various parts are much more self-sufficient and less closely interrelated than in capitalism .... One sector of society simply lives out its "natural" existence in what amounts to a total independence of the fate of the state.'[56] The state is bound to be insecurely anchored in such societies. Unlike industrial societies, capitalist and socialist alike, where the base is solidified and integrated but the superstructure is fragmented into a pluralist pattern, in the agricultural societies of Africa, the economic base is fragmented. The most common political response to these structural contradictions has been to create a unified, usually coercive political superstructure. It is no coincidence that the experiments in pluralist democracy introduced as part of the transition to political independence were shortlived. Once the state was taken over by people responsive to the forces generated by the peasant mode of production, the nature of political action changed accordingly. For them the structural contradictions of the fragmented economic base were becoming primary determinants of social and political action. Those in power had no choice but to create political structures capable of containing the divisive effects of these contradictions.

The coercive nature of the state is often used as a factor explaining the powers of the African political leaders. It is wrong, however, to assume that power only stems from lack of opposition, or suppressed opposition. In the case of the African societies, the main problem are the limits of state action: the difficulty of using the state as a regulatory and developmental instrument. This issue has been discussed by many scholars, for example, Peter Ekeh.[57] The 'public realm', that is, the sphere of state action, he maintains, lacks legitimacy in Africa. In this respect the African societies differ from the Western ones where the private and public realms share a common moral foundation – that is, what is considered morally right or wrong in the private realm is also considered morally right or wrong in the public realm. For centuries, his argument goes, Christian beliefs have provided a common moral foundation for both private and public ethic. There are, of course, exceptions, such as that presented in Banfield's study of 'amoral familism' in southern Italy.[58]

In Africa, by contrast, there is no monolithic public realm morally bound to the private realm. Instead, there are two public realms in post-colonial Africa with different links with the private realm. At one level is the public realm in which primordial groupings, ties and sentiments influence and determine the public behaviour of individuals. This primordial public realm is moral and operates on the same moral imperatives as the private realm. At another level there is a public realm which is historically associated with colonial rule and which is based on civic structures: the military, the civil service, the judiciary, the police, etc. Its chief characteristic is that it has no moral links with the private realm. This civic public realm, as Ekeh calls it, is amoral and lacks the generalized moral imperatives operative in the private realm and in the primordial public realm. The latter is a reservoir of moral *obligations* which one works to preserve. The civic public realm, however, is a place from which one seeks to gain, if possible in order to benefit the moral primordial public realm.

Others, such as Whitaker[59] and Price[60] have presented a similar argument, stressing that change is by no means unilinear and continuous. It is 'dysrhythmic' and, above all, a good deal of the structure and behaviour of pre-existing social systems has sustained itself in the face of penetration by Western institutional forms.

It is a great pity that political economists have not shown any interest in these issues, because they ought to be able to offer an explanation of this problem. The primordial public realm and the sustenance of traditional society is only possible in a situation where there is a mode of production supporting it. The social logic of the peasant mode gives rise to exactly those phenomena discussed by Ekeh and the others. The limits placed on state action in contemporary African societies are best explained in the context of a political economy approach. This study is a first attempt in that direction.

Political economists, like other social scientists, need to increase their competence to deal meaningfully with 'historically deviating' cases such as contemporary Africa. We have had very little to say that does not reflect our own Western experience. Take, for instance, this issue of civic morality and citizenship. It is natural for us to discuss these issues primarily in terms of the rights of the individual. Our own historical experience dictates this orientation of the debate. When discussing what is good for the development of African countries it is the same historical experience of ours that influences theorizing and policy advice. That the historical premises are different is usually overlooked because of our conviction that the rights of individual citizens are universal. Thus, we automatically miss that in Africa, for instance, the problematic issues relate to duties rather than to rights. The civic public realm is starved of morality and attempts to rectify this situation cannot be based on political education measures alone. The reason why the individual in African societies continues to see his primary obligation as being towards the primordial public realm is structural. The fragmentary economic base that characterizes a society where the peasant mode is strongly articulated gives rise to social formations in which primordial orientations are highly rational.

This orientation is well-documented in the writings of Frank Holmquist whose work focuses on how people in rural communities group together and with the help of well-placed individuals with ties to the community – political patrons – try to secure benefits and resources for themselves.[61] Although it is wrong to expect that these benefits are equally shared within the communities, people do make a contribution, whether in the form of money or labour. This is a form of local taxation, which is far more acceptable than government taxation, because it is usually more progressive – the big men in the communities make the largest contributions – and above all, because it is locally approved and administered. By making these contributions, which often go under the name of self-help, members of the rural communities hope to twist the arm of government so as to obtain a matching contribution to their efforts. Thereby they also try to prevent the use of government funds on other projects in other communities. Faced with competition from local communities engaging in this type of pre-emptive strategy of development, government officials find it difficult to defend or strengthen the civic public realm. The latter objective can only be achieved by increasing the tensions between state and peasant. It is a common task of these local political patrons to divert controversial state action away from their communities. Success in such efforts increases their status and power within the local community, and potentially also elsewhere.

Other studies have demonstrated similar findings. Cruise O'Brien has pointed to the crucial role that local patrons play in the decision-making system in Senegal.[62] Peel has shown how communal action often takes precedence over class action in Western Nigeria.[63] The present author has identified the same articulation in a study of co-operative organizations in East Africa.[64] What all these studies show is that the peasant mode of production gives rise to an 'invisible' economy of affection that provides opportunities for social action outside of the framework of state control. These ties are personalized and very difficult to change, short of an effective transformation of the economic structures that support them.

The petty-bourgeoisie and the post-colonial state

The debate about the post-colonial state in Africa has suffered from the same shortcoming as much of the other arguments inspired by political economy: it has prematurely accepted that the capitalist mode of production is dominant in Africa. The argument by Colin Leys that 'in post-colonial societies in Africa there can be little doubt that the *dominant* class is still the foreign bourgeoisie'[65] and von Freyhold's point that the African petty-bourgeoisie only constitutes a *governing* class but the metropolitan bourgeoisie remains the *ruling* class[66] miss the most important dimension of the relationship of state to society in Africa. By taking for granted that those who control the state also control the society, they offer a misleading picture of the power structure in Africa. John Saul comes closer to the real problem by emphasizing the relative autonomy of the post-colonial state.[67] By this he has in mind the power of the petty-bourgeoisie in African societies to break with the metropolitan bourgeoisie and attempt a revolutionary transformation of their societies. The former has a revolutionary potential which is not acknowledged in the analyses of Leys and von Freyhold. Saul, however, falls into the same trap as the other two by not realizing the autonomy of the state also vis-à-vis the peasants. The latter are not caught in relations with the bourgeoisie, be it the metropolitan or the African variety, which force them into effective subordination. That the bourgeoisie attempts to achieve such a subordination is not denied, but it is misleading to argue as if the peasants are already caught. Capitalist reproduction in Africa is only at a very initial stage. Thus, the classes to which capitalism gives rise are far from the position which they may attain in societies where the capitalist mode of production is effectively dominant.

Much of the power of the small peasants in Africa stems from their control of the means of subsistence. The production of the basic necessities is still controlled by peasants who are difficult to get at, not only because of their numbers but also because they are capable of securing their own subsistence and reproduction without the assistance of other social classes. The latter, on the other hand, cannot in the contemporary development context of Africa reproduce themselves without a strong dependence on peasant produce. Samir Amin is one of the few political economists who has recognized this as a weakness of the African petty-bourgeoisie. He has argued that even a progressive government has to break the traditional agricultural sector through capitalist development.[68] Greater productivity in the use of the means of subsistence is a precondition, above all for a regime committed to national self-reliance.

Neither the metropolitan bourgeoisie, nor the African petty-bourgeoisie, have been very successful in achieving such a transformation of the means of subsistence. This is because they lack effective instruments of power to influence peasant action. Price incentives, administrative supervision, political education, etc., do not get to the root of the problem.

This problem also becomes comprehensible if we do not take it for granted that there exists an automatic affinity between the metropolitan and the African petty-bourgeoisie. The latter, which in addition to businessmen and administrators in the urban-based sectors also consists of the petty-capitalist producers in the rural areas, are not supporters of international capital by design but only by default. Although the petty-bourgeoisie objectively are placed in a contradictory position to the peasants, the economy of affinity is used to transcend this and reduce the social tensions that otherwise would arise. The economy of affection links the African petty-bourgeoisie with the peasants in a manner that holds back capitalist expansion. This behaviour among the African petty-bourgeoisie is by no means historically unique. Lukacs' study of the peasantry and the petty-bourgeoisie in Europe led him to the following conclusion: 'Their aim is not to advance capitalism, nor to transcend it, but to reverse its action or at least prevent it from developing fully.'[69] If this observation carries any weight it would be wrong to assume that the co-operative relations between the African petty-bourgeoisie and the agencies of international capital stem from a shared interest. The petty-bourgeoisie is not a priori a supporter of international capital. It would like to develop its own economic base, either through private or collective ownership of the means of production. In doing so, however, it comes into conflict with the peasantry to whom its members are closely linked through the economy of affection.

It would be wrong to assume that the demands of capitalism always prevail over the needs of the economy of affection. The petty-bourgeoisie does not always operate from a position of strength. In fact, in the context of contemporary Africa, this is more often the exception than the rule. The relative autonomy of the peasantry forces the political leaders to adopt a patronage type of approach. In the absence of effective means to control the economic activities of the peasants, the petty-bourgeois leaders are obliged to buy the support of the peasants with political currency, for example, schools, health dispensaries, and other such amenities that peasants value. They must offer a tangible benefit in order to get the peasants interested in their own schemes, but even so they cannot be sure that peasant support is forthcoming. The peasants may decide to ignore the policy demand if it is too controversial or too demanding.

Where it has been difficult to get at the peasants through the market forces, African politicians have tried to replace the market forces with a political market-place. In this, contracts are essentially social or political, that is, they do not carry any objective economic values. The political market-place, unlike the economic market, is a typically pre-modern institution. Many of the deals that are entered into are expensive, at least as seen from the perspective of the capitalist or socialist modes of production. There is no emphasis on efficiency. In that respect politics in Africa is not subordinated to the demands of the relations of production. It is this pre-modern articulation that makes it possible to claim that in Africa economics feeds politics, as opposed to capitalist (and modern socialist) societies where economics breeds politics. These variations in the articulation of social relations have structural roots, notably the discontinuity caused by the existence of two contending modes of production, neither of which really prevails.

So common is this situation in sub-Saharan Africa that it is not an exaggeration to claim that the principal structural constraint to development are the barriers raised against state action by the peasant mode of production. To subordinate the peasants to the demands of state policies, carried by the political leadership, is a controversial task that all regimes face in Africa. The Marxist–Leninist in Africa has the same need to get the peasant involved in the cash nexus as the capitalist-oriented leader. In order to appropriate the surplus product from the peasant more effectively there is no other way available but to raise peasant productivity and make him produce more than for his own domestic needs. 'Exploitation' in this sense of the word, is inevitable in the African societies if they are to develop. Such has been the road to progress in all other societies.

Power, dependence and development

Development is inconceivable without a more effective subordination of the peasantry to the demands of the ruling classes. The peasants simply must be made more dependent on the other social classes if there is going to be social progress that benefits the society at large.

The concept of dependence is crucial to the analyses of both power and development. It lies at the base of both, and indicates that both are closely interrelated. Development is largely a matter of power, not only the use of power but also the creation of power structures that facilitate development. This is particularly true of Africa where interdependencies that create a social dynamic are very weak.

Such interdependencies are a precondition for the effective use of power.[70] A person's ability to control or influence somebody else resides in control over the things that the latter values or needs. The same applies to the power of social classes. It presupposes that one class controls what the other wants or needs. Much of the colonial and post-colonial history in Africa has centered on this problem. The petty-bourgeoisie has been in strong need of the surplus product of the peasants. The peasants have been primarily interested in measures that facilitate their social reproduction, that is, schools, dispensaries, water and roads. It is not difficult to see who starts from the most advantageous position in this power struggle. Increased returns on land is an absolute necessity for the petty-bourgeoisie, as it cannot strengthen its own position without such an achievement. The things that the peasants value, by contrast, are not absolutely necessary, only desired. Furthermore, the peasants have power as long as they can stay indifferent to what the ruling classes offer, or can secure these through alternative channels. This way they retain their autonomy and deny the rulers the opportunity to exercise power over them. Peasants in Africa have largely succeeded in exercising their own power by denying the officials controlling the state the opportunity to establish effective relations of dependence. Subsequent chapters will show how the peasants have remained indifferent to official policy demands placed on them, either because the proposed measures have made no sense in the local development context or because the peasants have been aware of alternative means to deal with the issue. In those cases where the rulers have threatened the reproductive capacity of the peasant mode, the rural producers have often rioted or in any other way shown their opposition. Inappropriate policy measures to get at the peasantry have often intensified the difficulties of creating such relations of dependence that facilitate development.

The extent to which peasant autonomy has been reduced obviously differs from one African country to another. Still, evidence suggests that the peasants by and large remain uncaptured by other social classes. Existing relations of dependence are still feeble. Although the peasants are incorporated into the larger world economy, and thus interact with other social classes in that context, their dependence on the system is marginal. They live in the boundary region of this system and there they have the unique prerogative of choosing to withdraw. They have a true exit option.

In order to understand the political situation in Africa, then, it is important to recognize that a large group of social actors are still to be drawn firmly into ties of dependence with the ruling classes, a precondition for effective exercise of state power. It is perhaps our gravest analytical mistake in the study of Africa to assume a priori that the peasants are already caught in such relations of dependence.

The interesting thing about the African situation is that despite strenuous efforts both by the colonial powers and the independent governments, peasants in many parts of the continent have retained a considerable measure of autonomy vis-à-vis other social classes. Small has proved its power by remaining economically independent. We are faced with what must appear to most people as a paradox: those with power in Africa are not necessarily those in control of the state but those who remain outside its control. As long as large numbers of producers are unaffected by state policies, the power of those who rule is largely illusory. The most obvious manifestations of the use of power, such as the legislative control, formulation of policies and implementational responsibility, are not really decisive. Even such examples as intimidation of the peasants, in which officials often engage, are not really proof of power. Such measures do not alter the developmental premises and certainly do not lead to the strengthening of the position of the rulers. On the contrary, such measures are often indications of the lack of real power on the part of the officials. It must also be recognized that among the rural producers the smallholder peasants who cultivate their land without any significant inputs from outside are usually more powerful than those who have been effectively absorbed by the capitalist economy and respond to its demands. The peasants often have a definite bargaining power vis-à-vis the latter which they can use to defend or even improve their own position.

In the analysis of the African situation there is good reason to remember Shanin's observation that 'not only victors and rulers determine political reality'.[71] In Africa the course of events is determined as much by those with power to withdraw from state policies as it is by those who actually make and execute these policies. Peasants can often trade the threat of withdrawal of support for the regime for resources the state commands. This is a smart form of politics on the part of the peasants that most observers have been late in recognizing. From the point of view of those who rule the African countries, this is a *negative* form of power they wish to erase. If these countries wish to become more self-reliant, a strategy based on agricultural modernization is in most cases the only feasible option. Yet to make the many smallholder peasants move along the lines of such a strategy has so far proved very difficult and costly.

The principal constraint to development of the African economies is not the dependence of the petty-bourgeoisie on international capital, an issue which has been given excessive prominence by writers on the political economy of Africa. The main problem is that this dependence does not extend beyond the state level – the African rulers have been unable to make the peasants effectively dependent on their policy measures. What is politically interesting, therefore, is not the dependence of the peasants, but their relative autonomy: their ability to avoid getting caught in relations of dependence. Small is powerful in Africa because it is sustained by an active peasant mode of production with its own alternative economy. The root of peasant power is economic; the issue at stake, therefore, is one of political economy and not just a matter of cultural traditionalism. To deal with it, however, it is necessary to transcend the boundaries of conventional paradigms used in the study of political economy. While political economy studies of societies in other parts of the world have been able to ignore studies written in the tradition of the peasant society approach simply because the peasantry in those societies have already been reduced to political insignificance, such a view is highly mistaken in the context of African studies. The capitalist mode of production is by no means so dominant that peasant power is irrelevant for the development issues at large.

Nowhere has this been better proven than in the case of Tanzania, where after the Arusha Declaration of 1967 the political leadership placed virtually all their eggs in the rural development basket. The development strategy was based on the transformation of the peasant mode of production in such a manner as to achieve a social transformation of society at large. This situation highlights the issues to which this book is devoted.

References and notes

1. Barrington Moore Jr., *The Social Origins of Dictatorship and Democracy: Lord and Peasant in the Making of the Modern World* (Boston: Beacon Press, 1966).
2. John Markie, 'Ujamaa villages in Tanzania: a possible solution to the problems of the rural poor', *Land Reform*, vol. 1 (1976), p. 56.
3. M. A. Zaman, 'Bangladesh: the case for further land reform', *South Asian Review*, vol. 8, no. 2 (1975), pp. 97–115.
4. See, for example, Albert F. E. van Binsbergen, 'The contribution of small farmers and rural workers to food production and development in Latin America', *Land Reform*, vol. 1 (1977), pp. 15–24.
5. W. Allen, *The African Husbandman* (Edinburgh: Oliver & Boyd, 1965).
6. See Lloyd Fallers' articles 'Are African cultivators to be called "peasants"?' *Current Anthropology*, vol. 2, no. 2 (1961), and his chapter 'Equality, modernity and democracy in new states', in Clifford Geertz (ed.), *Old Societies and New States* (New York: The Free Press, 1963). It is only in the latter that Fallers is prepared to refer to the rural cultivators as 'proto-peasants'.
7. The writing of Eric Wolf has been particularly influential. See his *Peasants* (Englewood Cliffs, N. J.: Prentice-Hall, 1966).
8. This does not differ from any of the authoritative definitions that are found in Teodor Shanin, *Peasants and Peasant Societies* (Harmondsworth: Penguin Books. 1971).
9. John Saul and Roger Woods, 'African peasantries', in Shanin, op. cit.
10. Wolf, op. cit., p. 10.
11. Ken Post, '"Peasantization" and rural political movements in Western Africa', *Archives européennes de sociologie*, vol. 13, no. 2 (1972), pp. 223–54.
12. This claim is made by Mahmood Mamdani, *Politics and Class Formation in Uganda* (New York: Monthly Review Press, 1976) who argues that northern Uganda was 'proletarianized' to serve the interests of 'kulak' farmers in southern and eastern Uganda. The same point is also made by Samir Amin in his paper, 'Capitalism and ground rent: the domination of capitalism over agriculture in tropical Africa' (Dakar: IDEP, 1974). With reference to Tanzania it is reiterated, for example by Marjorie Mbilinyi, 'Peasants' education in Tanzania', mimeo. University of Dar es Salaam, Department of Education, 1977.
13. A. V. Chayanov, *The Theory of the Peasant Economy* (Homewood, Ill.: Richard D. Irwin, Inc., 1966).
14. See Jan Rudengren, 'Regional development: case study of Kahe–Msaranga–Mandaka Area, Tanzania', Ph.D. dissertation, Ekonomiska Forskningsinstitutet vid Handelshögskolan i Stockholm (EFI), forthcoming). The correlation is 0.48 at the 0.001 level of significance.
15. John C. de Wilde, *Experiences with Agricultural Development in Tropical Africa*, vol. 1 (Baltimore: John Hopkins Press, 1967), pp. 21–2.

16. Jørgen and Karen Rald, *Rural Organization in Bukoba District, Tanzania* (Uppsala: Scandinavian Institute of African Studies, 1975), p. 108.
17. Jannik Bosen, Birgit Storgård-Madsen and Tony Moody: *Ujamaa – Socialism from Above* (Uppsala: Scandinavian Institute of African Studies, 1977).
18. Chayanov, op. cit.
19. Karl Polanyi, *The Great Transformation* (Boston: Beacon Press, 1957), pp. 163–4.
20. Hans Ruthenberg, *Farming Systems in the Tropics*, 2nd edn (Oxford: Clarendon Press, 1976), p. 73.
21. J. H. Monyo, A. D. R. Ker and Marilyn Campbell (eds), *Intercropping in Semi-Arid Areas* (Ottawa: International Development Research Centre, 1976).
22. Andrew M. Kamarck, *The Tropics and Economic Development* (Baltimore: Johns Hopkins Press, 1976).
23. Jacques Ellul, *The Technological Society* (New York: Vintage Books, 1964), p. 97.
24. Florian Znaniecki, *The Social Role of the Man of Knowledge* (New York: Octagon Books, 1965).
25. Barry Hindess and Paul C. Hirst, *Pre-Capitalist Modes of Production* (Routledge & Kegan Paul, 1975), p. 197.
26. James C. Scott, *The Moral Economy of the Peasant: Rebellion and Subsistence in Southeast Asia* (London and New Haven: Yale University Press, 1976), p. 40.
27. Emmanuel Terray, *Marxism and 'Primitive' Societies* (New York: Monthly Review Press, 1972), p. 147.
28. Kenneth Jowitt, 'The Leninist response to neocolonialism', (Institute of International Studies Monograph, University of California, Berkeley, 1978).
29. This concept is meant to convey the same meaning as implied in the reciprocal mode of economic organization identified by Polanyi as typical of simple agrarian societies.
30. Claude Meillassoux, *L'Anthropologie Economique des Gouro de Côte d'Ivoire* (Paris: Mouton, 1964). This argument is also analysed in the volume edited by Maurice Bloch, *Marxist Analyses and Social Anthropology* (Malaby, 1975).
31. Sara S. Berry, 'Risk and the poor farmer', mimeo., Boston University, August 1977.
32. Polanyi, op. cit.
33. P. P. Rey and G. Dupré, 'Reflections on the pertinence of a theory of the history of exchange', *Economy and Society,* vol. 2, no. 2 (1973), pp. 131–63.
34. Catherine Coquery-Vidrovitch, 'The political economy of the African peasantry and modes of production', in Peter C. W. Gutkind and Immanuel Wallerstein (eds), *The Political Economy of Contemporary Africa* Beverley Hills: Sage Publications, 1976) pp. 90–111.
35. V. I. Lenin, 'Imperialism: the highest stage of capitalism', in *Collected Works*, vol. 22 (Moscow and London: Lawrence & Wishart, 1964).
36. André Gunder Frank, *Capitalism and Underdevelopment in Latin America* (Harmondsworth: Penguin Books, 1969).
37. Arghiri Emmanuel, *Unequal Exchange: A Study of the Imperialism of Trade* (New York: Monthly Review Press, 1972).

38. Samir Amin, *Accumulation on a World Scale* (New York: Monthly Review Press, 1973).
39. cf. Charles Bettelheim, 'Theoretical comments', in Emmanuel, op. cit.
40. Jairus Banaji, 'Backwood capitalism, primitive accumulation and modes of production', *Journal of Contemporary Asia*, vol. 3, no. 4 (1973), pp. 393–411.
41. Rey and Dupré, op. cit.
42. Lionel Cliffe, 'Rural political economy of Africa', in Gutkind and Wallerstein, op. cit., pp. 112–30.
43. Ernesto Laclau, 'Feudalism and capitalism in Latin America', *New Left Review*, vol. 67 (May–June 1971), p. 35
44. V. I. Lenin, 'A characterization of economic romanticism', in *Collected Works*, vol. II (Moscow: Progress Publishers, 1972), p. 217.
45. Geoffrey Kay, *Development and Underdevelopment: A Marxist Analysis* (Macmillan, 1975), p. 55.
46. Elisabeth Dore and John Weeks, 'Class alliances and class struggles in Peru', *Latin American Perspectives*, vol. 4, no. 3 (Summer 1977), pp. 4–17.
47. Food and Agriculture Organization of the United Nations (FAO), 'Special feature: FAO indices of agricultural production – agriculture, food, crops, cereals and livestock products', *Monthly Bulletin of Agricultural Economics and Statistics*, vol. 26 (1977), pp. 20–9.
48. Michael Lipton, *Why Poor People Stay Poor* (Temple Smith, 1977), pp. 30–5.
49. Göran Djurfeldt and Staffan Lindberg, *Behind Poverty: The Social Formation in a Tamil Village* (Lund and London: Studentlitteratur and Curzon Press, 1975).
50. Rudengren, op. cit.
51. David K. Leonard, *Reaching the Peasant Farmer* (Chicago: University of Chicago Press, 1977), p. 245.
52. Jerzy Tepicht, *Marxisme et agriculture: le paysan polonais* (Paris: Armand Colin, 1973).
53. This argument is made by Milovan Djilas, *The New Class* (New York: Praeger, 1957) with reference to Eastern Europe after the establishment of Communist regimes there.
54. Frances Hill, 'Experiments with a public sector peasantry: agricultural schemes and class formation in Africa', paper presented to the African Studies Association Conference, Boston, November, 1976.
55. Albert Hirschman, *Exit, Voice and Loyalty: Responses to Decline in Firms, Organizations and States* (Cambridge, Mass.: Harvard University Press, 1970).
56. Georg Lukacs, *History and Class Consciousness* (M.I.T. Press, 1968), p. 55.
57. Peter Ekeh, 'Colonialism and the two publics in Africa: a theoretical statement', *Comparative Studies in Society and History*, vol. 17, no. 1 (1975), pp. 91–112.
58. Edward C. Banfield, *The Moral Basis of a Backward Society* (New York: The Free Press, 1958).
59. C. S. Whitaker Jr., 'A dysrhythmic process of political change', *World Politics*, vol. XIX, no. 2 (January 1967), pp. 190–217.
60. Robert M. Price, *Society and Bureaucracy in Contemporary Ghana* (Berkeley: University of California Press, 1975), pp. 205–19.
61. Frank W. Holmquist, 'Implementing rural development', in Goran Hyden,

Robert H. Jackson and John J. Okumu (eds), *Development Administration: The Kenyan Experience* (Nairobi: Oxford University Press, 1970).

62. D. C. Cruise O'Brien, *Saints and Politicians: Essays on the Organization of a Senegalese Peasant Society* (Cambridge University Press, 1975), p. 141.

63. J. D. Y. Peel, 'Inequality and action: the forms of Ijesha social conflict', Conference on 'Inequality in Africa' of the Social Science Research Council at Mt. Kisco, New York, September 1976, p. 41.

64. Goran Hyden, *Efficiency Versus Distribution in East African Cooperatives: A Study in Organizational Conflicts* (Nairobi: East African Literature Bureau, 1973).

65. Colin Leys, 'The "over-developed" post-colonial state: a re-evaluation', *Review of African Political Economy*, no. 5 (January–April 1976), pp. 39–48.

66. Michaela von Freyhold, 'The post-colonial state and its Tanzanian version', *Review of African Political Economy*, no. 8 (January–April 1977), pp. 75–89.

67. John S. Saul, 'The state in post-colonial societies – Tanzania', *The Socialist Register 1974* (The Merlin Press, 1974).

68. Samir Amin, 'The class struggle in Africa', *Revolution*, vol. 1, no. 9 (1964), p. 43.

69. Lukacs, op. cit., p. 59.

70. For illuminating analyses of the concept of power as stemming from dependence, see Richard M. Emerson, 'Power–dependence relations', *American Sociological Review*, vol. 27, no. 1 (February 1962), pp. 31–40, and Steven Lukes, *Power: A Radical View* (Macmillan, 1974).

71. Teodor Shanin, 'The peasantry as a political factor', *The Sociological Review*, vol. 14, no. 1 (March 1966), p. 18.

CHAPTER 2

Small rebuffs modern and big: peasants in colonial Tanganyika

It is now generally accepted that pre-colonial Africa had a long and varied history of its own. Africa had its own empires, its powerful kingdoms. Even where the societies lacked ruling hierarchies and their social organization was acephalous there was an active legend to keep society together and give its people a sense of dignity. As contacts with outside powers increased, economic and political relations began to change. In West Africa empires that prospered from trans-Saharan trade gave way to coastal kingdoms as Portuguese and other European traders became a more powerful influence. It was the rulers of these coastal kingdoms that were instrumental in securing slaves from the inland societies.

In East Africa there was once the powerful kingdom of Kitara in the interlacustrine highlands. When Arabs and European explorers reached this area in the nineteenth century Kitara was giving way to another powerful kingdom – Buganda. These societies did not consist of primitive subsistence producers alone, but had developed their own technology for a range of products. Many of these were used locally but others were exchanged in barter trade with people from far away. It was the goods obtained from such long-distance trade rather than regularized extraction of surplus from the local peasantry that enabled the development of embryonic states in these societies. Booty secured in warfare also became instrumental in facilitating the emergence of ruling hierarchies. Societal stratification bore witness of active economies.[1]

Colonial history never acknowledged pre-colonial developments. History began with the white man's arrival on the black continent. Progress started with the establishment of colonial rule. In the eyes of European observers of the time it implied a radical break with the past. It was the application of the advanced principles of capitalism that would bring Africa out of backwardness. Much of Africa's history has been written as if this were also what happened. We have generally accepted the point that colonial rule did exercise a powerful influence on the course of events in Africa. Consequently it is not surprising that even those who in recent years have attempted to rewrite African history have accepted this premise. The struggle against the colonial power is only important if the latter is presented as strong and dominant. The same point is readily adopted also in the Marxist perspective on Africa: capitalism destroyed existing modes of production. Still, if we extend history beyond its specific political expressions, Africa's history needs to be re-examined from the premise that capitalism did *not* exercise such a strong influence on Africa. Political resistance in Africa is evidence not of the strength of capitalism but of its failure to penetrate the African economies. Anti-colonialism was articulated by social classes with roots in a pre-capitalist mode of production, not by classes who had already been irreversibly incorporated into the capitalist mode. Such is certainly the evidence from Tanzania. *This is true, but what you seem to overlook is that the resistance of the africans was broken by force and some degree of transformation has occurred despite resistance.*

issue

NB

True

The effects of early colonization

The early explorers brought back reports to Europe that give the impression of bounty and relative affluence in many of the societies which they passed through in East Africa. Parts of the picture they convey may be exaggerated: given the prevailing image of Africa as the 'dark' and 'primitive' continent, explorers were often pleasantly surprised by what they saw. Thus, for instance, Burton and Stanley produce subjective images of Africa that are clearly in reaction to prevailing conceptions of the continent among contemporary Europeans.

Even if this bias in their accounts is considered, it is clear, as recent work by Ford and Kjekshus demonstrates[2], that the pre-colonial economies of the societies that nowadays constitute Tanzania were well adapted to the ecological conditions, thus offering the local people optimal returns from their efforts. People had devised methods by which they could not only protect themselves against vermin and attacks from wild animals but also use the laterite soils in a productive manner. As Kjekshus concludes:

> the pre-colonial economies developed within an ecological control situation – a relationship between man and his environment which had grown out of centuries of civilizing work of clearing the ground, introducing managed vegetations, and controlling the fauna.[3]

This conclusion stands in great contrast to the impressions by some of the early colonial writers who saw in East Africa nothing but 'blank, uninteresting, brutal barbarism.'[4] The reason why such writers produced a wholly negative picture of East Africa is that they experienced the African economies at a time of extreme crisis brought about by the contacts with forces that ruined the existing ecosystems.

NB - political resistance may not necessarily be interpreted to mean resistance to capitalism, but resistance to land alienation, surplus labour extraction in form of taxation, labour service etc

Colonization was largely a trial-and-error process. It set in motion many unknown forces over which the human actors had little control. The rinderpest was one such factor that caused the breakdown of existing man-controlled ecological systems. We know through Franz Stuhlmann, who travelled with Emin Pasha to Uganda in 1890, that the Karagwe kingdom in what is now north-western Tanzania had a flourishing economy based on large herds of Sanga (long-horned) cattle. He tells us about local cattle-breeding techniques and the use of smoke from cow-dung as a repellent against flies. He estimates the Karagwe herds to have exceeded 100000.[5] Soon after Stuhlmann had passed through the area, a rinderpest epidemic wiped out the herds. Another observer, who travelled through the same area in 1896 confirms the economic ruin caused by the pest.[6] The same impressions of economic ruin are conveyed from other parts of the colonial territory.[7]

The arrival of European colonizers also led to other epidemics. Particularly serious was the smallpox epidemic that hit East Africa in the 1890s. In Karagwe, it coincided with the rinderpest, and local people used the same word – *Mubiamo* – to describe the disease.[8] It struck people in all parts of the colony. Areas which had previously been densely populated were abandoned. One estimate suggests that as many as 150000 people may have died of smallpox and dysentery in 1898 alone. In addition to these diseases over which no effective control existed at the time, some areas of Tanganyika were hit by a sand-flea plague. Although attacks by sand-fleas nowadays are easily controlled, it took on the proportion of a plague when it first struck.

Large parts of Tanganyika suffered depopulation and famine was experienced in certain areas during the 1890s. To the local population these were dark years when they suffered a drastic decline in living standards and social security. The image of despondency and inability, even laziness, that characterized so much of the writings by Europeans about East Africans at the time is created from a people undergoing a severe crisis. The dislocations in production were largely caused by epidemic diseases about which neither the colonizers nor the colonized could do very much. Drought and locust swarms contributed to making conditions catastrophic in some areas. On top of all this was the German policy of procurement of food for its troops that was ruthlessly executed as colonial rule was established. Villages were ransacked and left with insufficient food supplies for their own populations.

Early German administration in Tanganyika was primarily carried out by military personnel. After having secured occupation of the coast they sent military expeditions inland to establish control over the many populous kingdoms there. The Germans were few and their troops often inadequate to secure control. Austen has described how in both Bukoba and Mwanza the German administrators faced one crisis after another as a result of failure to secure compliance from local chiefs.[10] It was a frail authority and eventually only established by playing off one local ruler against the other. Thus, centres of European power emerged around these accommodating rulers: Kahigi of Kianja in Buhaya, Masanja of Nera and Makwaia of Usiha in Sukumaland and Karunde in the central Nyamwezi chiefdom of Unyanyembe.[11]. Comparative advantages to be gained from access to new resources and stronger defence against rivalling kings and princes were the main reasons for accommodation to German rule. Inconsiderable and weak contestants were often able to turn the course of events in their favour by seeking German support. This is true of Marealle in Kilimanjaro and Kibanga in Usambara, who were both instrumental in opening up these areas for German settlement. They offered the necessary services for the settlers who entered the area.[12]

The agricultural development pattern in Tanganyika differs from neighbouring Kenya and Uganda. In Kenya, European capitalist interests tended to be paramount to the point where most cash-crop production by peasants was prohibited. In Uganda, instead of promoting a settler economy, the British colonizers sought to induce the sedentary cultivators to engage in cash-crop production for export. In Tanganyika, by contrast, the Germans opted for a mixture of settler and plantation agriculture on the one hand, and a cash-crop oriented peasant agriculture on the other.[13] With the assistance of collaborative chiefs land was alienated to German settlers on the fertile slopes of Mount Kilimanjaro and Mount Meru and in the Usambara Mountains. Sisal plantations were established along the coast. Labour recruitment was organized for the newly established commercial interests and to secure the completion of public projects, notably the railway from Dar es Salaam to Ujiji/Kigoma.

In brief, it can be said that the German colonization of Tanganyika effectively put an end to the prosperity of the indigenous pre-colonial economies. A combination of epidemic diseases, natural catastrophes and German colonial policies wrecked the fragile balance between man and nature on which these economies had rested. The conventional explanation of the effects of colonial policies is to emphasize the subordination of the local population to control by a group of foreigners, the exposure of the rural producers to unpredictable market forces, and their subservience to the needs of a large capitalist sector. In short, their incorporation into the capitalist mode of production.

The evidence supporting this conclusion is generally exaggerated. The most important thing that happened at the time of colonization was the disruption, by default as much as by design, of the man-controlled ecological systems that supported the pre-colonial economies. By undermining these, the colonizers forced the producers into a defensive posture vis-à-vis nature. The local know-how no longer secured their reproduction. The relative and absolute deprivation that the rural peoples of Tanganyika suffered was largely caused by being unable to secure the necessities of life in a regular and familiar fashion. They

Colonisation destroyed pre colonial MP & generated a new pre-capitalist based in dependent peasant prod.

42   SMALL REBUFFS MODERN AND BIG

became more dependent on the vagaries of nature than they ever were before. Survival was made more difficult with the coming of the white man. To the European observers the African producers appeared lazy and despondent mainly because they had to concern themselves so heavily with the problem of producing the necessities of life. Much of their own knowledge was no longer valid and the Germans often aggravated their situation by compelling them to grow crops that were not very suitable for the local conditions. The rural producers were quite rational in their 'inward' orientation. They had little opportunity to respond to pressures from the capitalist sector.

In the light of what happened to the rural producers, it seems awkward to argue that colonial conquest laid the foundation for capitalist penetration in Africa. It destroyed the *pre-colonial* modes of production but it did not pave the way for capitalism – with the exception of the plantation and settler enclaves. Instead, it helped to create a *pre-capitalist* peasant mode of production, in which the integration of the rural producers into a wider national economy was an essential element. This integration, however, was marginal and the needs of the capitalist sector did not impinge on the peasant producers to the extent that they were absorbed by it. Even in Kenya, where the capitalist sector was much more extensive and its demands on the local peasants much more far-reaching, it would be premature to argue that the capitalist mode totally wiped out any traces of pre-capitalism. The Mau Mau uprising was a rude awakening to the fact that despite a capitalist dominance of the countryside for two generations, a regeneration of the peasant mode was still possible. Colonialism did not erase the pre-capitalist modes of production. It did destroy the pre-colonial ones but it generated a new pre-capitalist mode based on independent peasant production. The latter survived even in those areas where it was forcefully submerged, for example, in Kenya. Most political conflicts of importance in colonial Africa are best conceived of, not as a class confrontation within a cohesive, capitalist mode of production, but as confrontations between social classes originating in two separate modes. These confrontations do not revolutionize the means of production but may lead to changes in the political regime.

Peasants under German rule

Becoming a peasant in Tanganyika meant trading the security and self-sufficiency of the pre-colonial economy for uncertainty and cash-crop production in the context of the wider colonial economy. Although elements of traditional forms of social organization survived in the rural areas, the new situation created a more direct concern with the needs of the individual household. The customary knowledge generated within the indigenous economies could no longer guarantee collective survival.

NB – The question is not whether the pre-colonial structure is totally wiped out or not, but its restructuring as a result of capitalist penetration.

The peasant status was forced upon the rural producer by the break-down of the pre-colonial economy. As long as he was left to cater for his own needs, the peasant had no reason to be worried. The problem, however, was that the colonial state could not generate enough revenue outside the peasant sector. It had to turn to the peasants for its revenue.

Taxation of the African population in Tanganyika – at a rate of three rupees per rural dwelling – was originally introduced in 1897. The objective then was more 'educational' than the direct generation of revenue; it was expected that the effect of taxation would be the incorporation of the indigenous producers into the monetary economy. Payment was possible both in kind, cash and public labour.

One way of entering the cash economy was to become an employee on the plantations and estates set up by Europeans. The beginnings of capitalist agriculture in Tanganyika, however, were very discouraging. The settlers did not experience immediate success in their efforts at tropical agriculture, and at the turn of the century European agriculture in Tanganyika was highly depressed. At the same time the revenue demands of the colonial state kept growing. It was impossible to treat the hut tax as purely an educational measure.

Götzen, who became governor in 1901, decided to force Africans to grow cotton as a revenue-generating measure. Cotton cultivation had already been tried in northern Tanzania with little success but the new governor did not hesitate to initiate a cotton-growing scheme in the southern coastal belt of the colony. He believed that cotton cultivation on individual smallholder plots would be ineffective and thus ordered that the crop be grown on a large communal plot – *Dorfschamba* – established at the headquarters of each headman in the experimental area. The headman was ordered to make all adults in his area work on this plot for twenty-eight days a year. This form of peasant agriculture by conscription was a disastrous failure. The work was very poorly rewarded and its scope grew far beyond original expectation. As a result the conscription conflicted with the demands of subsistence farming. Cotton became a common cause of grievance in the area and a rebellion broke out in the Rufiji Valley in 1905.[14] It was one of several local rebellions that sparked off the Maji Maji War, keeping the German rulers busy for over a year. The leaders of the Rufiji rebellion were often headmen who refused to accept the unreasonable demands of the Germans.

Resistance to taxation and forced labour was particularly evident in those areas where these interfered with the demands of the local peasant agriculture. For instance in the Makonde area in southern Tanzania where the threat of famine is recurrent, the imposition of tax was considered an unfair obligation. Liebenow tells us about at least one tax revolt that occurred in the area.[15] The leader was a certain headman who told his followers that anyone who paid his taxes would fall victim of smallpox. A quick dispatch of troops from the provincial headquarters and the immediate execution of the headman and his closest supporters terminated the revolt.

It appears that the indigenous reaction to 'peasantization' in the up-country areas of the colony was more peaceful, the main reason being that they had access to sources of income that did not conflict with the demands of subsistence farming. One important source was porterage. This attracted many male adults from the Nyamwezi and Sukuma areas. As a result, the hut tax began to generate considerable revenue in these areas without much disturbance of the local economies. The same was true of Buhaya, where porterage and later commercial production of coffee – a traditional crop in the area – was encouraged by the Germans. As Austen notes, by 1901 large parts of Bukoba and Mwanza Districts were already paying their tax in cash.[16]

Although land alienation in Tanganyika never reached the same extent as in neighbouring Kenya, colonial policy aimed at establishing plantation and settler agriculture as the mainstay of the economy. Unwilling to trust the African peasant contribution on his own land, the German administration secured recruitment of able-bodied adults for the plantations and estates. Götzen, for instance, endorsed a programme for resettling up-country people – particularly the Nyamwezi – nearer to the coastal plantations. This planned attempt to integrate the peasants into the emerging capitalist economy, labelled *Koloniale Lebensaufgabe* ('colonial life-work'), was a failure. Within less than two years virtually everybody had gone back to their homes, sought employment on the railway construction or, in a few cases, moved on to Kenya to work for a higher pay on the plantations there.[17]

Although the German planters and settlers experimented with many crops, they were not very successful. At the time of the First World War, only sisal could show an uninterrupted growth. Mechanized cotton cultivation in Sukumaland had proved unadaptable to local soil and climatic conditions. Arabica coffee cultivation was restricted by shortages of suitable land – the Germans having been unable to occupy the more fertile slopes of Mount Kilimanjaro and Mount Meru and instead being confined to the lower slopes of these mountains. African rubber production also proved not to be viable after having lost out to the higher-grade South Asian variety.[18] Large-scale agriculture was only a moderate success in Tanganyika, and during this first period of colonization more money is likely to have gone into such agriculture than was actually taken out of it.

A few individual officers in the German colonial administration believed in the promotion of African smallholder agriculture. One such person was Major Willibald von Stuemer, who worked in Bukoba in the early 1900s. He was responsible for introducing commercial coffee production in the area in 1904. It was part of the administration's plan to increase its tax revenue and conceived as a viable project given the tradition of coffee cultivation in the area. According to Haya customs, consumption of coffee had been ritual rather than nutritional. Its production as well as consumption had been controlled by the royal clans. To extend it to the commoner, therefore, was regarded with suspicion by the local chiefs. Yet this is exactly what von Stuemer asked the chiefs to do. Rather than engaging in direct rule he worked through the chiefs. By threatening the reluctant ones with European settlement in their chiefdoms he got them to apply their coercive powers to make commoners engage in commercial coffee production. This effort soon paid off for a variety of reasons. The growing of coffee did not interfere with the subsistence cultivation which in this area is a mixture of bananas and vegetables grown on an intercropping basis. It could be accommodated without much extra work. The growing of coffee among existing banana groves, in accordance with customary practices, greatly enhanced the value of the land, control over which had always been in the hands of the chiefs. The chiefs declared some of the land grown with coffee to be their estates – nyarubanja – a traditional prerogative that was now producing the emergence of a semi-feudal economy. There was the additional incentive to production of coffee – a major rise in the world market price of the Bukoba variety of robusta coffee between 1905 and 1906.[19]

Despite the relative success of the effort to introduce coffee on a commercial basis among the Haya people, the peasant mode in Tanganyika was by 1914 still suffering from the dislocations caused both by nature and arbitrary German policies. The limited success of the development of capitalist forms of agriculture, however, meant that the absorption of rural producers into wage employment was limited. The wage labourers in the agricultural sector were still migratory. They retained their access to land. Although allowed a position only in the shadow of the capitalist sector, peasant agriculture survived during the German period. When some of the demands on the peasants became too harsh, they resisted colonial policies, particularly in agriculturally critical years. The Maji Maji War shook the whole regime and led to a serious reconsideration of colonial policies in Africa.[20] Their impact, however, was never to be fully felt because of the outbreak of the First World War that put an end to the German presence in East Africa.

British agricultural policies

The war between the Germans and the British in East Africa forced the peasants on the defensive. Many were conscripted into the army and supplies for the soldiers commandeered from the peasant households. Although the actual physical damage caused by the war was comparatively limited, it left the colonial economy in disarray. All the German property was seized by the British; peasant agriculture was reduced to subsistence cultivation. Whatever gains the peasants had made during the German time were wiped out. In some respects the British followed in the footsteps of the Germans, in others they differed. Tanganyika never became as important to the British as it was to the Germans. Of all its colonies in Africa, Tanganyika was the most important to Germany. To the British Tanganyika was just another colony, over which, moreover, it had only limited control after the League of Nations declared it a territory under its mandate. This is not to deny that Tanganyika represented a major gain to the British who now could claim a continuous stretch of land from the Sudan to Rhodesia.

The initial British presence in Tanganyika was low-keyed. First, it gave priority to the task of winning over to its side the local rulers – traditional or appointed by the Germans. Secondly, it tried to 'retribalize' the Africans by allowing many of them to resettle in their home areas. Once these twin tasks had been accomplished, the British under Governor Cameron put into practice a more systematically conceived 'indirect rule'. This presupposed British control in a paternalistic fashion and limited consultation with the local chiefs on policies that would affect the welfare of the people in their areas. Priding themselves on being experienced colonizers they were convinced that they could avoid the mistakes of the Germans.

The British, however, laboured under the same mistaken view of the 'native' as the Germans. He was seen as an idler, unwilling to make his contribution to the development of the colonial territory. Joseph Chamberlain, the Colonial Secretary, said in the House of Commons in 1901: 'It is good for the native to be industrious ... Under all circumstances the progress of the native towards civilization is only secured when he should be convinced of the necessity and dignity of labour'.[21] A similar perspective is echoed in the Ormsby-Gore Commission of 1925, in which the subsistence producer is seen as not making a legitimate contribution to the development of the colonial territory like other groups are called upon to do.[22] Thus the British, in the same vein as the Germans, tried to make the peasants more effectively incorporated into the cash economy. It was only in the context of the modern economy that he would become industrious. Here the British revealed their narrow understanding of the African peasant economy. They discounted all the time that the peasant spent on his own reproduction and labelled him idle or lazy for not making a larger contribution to the colonial economy. To be sure, the peasant spends his time primarily on productive activities that meet the needs of his household. It was as much the mistake of the Germans as of the British to disregard the indirect benefits of these efforts to the colonial economy. Work was only conceived as beneficial in relation to the demands of the capitalist mode.

Capitalist production in the agricultural sector was not really expanded during the British era. Land alienation increased somewhat, but remained small in terms of the area covered. By 1958 the estate and plantation sector covered approximately 2.5 million acres, or 1.1 per cent of the land area. Only a third of this area, however, was actually used for plantation crops or other farming. Another third was used for grazing. The remainder was fallow land, forest and unspecified areas.[23] Of the plantation crops sisal was singularly important, leaving maize, coffee, tea and sugar as next in significance.[24] Most of the estate and plantation owners were British or Greek but a substantial number of Indians and Pakistanis had acquired former German property when it was auctioned after the First World War.

The plantation sector depended on hired labour, often recruited from far away to ensure that family demands would not easily interfere with their work. Thus workers for the coastal sisal plantations were recruited in the western and southern areas of the country, even from neighbouring colonies. The intention was clearly to uproot these people and turn them into a class of workers who would be available to meet the demands of the growing capitalist sector. In Tanganyika recruitment for work in the capitalist sector had to be done by compulsion. There was no shortage of land that forced peasants to seek wage employment on the plantations. Every family had access to land in their home areas. It was easier for them to cater for their needs there than it was as wage earners on the plantations, even if housing was provided. The instability of the working conditions on the plantations also contributed to making wage employment unattractive. Workers were often arbitrarily dismissed and during the economic slumps they could easily be laid off. At the time of the great depression the settlers and planters suffered economic ruin. Their production took place firmly within the capitalist sector and responded very directly to the economic crisis.

The crisis in the plantation sector stands in sharp contrast to what happened in the peasant sector. Table 2.1 shows the production for export of coffee and cotton in Bukoba and Mwanza respectively.

Production statistics from the peasant sector are always based only on quantities that pass through the formal channels of marketing. Thus they are never wholly reliable. Even so, it is clear from the table that the peasants are more immune to world market price changes. During the depression when prices slumped their production did not go down. Both Iliffe and Datoo are inclined to see this as a result of their wish to make as much money as before.[25]

In the early days of colonial rule in Tanganyika, the British showed little interest in expanding large-scale agriculture. One reason is likely to have been the problems and subsequent failure of settler agriculture in Uganda in the 1920s.[26] In line with the British policy of indirect rule, therefore, they tried to expand peasant agriculture. In the 1920s and 1930s it was primarily a matter of introducing new crops. This was often done in a haphazard manner with little consideration of the effects on the existing farming systems. Moreover, no effort was made in those days to improve the production techniques. The agriculture extension

TABLE 2.1. Production of coffee in Bukoba and cotton in Mwanza, 1924–34

Year	Bukoba coffee (tons)	Mwanza cotton (lb)
1924	3 535	2 128 694
1925	4 150	2 975 300
1926	4 637	4 290 300
1927	3 943	2 848 000
1928	7 826	2 880 000*
1929	6 794	2 961 602
1930	7 368	3 325 600
1931	6 586	2 604 597
1932	7 111	3 100 000
1933	7 922	6 060 000
1934	10 210	10 585 200

* First year of rail connection to Mwanza, and figures are incomplete.
Source: Tanganyika Agriculture Department Reports, reprinted in Ralph A. Austen, *Northwest Tanzania under German and British Rule: Colonial Policy and Tribal Politics, 1889–1939* (New Haven: Yale University Press, 1968).

service was forced to follow a trial-and-error approach in the absence of reliable research data. While peasants often found no difficulty in adopting new crops, except in those cases where their cultivation was in conflict with the demands of existing production cycles, they were generally more sceptical of the ability of the extension service to offer them advice on how to farm. The prevailing peasant attitude was that by learning from the older generations they became capable of effective farming. In the context of the traditional farming systems this was true. The best instructor was not the science-educated agricultural officer but the father of the peasant. The 'hub-and-wheel' approach of the extension service, that is, one omniscient European agricultural officer surrounded by local assistants totally dependent on his orders, served to reinforce this attitude.[27]

With the introduction of new crops the agricultural officers could secure themselves a niche in the local farming systems that made them more relevant to the peasant. Still there was a limit to how far the peasants would allow the agricultural extension officers to influence their practices. This became apparent as the British began to realize that the introduction of new crops often led to soil erosion, crop diseases, etc. To cope with these problems, the colonial authorities introduced by-laws and regulations that forced the local peasants to adopt new farming practices.

In line with indirect rule, these policies were implemented through the Native Authorities, that is, the chiefs, who were expected to serve as buffers between the colonial authorities and the local population. Because these new regulations were asking the peasants to trade local know-how for knowledge produced by a group of strangers, the colonial policy of improving peasant agriculture became very unpopular. That it was carried out with an element of coercion only reinforced these sentiments. Many chiefs were not very anxious to go along with the British since it was likely to undermine their local legitimacy. Still, they often had no choice. Thus tension began to emerge in the rural areas between the peasants and the authorities. As Ruthenberg shows in his overview of agricultural development in Tanganyika, administrative ordinances were, in the eyes of the British, the proper means to achieve peasant development.[28] Many of the colonial officers believed that the local peasants did not know what was in their best interest.[29] Many peasants engaged in passive resistance and British impatience grew as the quality of peasant agriculture continued to be low. Being captives of their own prejudice that the peasant lacked a perception of what was good for him, the British officers created a political situation over which they gradually began to lose control. Pratt reports that as a result of the colonial policy of agricultural development through coercion some 75 000 persons were convicted before native courts in 1946 alone.[30] Some of the administrative officers were concerned about the effects of the agricultural policies and this produced a conflict in some districts between the generalist administrators and the agricultural officers and a retreat from the most unpopular aspects of the policies.

It was not until the mid-1950s that the British shifted their attitude towards the local peasants and adopted the approach of 'persistent persuasion'.[31] By that time, however, the effects of the earlier policies to improve peasant agriculture in Tanganyika had already changed the political situation in favour of the nationalist movement. The British had set in motion a process over which they lost control. The key actor in this process was the peasant.

Peasant reactions to enforced agricultural change

BUHAYA

As indicated earlier, Buhaya is a coffee-growing area on the western side of Lake Victoria. The crop was traditionally grown together with bananas by the royal clans in the area, but the Germans introduced commercial coffee production among commoners by 1904. Thus the British found an already established system of commercial production based on bananas and coffee existing on an intercropping basis. Throughout the 1920s coffee production kept expanding (see Table 2.1). Most of this was achieved with only a minimum of European assistance. In the latter part of the 1920s, however, there was a growing pressure among European officers to ensure improvement of coffee cultivation techniques, the belief being that without such an improvement diseases could strike the coffee trees of the peasants. This proposal, however, was very unpopular with the local producers as it implied government interference in their farm operations. Having experienced an unprecedented prosperity due to high coffee prices in the 1920s, peasants did not see the cause for alarm. In their view it was a subtle way of getting them into relations of dependence that would enable the local agricultural officials to control their farming. In 1928 the Native Authority had to be pressed by the British to adopt a set of rules making it mandatory for the coffee farmers to adopt new techniques. There is no evidence, however, that the local chiefs actually enforced these rules. Their reluctance created a political issue, which reached the highest levels of colonial administration. Rather than making a confrontation between the Native Authority and the Agriculture Department, the Governor ruled that the issue should be dropped. In justifying his action, Cameron argued that 'the Native is, after all, greater than his coffee.'[32]

Coffee production in Bukoba did not decline during the depression years but continued to rise. In 1935 a record of 10·881 tons of robusta coffee were exported from Bukoba.[33] Peasant autonomy, however, was soon to be threatened again in Bukoba. The colonial administration tried to use the fall in prices as an excuse to achieve more direct control of growing methods. The rules that had been passed earlier were considered inadequate and the administration tried to convince the chiefs to pass new legislation.

To bolster their attempts to modernize agriculture the colonial administration transformed a secondary school – Nyakato Central School – into a coffee training centre. The idea was to train both African staff for local agricultural administration and more enlightened coffee growers. However, the effort backfired. Students failed to report to the training centre, complaining that the curriculum placed too much emphasis on practical agriculture rather than academic work. Nor did it assure the graduates of government employment.[34] In the end the Agriculture Department decided to focus its efforts on the 'progressive' farmers, that is, those who showed a spontaneous interest in improving their practices.

There were a number of such farmers in Bukoba District, many of whom were active members of the local branch of the African Association, a quasi-political organization with the objective of promoting the welfare of the African population.[35] It was dominated by individuals who saw modern education and improved farming as beneficial to the indigenous people. They were hostile to the chiefs whom they saw as standing in the way of progress. The leaders of the African Association, however, were not only satisfied with improved cultivation. They wanted a greater share of the lucrative coffee trade, controlled by expatriate, primarily Asian, businessmen. In 1934 the African Association submitted a request to that effect but it was flatly refused by the administration. The British were primarily interested in 'de-politicizing' the African Association and turning it into a native planters' association. An offer by the Provincial Commissioner, C. MacMahon, of economic support in return for abstention from political intrigues was accepted by a group of AA leaders who agreed to form the Native Growers Association. MacMahon had promised the NGA a loan from the Central Native Treasury to enable the growers to purchase metal hand hullers for basic processing of the coffee. The financial situation of the Treasury, however, ruled out such a loan and the NGA leaders felt that they were being let down by the administration. This feeling was reinforced when in 1935 the Provincial Commissioner refused to accept a request from the NGA that the organization be given a monopoly of the Bukoba coffee trade. MacMahon saw the Africans as producers and accused the two principal leaders of the NGA, Kiiza and Rugizibwa, of being profiteers.[36]

Given the opposition by the chiefs to new coffee rules, the NGA was still the most effective link with the native growers. The provincial administration, therefore, was anxious not to sever the ties with the Association. Keeping that relationship gave them an advantage in negotiations with the Chiefs Council, where only one of the eight local chiefs was really interested in improved coffee cultivation. The British, however, failed to appreciate fully the local tensions, and in 1937 a major political crisis erupted.

The direct cause of this crisis was an attempt by British officers and the chiefs jointly to introduce new coffee rules. The chiefs had reluctantly been talked into accepting the new rules by being promised that coffee inspection, instead of being carried out by Agricultural Department employees, as originally proposed, would be done by supervisors hired by the Native Authorities. The rules which the British agricultural officers considered necessary to prevent disease from affecting the coffee trees planted in the banana groves, allowed the inspectors the right to uproot 'sick' trees and interfere in the local intercropping system by preventing the use of old banana stems for mulching. Since for generations the quality of the soil in the area has been sustained by this form of traditional mulching, the rules posed a threat to the peasants at large. They resisted and even rioted against the colonial administration.[37] As Austen writes about the event: 'To the Haya peasants who demonstrated against these laws and resisted, even to the point of taking up arms, the inspection of their plots, the new regulations represented not only an unwarranted interference with their cash coffee cultivation, but also a positive threat to their subsistence banana crop.'[38] An anonymous peasant wrote to the Provincial Commissioner at the time: 'We do not need to be taught how to grow coffee or banana trees or to stop from growing anything on our *shambas* [plots] or on our soil.'[39]

The events in 1937 were further proof to the British that 'progressive' agricultural policies could not be implemented through the Native Authorities, but even more alarming to them was the stand taken by the AA. Its leaders, who had not joined the NGA, made no secrecy of their opposition to the new rules. Most of the heckling against the chiefs and the colonial officers at the scenes of the various riots was in fact led by AA leaders. The NGA leaders, who by and large accepted the rationale of the British agricultural officers, had no chance of influencing local opinion. The opposition to the new rules was massive among the peasants.[40]

The British had no difficulty in containing the disturbance but its effect was quite extensive. To begin with the British suspended, and later deposed, two of the chiefs who had proved most ineffective during the crisis. All the chiefs in Bukoba District suffered a cut in their personal income[41] and after an investigation of the land tenure rules, their *nyarubanja* holdings were cut by almost a quarter.[42]

There is evidence, however, that the British nevertheless preferred to deal with the local chiefs rather than the leaders of the AA and the NGA. By interfering in the process of selecting new chiefs they tried to assure themselves of getting the most enlightened and effective ruler. They hoped that with the help of more effective chiefs the authority of native administration could be enhanced. This policy was pursued at the cost of collaboration with the progressive elements in the NGA. Some of those in the NGA lost their licence to hull coffee and the experiment with Nyakato School as an agricultural training centre was abandoned by MacMahon in 1939. It was returned to the Education Department to be run as a middle school. Thus, unlike Uganda where the British at that time had turned away from the local chiefs and begun to give support for the commercialization of smallholder farming, in Bukoba (just across the border) the same colonial authority decided to continue supporting the chiefs at the cost of other emerging petty-bourgeois groups.[43]

The AA was unable to play an active role in Bukoba District in the years after the riots. The British had originally thought of deporting its principal spokesmen, but decided to leave them in the district and limit their movements. The riots in Bukoba are significant in that they constituted the first active resistance to colonial rule since the Maji Maji War. The significance of the events in Bukoba lies particularly in the fact that the peasants were the key actors. It was the decision by the ordinary peasants to resist the new rules that forced the British to retreat. Although it did not lead to an immediate strengthening of the AA, the incident set a precedent for subsequent anti-colonial forms of resistance.

KILIMANJARO

Land on the lower slopes of Mount Kilimanjaro and Mount Meru in Tanganyika's Northern Province had been alienated to European settlers already during German rule. The colonial policy did not dispossess the indigenous population of land already under cultivation, but it put an effective brake on their ability to open new farms in the area. The ring of white settlers on the lower slopes intensified the pressures on the land held by the indigenous population. To cope with this situation in the context of the colonial economy they could either seek employment on the settler estates or intensify their production on the existing land holdings.

The British settlers who took over the former German estates after the end of the First World War were anxious to secure cheap labour from the population on the mountains. In Kilimanjaro they were particularly strongly opposed to any policy that encouraged the local peasants to produce cash crops. They had come to appreciate the strength and hard work of their Chagga labourers and they did not want to lose them. Thus, unlike Bukoba, there was no conscious colonial policy to stimulate the cultivation of coffee among the local peasants. The taste of cash-crop production in Kilimanjaro came through the missionaries who encouraged, on a limited scale, the local peasants to grow coffee for sale.

The new crop tended to catch on much quicker than was politically acceptable. The Chagga peasants preferred their autonomy to dependence on the estate owners. Growing coffee for somebody else was not really an option when coffee could be grown for oneself. The presence of the European settlers in the vicinity of the Chagga peasants most probably accelerated the adoption of the new cash-crop. Another reason that also contributed to the rapid expansion of coffee among the peasants was the relative ease with which the coffee trees could be interplanted with bananas. It did not require new land and was not too labour-demanding. The new cash-crop could be incorporated into the existing farming system without any evident disturbance.

Charles Dundas, who was the local District Commissioner in Kilimanjaro in the 1920s, took an immediate liking to the Chagga people and was instrumental in shifting official policy in favour of smallholder production of coffee in the District. The rapid expansion of coffee cultivation that followed in the wake of this decision, however, invited the colonial authorities to take a more direct interest in regulating both production and marketing. Thus a confrontation between peasants and authorities developed also in Kilimanjaro. Unlike Bukoba, however, the conflict centred less around rules regulating production. In Kilimanjaro the crop was new and the British had ensured that the local peasants followed production techniques acceptable to them. Instead the main issue was coffee marketing.

The colonial administration provided the local coffee growers with their own association, Kilimanjaro Native Planters Association, started in 1925 when the British initiated their efforts to promote smallholder cultivation of coffee. The first President of KNPA was the Senior Commissioner in the district administration. The British policy was that all coffee should be sold through the KNPA. By making the growers pay a token membership fee they were expected to stay loyal to the organization. But the peasants, had no vested interest in an organization that had been set up by somebody else and they generally preferred to sell their coffee to whoever offered the best price. In other words, they refused the monopolization of marketing that the British tried to introduce.[44]

Coffee was sold outside the KNPA and the 2 per cent levy to pay for the overheads of the association could not be collected. The financial difficulties were so grave that in 1931 the District Commissioner had to decide whether there was any point of continuing the organization. His recommendation was that the KNPA be registered as a co-operative society according to the new Co-operative Societies Ordinance that was being introduced. This was accepted. KNPA folded and was replaced by Kilimanjaro Native Co-operative Union, the first of its kind in East Africa.

Contrary to most accounts of the KNCU, it must be pointed out that its beginnings were hard. The Chagga peasants remained suspicious of the new organization. They had not been consulted and, in the absence of proper information about its objectives, there were many who believed that it was a conspiracy by the settlers and some of the chiefs to discourage coffee growing on the mountain by lowering the prices of the product. The formation of the KNCU coincided with a drop in coffee prices on the world market and many peasants were prepared to attribute the price decline to actual government intervention. The interesting thing is that the peasants in Kilimanjaro continued to expand production, although prices kept falling as indicated in Table 2.2.[45]

TABLE 2.2. Coffee production statistics for Kilimanjaro District, 1932–36

	1932/33	1933/34	1934/35	1935/36
Cents paid per lb	29	27	20	15
Crops (in 100 tons)	10–11	11–12	16	18
£1000s paid to growers	over 35	over 35	over 35	30
Growers (1000s)	12–13	16–17	18–19	21–22
Coffee trees (millions)	4–5	5–6	7–8	9–10

The table suggests that the increase in production was principally achieved through an expansion of coffee cultivation to new growers. The number of growers, like that of coffee trees, nearly doubled during the four-year period covered in the table. Iliffe's and Datoo's point that peasants produced more to maintain their income loses much of its validity.[46] There is little evidence that the peasant growers individually responded very significantly to the price fall. The main issue in Kilimanjaro at the time was the new co-operative. The petty-capitalist growers, in particular, saw it as a disadvantage to be compelled to sell through the KNCU where a uniform government price was offered. This became particularly evident in 1935 when it was rumoured that there would be no final payment to the members.[47] The KNCU management refused to make an official statement on the matter fearing that it might discourage farmers from selling to the co-operatives. Suspicion rose high and led to a riot in 1936, and a court case in which a group of coffee growers questioned the legality of the rule, passed by the Native Authority, that all coffee should be sold through the KNCU. The aggrieved coffee growers maintained that as they could grow their coffee without the aid of the chiefs and the co-operative society, they should also have the right to sell it on the market through competition rather than through the government-controlled co-operatives. The court did not support the petitioners and the outcome of the case reinforced the belief among the peasants that their chiefs were closely aligned with the colonial administration.

Many of the incumbent Chagga chiefs were discredited as a result of their close collaboration with the British. This sentiment grew stronger as land shortage among the indigenous population became a sensitive issue. It took on particular importance after the Second World War when a Commission was appointed to look into what to do with the 'enemy' (former German) property.[48] German settlers had been reinvited in the inter-war years but chased out of Tanganyika at the inception of the Second World War. In 1946 the Chagga people were advocating a return of some of the alienated land to them. The Commission also recommended the return to them of land previously occupied by German settlers. It even proposed the return of some land alienated to the church missions.[49] The implementation of the recommendations contained in the Commission report did not satisfy the Chagga people. Most of the good land was given to European settlers while the local people were offered expansion on the dry plains below the mountain.

The land issue in Kilimanjaro remained essentially a local political issue. It divided the Chagga people into different political organizations, some trying to settle their grievances by co-operating with other nationalist groups, others attempting to achieve the same thing through the establishment of a paramount chief.[50] The Chagga people did not, like the Meru people, take their land case to the United Nations.[51] In the case of the demands of both these tribal groups, however, the British never yielded. They believed that the settlers made more productive use of the land than the indigenous people and viewed their problem rather in terms of resettlement.

The introduction of modern techniques was facilitated in Kilimanjaro by the fact that coffee was a new crop and that coffee cultivation was so much more attractive than working on the settler estates. Thus, even if coffee growing meant more work, 'self-exploitation' was far more acceptable to the Chagga peasants than exploitation by capitalist farmers. Chagga incorporation into the world capitalist system was not even, but in comparison to most other tribes in Tanganyika, it was more extensive. This was largely achieved during the colonial period due to the introduction of modern small-scale farming in competition with large-scale farming. The creation of estates accelerated the pressures on the land in Kilimanjaro and forced the Chagga peasants to be more outward-looking. They were generally more open to advice concerning modern farming. They were more inclined to move outside the agricultural sector in pursuit of a career. To some extent, this entrepreneurialism was the product of the indigenous social system among the Chagga people. Increasing land shortage and settler competition reinforced this orientation. Nowhere in Tanganyika was petty-capitalism more easily developed than among the Chagga people.

SUKUMALAND

Ever since the Germans colonized Tanganyika cotton had been considered the most suitable agricultural crop for the lands east and south of Lake Victoria. However, attempts by the Germans to establish large-scale cotton farms had failed. Efforts by Gunzert, the *Bezirksamtmann* in Mwanza from 1906 to the German capitulation in 1916, to spread cotton (and peanut) cultivation among African small-holders had also been unsuccessful. Drought and ineffective supervision by the local chiefs had contributed to this. Unlike Bukoba where the chiefs had a fairly close relation to each village, in Sukumaland the system of land holding and labour distribution gave the villages a large measure of autonomy vis-à-vis any political authority.[52] Gunzert's use of military personnel to enforce cotton cultivation led to an increase in production but did not make the local peasant more inclined to adopt the new crop on a permanent basis. Thus when the British took over administration they had to start anew.

Sukumaland, the area south of Lake Victoria, is large, but in the colonial days vast stretches of land were uninhabitable because of tsetse flies. In pre-colonial days when the balance between man and nature appears to have been more favourable, there was no real shortage of usable land.[53] This became an issue in the 1920s and 1930s when, in addition, modern medicine helped to improve not only human health

but also that of domestic animals. The Sukuma people have traditionally kept herds of cattle. In the 1920s it was becoming clear to the British
that it was only by reclaiming land through anti-tsetse campaigns that
cattle-herding and agricultural production could continue to coexist.
The British also tried to convince the Sukuma to sell off some of their
cattle – largely to prevent soil erosion – but this proposal met with
immediate resistance from the local chiefs. While the policy to open up
new land met with positive response, any scheme to control livestock
was instantly rejected.[54]

Although cotton continued to be the main crop in Sukumaland
throughout the inter-war period, there was very little that the British did
to alter the parameters of the farming system. If the area had been
relatively ignored during all these years in favour of development
programmes in Bukoba and Kilimanjaro, the main thrust of colonial
agricultural policies after the Second World War was directed towards
Sukumaland. Soil erosion and pressure on the land had grown to
become such big problems that, according to some colonial administrators, only through a more comprehensive effort could it be solved.
The colonial administrators began to plan the Sukumaland
Development Scheme, a predecessor to the many 'integrated' development programmes that occupy rural administrators in Third World
countries today. Experiments in local government went hand-in-hand
with resettlement of people on new land and the introduction of new
production techniques. In short, the scheme was designed to maximize
the possibilities for productive use of the land by redistribution of what
appeared to be surplus populations of people and livestock. A population density of 100 per square mile was seen as critical in order to
allow for a rational and consistent use of the land for both cultivation
and animal husbandry.[55]

A pyramid of representative councils, all brought together under the
Sukumaland Federal Council, was created, but it soon became an issue
as to how far democracy was practical in the context of the scheme's
economic objectives. The most influential person within the scheme, N.
V. Rounce, firmly believed that compulsion was necessary. His prime
concern was agricultural improvement and he pleaded for an understanding by his colleagues of the fact that 'in place of the stress which
forces Europeans to do things, the African must be compelled – and
forcibly too – to improve the conditions under which he lives, with his
own hands.'[56]

Rounce and those who shared his belief in compulsion found little
support for their views in Dar es Salaam. The senior administrators
there did not agree to any legislation that would permit the forcible
removal of people from overpopulated areas. Rounce, however, could
take pleasure in the fact that there already existed in Sukumaland
legislation of various sorts that required peasant farmers to improve
their agriculture. Thus the local administrators did not need the support

of Dar es Salaam. Rounce, and some of the other administrators involved in the scheme, believed that they could achieve what they wanted by depending on existing legislation and the support of the chiefs.[54] The colonial administration decided to use the Native Authorities as much as possible, hoping that they possessed a greater measure of legitimacy than themselves. What the British did not sufficiently consider, however, was the fact that with the implementation of the scheme's policies, the Native Authorities and their laws came increasingly under attack from the peasants. The interference in their farming system became too much to accept. In addition, they had to pay local hut tax, cattle tax and a levy on the cotton they were selling. The Sukuma peasants did not riot like they did in Bukoba and Kilimanjaro. They did not have to because local administration could not cope with the legislation and its necessary supervision. Therefore, Sukuma peasants conveniently ignored many of the regulations. They had good reason for doing so. As Collinson notes in his study of the Sukuma farming system, the mark of a sound farm manager is flexibility, particularly in the use of labour.[58] The unfavourable consequences of rain and other such factors have long since taught the Sukuma peasant to take one day at a time. The day-to-day management of the labour force is the key feature of that farming system and it is only by adapting the use of it to the situation of the day that he stands a reasonable chance of success. He does not see any reason to follow administrative or political decrees obliging him, for example, to observe 'correct planting times'.

In the early 1950s, as Maguire points out, Sukumaland was overlegislated and over-regulated.[59] Pratt mentions that there were over fifty different orders on an extraordinarily diverse range of matters, which included the eradication of witch-weed and periwinkle, the provision of ten days free labour a year on public works, the forbidding of the use of the hoe to decorate houses, except by chiefs, and the control of disorderly conduct.[60] This is certainly how the local peasants experienced the situation. Even some of the British officials shared this view, although their main concern was its impact on the system of indirect rule. The local councils simply could not carry the administrative burden that the Sukumaland Development Scheme imposed on them. However, at least one of the administrative officers at the time, Peter McLoughlin, admitted that the Sukuma resistance to the content of specific measures, as well as to methods of enforcement, was inspired by rational consideration and not ignorance as the conventional view in colonial circles suggested.[61]

On balance, it would be wrong to write off the Sukumaland Development Scheme as a failure. In fact, in some respects it was successful. It stabilized the population of central Sukumaland, enabled approximately 30 000 people to resettle in the neighbouring Geita District over a period of five years and permitted a fivefold increase in cotton output between 1947 and 1961. The production increases, however, were primarily achieved through extending the acreage under cotton cultivation rather than any changes in the farming systems. The intensification of agriculture was only marginal and, as Iliffe notes, there was an obvious contradiction in attempting simultaneously to intensify agriculture and open up new land in Sukumaland, since only the pressure of land shortage could make intensive agriculture worth while.[62] The opening of a new frontier of Sukuma expansion in Geita District meant that there was not the same pressure to accept new cultivation techniques.

The British were not very successful in achieving their objective of more effective livestock control. Liebenow discusses how peasant reaction to cattle destocking undermined the legitimacy of the native authorities charged with the responsibility to implement that programme.[63] Maguire relates the so-called 'battle of Simiyu', an incident when a European veterinary officer created a riot by compelling people to inoculate their cattle against rinderpest.[64]

There were other expressions of primary resistance in many parts of Sukumaland, although the main issue in the early 1950s was the marketing of cotton. It was dominated by Asian traders, who controlled both marketing and ginning. It was the relative effectiveness of this system rather than its ineffectiveness that made it a political issue. The British, particularly during the Second World War, had taken steps to ensure regular supplies of cotton. To avoid discouragement among the local growers, the Asian middlemen had been encouraged to set up buying points so that no grower had more than a maximum of five miles to the nearest market outlet. The local peasant farmers believed that they were exploited by the traders who, among other things, were said to cheat when weighing the cotton. There were also some petty-capitalist farmers who believed that marketing and ginning should be in African hands. To achieve their objective they formed a network of co-operative societies, partly inspired by the success of such organizations in Uganda. Unlike Kilimanjaro where the co-operative solution met with initial resistance from the wealthier farmers, in Sukumaland the same class of farmers seized upon it as the most appropriate instrument. They had the business experience to compete with the Asians. It was inevitable that the leaders of the Sukumaland co-operatives were not only good farmers but also good businessmen. The challenge of the co-operatives lay in marketing. As long as the co-operatives were able to reduce cheating and their business was growing, peasants gave their co-operative leaders unreserved support. In 1953, 13 per cent of the crop was purchased by the co-operatives. In 1956 the percentage amounted to two-thirds of the crop and in 1959 they obtained a monopoly for the purchase of cotton from growers.[65] The Victoria Federation of Co-operative Unions (VFCU) became the single largest co-operative organization on the continent of Africa.

There were other factors that supported the growth of the co-operative movement in Sukumaland. If the wealthier farmers provided the leadership in part to achieve their own ends, the ordinary peasant farmers had their own reasons to join the co-operative movement. Primary among these was a widespread feeling that the production of cotton did not benefit them enough.[66] Cotton was necessary to produce textiles but it was not easy for the Sukuma people to afford good clothing, and clothing is a basic need. Thus in this area the incorporation of the peasants into the world capitalist system raised their consciousness. They really felt deprived. Such sentiments did not develop in the coffee-growing areas, because coffee never became a popular local drink in the rural areas. There the cultivation of cash crops provided an opportunity to improve living without too much extra effort. In Sukumaland, by contrast, peasants felt that they got very little out of the labour-intensive cultivation of cotton. In no other area of Tanganyika were the anti-colonial sentiments so directly influenced by a sense of economic exploitation as they were in Sukumaland. The nature of the crop, the intensive marketing systems, dominated by non-African traders, and the general arrogance of the colonial administration, were all factors that made the area a hotbed of nationalism in Tanganyika.

OTHER AREAS

Peasant reaction to colonial agricultural policies was very similar in other areas. In Handeni District in Tanga Region both Germans and British had tried to introduce cotton cultivation, but the efforts had been largely in vain. One study of these programmes concludes:

> Cotton was grown in the years when either they were forced to as during the Second World War or when extensive cotton growing campaigns were carried on. During these 'pressure' periods production in the District increased and when the pressure was removed, production fell.[67]

The peasants in Handeni used their 'exit' option as soon as they could and the district never became a cotton-growing area. Available production statistics suggest that the peasants did not want to give up their concern with subsistence production for the uncertainties of cotton-growing.[68] In Handeni the colonial administration also engaged in regulating food crop production. The local preference was maize growing. In good years when there was a surplus, some of it could be sold to the workers on the nearby sisal plantations. The crop, however, was not drought-resistant and consequently famine was a recurrent phenomenon in the District. The British began to enforce the production of drought-resistant crops, notably cassava.[69] Handeni peasants, however, resisted growing it because they knew its flour was much less nutritious than maize flour. According to local tradition, eating cassava flour could cause sterility. They were also reluctant to grow the crop because it entailed more labour, notably to watch against vermin. In the case of maize, and sorghum, guarding against vermin was limited to a relatively short period, but with cassava it had to go on for months.[70] Cassava cultivation, therefore, was taxing on the peasant labour.

Because of peasant default in growing cassava, the British decided in 1949 that famine relief should only be supplied to those who had no means of producing on their own because of age or sickness or any other unexpected incapacity. All other persons were expected to pay in cash or supply labour free to compensate for the costs of the famine relief. Although this was not the official objective, it seems clear that the British laboured under the assumption that there were many lazy peasants who rather than growing food turned to the government for it. They were unwilling to admit that, in the light of their own policies, it was quite rational for the peasant to avoid growing cassava.

A primary concern of the British in the early 1950s was erosion control. While in earlier years the introduction of new crops had preoccupied the colonial administration, the 1950s saw an increasing concern with the problem of conserving available natural resources. As Ruthenberg notes, the belief of the time was that 'the health and the vigour of a nation depends on the health and vigour of its soil.'[71] In the Usambara Mountains in Tanga Region the colonial administration introduced a set of ordinances that made it compulsory for the peasants to: keep cattle only in stables; graze cattle only on flat land; not cultivate slopes exceeding 25 per cent; use slopes of less than 25 per cent only with ridging; refuse to burn weeds and crop refuse; plant elephant grass as a fodder crop; transport cow manure to the fields; plant elephant grass, sugar cane or bananas on a five-yard strip on both sides of all watercourses; irrigate only on flat land; and plant trees on steep or eroded slopes. Although extension officers were available to advise the peasants, policy implementation was usually forced on the peasants by administrative measures. In 1954 a total of 45 000 acres were ridged or terraced. The peasants, however, refused to go along any further. In subsequent years the administrative measures became more and more unpopular and after increasing unrest they had to be suspended in 1957.[72] Today only occasional remnants of the efforts to terrace and ridge remain. The only lasting improvement was the financially advantageous cultivation of bananas on steep slopes.

The erosion control measures that were introduced in the Uluguru Mountains in Morogoro District were equally controversial. They were ostensibly introduced to save the water flow off the mountains from what, in the view of one government report, constituted soil- and forest-destroying practices by the local peasants.[73] A government scheme was initiated in 1949 to improve land use, preserve and expand forests and stabilize the flow of water. After a few successful pilot schemes it was decided to introduce the measures all across the mountains. From 1950 to 1952 about 900 000 yards were terraced. From January to October 1954, a total of eleven million yards of terracing were completed.[74] Government reports hailed the efforts as successful.

By 1954, however, peasant resistance grew rapidly and culminated in a riot in 1955. Their main grievance was that terracing reduced their yields, a contention which in the short-term perspective of the peasant was quite correct. Consequently they only terraced the most infertile slopes. To get them to terrace the more fertile land, compulsion was necessary. Government officers forced them to work two to three days a week for something which peasants saw as reducing their incomes. In some cases they avoided it by bribing the officials, but the pressure on the peasants was sufficient to raise anger. The peasants also resisted the proposal that they stop burning crop refuse, an old custom in the mountains. Instead crop refuse was to be used for reinforcing soil fertility. This went against peasant rationality because they had learnt by experience that maize-borers breed in maize straws and damage the next crop. The British also tried to get peasants to use spades instead of hoes, which proved an unsuitable tool for terracing. Not all peasants, however, had shoes and the British had not invented a spade for bare-footers.

The latent discontent erupted into open riot when it was rumoured that the ultimate aim of the colonial administration was to force the peasants to settle on the plains below the mountains. Local politicians who had lived a timid existence in the shadow of the colonial administration seized the opportunity to propagate their case for freedom. One of the messages was that an African government would restore 'the ease of the old life'.[75] After widespread demonstrations, police were called in and one political organizer was shot to death. The most drastic effect of the riots, however, was the discontinuation of terracing. Those terraces which had already been completed were wilfully destroyed. Throughout the mountains bush fires burned as a symbol of protest. The Uluguru scheme ground to a complete halt. Trust in government had been seriously shaken and was not repaired by the demotion of the Agricultural Officers and Instructors in Morogoro to policemen.[76]

Colonial attempts at capitalist farming

In the early years of indirect rule the 'welfare of the native' had been reasonably well protected, albeit in a highly paternalistic fashion. In the 1950s it was becoming increasingly clear that the productive use of the land was the guiding policy principle. Peasant farming had proved difficult to develop in Tanganyika and many believed that it was time to try something different.

The first comprehensive effort by the British to launch new types of large-scale farming in the colony – the Groundnut Scheme – was a total failure. Initiated by the British Government in the belief that the food-oil shortage in post-war Britain could be solved by a massive scheme of mechanized cultivation of groundnuts in various parts of Tanganyika and other African colonies, large areas of land in the central and southern parts of the colony were opened up. Alas for the local peasants who had been recruited to work on these plantations, poor planning (particularly of soil conditions), unpredictable weather, and even the obstinacy of the baobab tree, contributed to doom the Groundnut Scheme to failure. Four years after its inception it was abandoned in 1951.[77]

Some of the land abandoned by the Groundnut Scheme became the beginnings of large-scale capitalist farming of other crops. In Urambo in western Tanganyika, tobacco was successfully introduced as a commercial crop and several capitalist farmers established themselves in the area. In Kongwa in the central part of the country, cattle ranches were set up to compensate for the failure of the Groundnut Scheme. Even in Nachingwea in southern Tanganyika, some large-scale capitalist farming began in the wake of the Groundnut Scheme.

Most of the surplus grain in the colony was by the 1950s produced on large-scale farms in the northern highlands, particularly in west Kilimanjaro and Mbulu, where wheat was successfully grown. In the Ismani area of Iringa, large-scale farming of maize developed rapidly in the 1950s and became the principal source of supply of maize for the growing urban populations.[78]

Settler agriculture had continued and even received a boost immediately after the end of the Second World War when retired military personnel came to settle in East Africa. The colonial government believed that the settlers were better equipped to use the land effectively than the local peasants. This led to a confrontation in Arusha where peasant farmers on the slopes of Mount Meru believed that the estates confiscated from German settlers who were forced to leave the colony at the outbreak of the Second World War should be given to them rather than to new immigrant settlers. The local population were also hostile to a government proposal to resettle Meru farmers in an area believed to be far less fertile than the land occupied by the settler estates. This led to the Meru Land Case which, although the Meru people were not very successful in changing government policies, served as a catalyst of anti-colonial sentiments in the area.[79]

Despite this expansion of capitalist farming in Tanganyika during the 1950s, it never became as prominent as in Kenya. It changed the parameters of social and economic action in adjacent peasant communities, but there is no evidence that it marginalized the peasants. If anything, the challenge of capitalist farming nearby served to make the local peasants improve their own cultivation. This is certainly true of both the Meru and the Chagga peoples where the adoption of

modern techniques of production was less problematic than in many
other parts of the country.

Peasant intractability and political independence

Since land alienation in Tanganyika never had the same dislocational
effects on peasant agriculture as it had in Kenya, the principal
confrontations were between the authorities and the smallholder
peasants on issues relating to the behaviour of the peasants. British
agricultural policy in Tanganyika was for a long time characterized by
failure to consider the intractability of the local soils. As Maguire notes,
this was one of the main reasons for the failure of the Groundnut
Scheme.[80] However, when the British became more concerned with the
soil question and began to treat it with care, they failed sufficiently to
allow for the intractability of the peasants. The latter refused to go
along with the colonial policies, either because they were invalid and
thus government action was reduced to a show of arrogance, or because
they implied a potential threat to the welfare of the peasant household.
Particularly objectionable were policies that aimed at regulating the use
of peasant labour time.

It would be wrong to view this peasant resistance as expressions of
their 'traditionalism' or 'laziness'. To be sure, there are peasants who
may be labelled traditional or lazy but the problem of rural
development in Africa is not adequately tackled along such lines. It is
important to accept that within the structural constraints of the peasant
mode of production, their behaviour is rational and quite
comprehensible. The agricultural policies pursued by the British often
did not make sense in the context of the resource-based peasant
agriculture in Tanganyika. The introduction of new production
techniques, moreover, threatened the local farming systems and
indirectly, therefore, the fulcrum of peasant autonomy. As Terence
Ranger has noted, all over Africa 'primary' resistance to colonial rule
centred around this issue. The widespread nature of these resistance
movements was clearly an important factor for the development of
nationalist party organizations.[81] It is true that spontaneous resistance
did not take place everywhere, but as Lionel Cliffe notes with reference
to Tanganyika, even in those districts where there was no organization
to channel peasant sentiments, there was a broad undercurrent of
resentment.[82] As he concludes, enforced agricultural change in
Tanganyika led to a crisis in colonial rule. The peasants thoroughly
disliked the idea, implicit in the British approach, that the fruits of
modern society could only be obtained by accepting the operational
premises of the capitalist mode of production. There is no better
evidence of the conflict between the latter and the peasant mode than
the incidents of primary resistance in the colonial period. The peasants

wanted access to modern goods and services without sacrificing the
economy of affection. This became increasingly unacceptable to the
British, when in the 1940s and 1950s they had to increase agricultural
productivity, largely as a means to finance expansion of education and
welfare facilities. The limits of the material base of the peasant mode
were becoming clearly visible as the British continued to push the idea
of the economic self-sufficiency of each colonial territory. Increased
self-reliance, however, would only be possible with a transformation of
the peasant mode of production. In this respect, the British had failed.
The incidents of primary resistance gave the emerging African petty-
bourgeoisie, who had largely accepted the development terms set by the
British but who had not totally defected from the economy of affection,
an opportunity to reduce their dependence on the colonial rulers. The
peasants provided an active base for anti-colonial resistance and an
increasing number of bourgeois leaders tried to capitalize on it. The
growth of Tanganyika African National Union (TANU) as a rural
mass organization in the latter part of the 1950s can only be understood
in such terms.

The most intensive efforts at enforcing agricultural change in
Tanganyika coincided, somewhat paradoxically, with the British plan
to initiate representative local government. This meant, on the one
hand, that the British provided institutional channels for African
grievances over their rule and, on the other, that they were able to
contain the expression of these grievances. The political message of
TANU was becoming increasingly populist and in the intelligent
interpretation of Julius Nyerere, the President of TANU, increasingly
convincing. His analysis of the indigenous peasant society made sense
not only to his local supporters but eventually also to many of his
colonial overlords. The fact that Nyerere was agreeable to playing the
political game along lines familiar to the British contributed to paving
the way for self-government and, eventually, full political independence
for Tanganyika in December 1961.

The peasants provided the base for the emergence of TANU and its
leadership skilfully used the colonial system to achieve its political
objectives. It would be wrong, however, to deny the fact that the British
colonial administration also tried to use TANU to secure some of its
ends. This became increasingly true in the latter part of the 1950s, as
Pratt's close account of the political negotiations leading to
independence suggests.[83] At least part of the TANU leadership,
including Nyerere himself, were quite close to the more liberal-minded
colonial officials. There was enough rapport to allow for a certain
amount of give-and-take in the political negotiations.

Particularly important is what happened in the field of agricultural
improvement. In spite of denouncements of enforced agricultural
change by individual politicians, TANU as an organization never
expressed any objections to the policies aimed at changing peasant

agriculture. This may in part be explained by a change in attitude by the British in the mid-1950s. Rather than relying on force they came increasingly to apply the principle of 'persistent persuasion'. The effect of this was essentially to benefit those who showed interest. Those with interest in modernizing their farming, and those who could afford it, were the 'progressive', petty-capitalist farmers. Many of these were also in leading positions in the co-operative movement and in TANU. They did not hesitate to take advantage of this new approach to agricultural improvement. Thus, TANU's stand on the issue must also be seen as reflecting the interests of its leaders. The ordinary peasant farmers, however, were only marginally affected by the 'persistent persuasion' approach. To them the issue was more complex than just a shift away from coercion. That became increasingly clear in the post-independence years.

References and notes

1. There is still much controversy over the principal pre-colonial patterns of history in East Africa. Helge Kjekshus, *Ecology Control and Economic Development in East African History* (Heinemann Educational Books, 1977) provides the most comprehensive review of the historical documents dealing with the nature of the pre-colonial economies.
2. John Ford, *The Role of Trypanosomiasis in African Ecology* (Oxford: Clarendon Press, 1971) and Kjekshus, op. cit.
3. Kjekshus, op. cit., p. 181.
4. Sir Charles Eliot, 'Report by His Majesty's Commissioner on the East African Protectorate', dated 18 April, 1903, Africa no. 6, cd 1626 (HMSO, 1903).
5. Franz Stuhlmann, *Deutsch-Ostafrika: Mit Emin Pasha ins Herz von Afrika* (Berlin: D. Reimer, 1894), p. 238.
6. V. Kollmann, *The Victoria Nyanza* (Swann, 1899), p. 48.
7. Kjekshus, op. cit., pp. 127–32.
8. Ford, op. cit., p. 138 and Israel K. Katoke, 'A History of Karagwe: Northwest Tanzania from circa AD 1400–1915', Ph.D. dissertation, Boston University, 1971.
9. M. Becker, *Über Bahuban in Deutsch-Ostafrika*, quoted in Kjekshus, op. cit., p. 134.
10. Ralph A. Austen, *Northwest Tanzania under German and British Rule: Colonial Policy and Tribal Politics, 1889–1939* (New Haven: Yale University Press, 1968), especially Chapters 3 and 4.
11. John Iliffe, *Tanganyika under German Rule 1905–1912* (Cambridge University Press, 1969), p. 16.
12. Kathleen M. Stahl, *History of the Chagga People of Kilimanjaro* (The Hague: Mouton, 1964).
13. For an overview of the colonial economic policies in the three East African territories, see E. A. Brett, *Colonialism and Underdevelopment in East Africa* (Oxford University Press, 1972). Lionel Cliffe traces the implications of these policies for rural class formation; see his article

'Rural class formation in East Africa', *Journal of Peasant Studies*, vol. 4, no. 2 (1977), pp. 195–224.
14. Iliffe, op. cit., pp. 22–3.
15. J. Gus Liebenow, *Colonial Rule and Political Development in Tanzania: The Case of the Makonde* (Evanston: Northwestern University Press, 1971), p. 81.
16. Austen, op. cit., p. 54.
17. Iliffe, op. cit., Chapter 4.
18. John Iliffe, *Agricultural Change in Modern Tanganyika*, Historical Association of Tanzania Paper No. 10 (Nairobi: East African Publishing House, 1971), p. 14.
19. Austen, op. cit., pp. 95–6.
20. Iliffe, *Tanganyika under German Rule*, op. cit., Chapter 3.
21. Quoted in R. F. Eberlie, 'The German achievement in East Africa', *Tanganyika Notes and Records*, vol. 55 (September 1960), p. 193.
22. The view of the Commission was that the subsistence farmer is a social parasite because unlike other social groups he does not make a contribution to the development of the economy of the colony. See Mahmood Mamdani, *Politics and Class Formation in Uganda* (New York: Monthly Review Press, 1976).
23. Hans Ruthenberg, *Agricultural Development in Tanganyika*, IFO-Institut Afrika-Studien No. 2 (Berlin: Springer-Verlag, 1964), p. 14.
24. ibid., pp. 15–16.
25. Iliffe, *Agricultural Change*, op. cit., p. 29 and Bashir A. Datoo, 'Peasant agricultural production in East Africa: the nature and consequence of dependence', mimeo., Department of Geography, University of Dar es Salaam, 1976.
26. Mamdani, op. cit. and Cliffe, op. cit.
27. See Jon Moris, 'Managerial structures and plan implementation in colonial and modern agricultural extension', in David K. Leonard (ed.), *Rural Administration in Kenya* (Nairobi: East African Literature Bureau, 1973), pp. 97–131.
28. Ruthenberg, op. cit., pp. 48–59.
29. For a review of British efforts to gain peasant compliance, see Dean E. McHenry Jr., 'Gaining peasant compliance: the colonial government's implementation of policies affecting rural Tanganyika,' mimeo., University of Dar es Salaam, 1974.
30. Cranford Pratt, *The Critical Phase in Tanzania 1945–1968* (Cambridge University Press, 1976), p. 25.
31. Ruthenberg, op. cit.
32. Austen, op. cit., p. 176.
33. T. S. Jervis, 'Bukoba coffee: inspection and grading', in Bukoba District Book (District Office, Bukoba, 1936).
34. Austen, op. cit., pp. 221–2.
35. The activities of the African Association are further discussed by George Bennett, 'An outline history of TANU', *Makerere Journal*, no. 7, (1963) pp. 15–32, and also by the present author, with specific reference to Bukoba, in *Political Development in Rural Tanzania: A West Lake Study* (Nairobi: East African Publishing House, 1969).
36. Interview with Herbert Rugizibwa, Bukoba, 23 February, 1965; see also Austen, op. cit., pp. 216–32.

37. See Lionel Cliffe, 'Nationalism and the reaction to enforced agricultural change in Tanganyika during the colonial period', paper presented to the East African Institute of Social Research Conference, Kampala, December 1964.
38. Austen, op. cit., p. 225.
39. Letter from anonymous peasant to the Provincial Commissioner, February 1937, Mwanza Provincial Minute Papers.
40. Interview with Suedi Kagasheki, Bukoba, 12 June 1965.
41. It is worth noting that Chief Kalemera of Kianja chiefdom in Bukoba District was the highest paid official in Tanganyika with the exception of the Governor.
42. Gelase Mutahaba, 'The importance of peasant consciousness for effective land tenure reform', undergraduate dissertation, Department of Political Science, University of Dar es Salaam, 1969.
43. cf. Austen, op. cit., and Mamdani, op. cit.
44. Oliver J. Maruma, 'Chagga politics: 1930–1952', undergraduate dissertation, Department of Political Science, University of Dar es Salaam, 1969.
45. ibid. p. 9.
46. cf. note 25.
47. According to the system, farmers are usually paid twice, first when they sell their coffee to the marketing organization and the second time when the coffee has been sold on the world market and the official price is known. The first payment is calculated in such a way as to ensure, under normal circumstances, a second payment. In 1935, however, the price dropped so drastically that a second payment could not be made.
48. The Commission's findings were published as *Report of the Arusha-Moshi Land Commission* (Dar es Salaam: Government Printer, 1947).
49. Stahl, op. cit. and Maruma, op. cit.
50. Basil Mramba, 'Kilimanjaro: Chagga readjustment to nationalism', paper presented to the East African Institute of Social Research Conference, Kampala, December 1966.
51. Kirilo Japhet and Earle Seaton, *The Meru Land Case* (Nairobi: East African Publishing House, 1967).
52. Austen, op. cit., pp. 83–108.
53. Kjekshus, op. cit.
54. M. K. McCall, 'Peasant rationality under imperialism: the case of Usukuma', paper presented to the 12th Annual Social Science Conference of East African Universities, Dar es Salaam, December 1976.
55. G. Andrew Maguire, *Toward 'Uhuru' in Tanzania: The Politics of Participation* (Cambridge University Press, 1969), pp. 27–8.
56. Quoted by Ruthenberg, op. cit., p. 50.
57. Maguire, op. cit., p. 30.
58. M. P. Collinson, 'The economic characteristics of the Sukuma farming system', Economic Research Bureau Paper 72.5, University of Dar es Salaam, 1972, p. 12.
59. Maguire, op. cit., p. 31.
60. Pratt, op. cit., p. 26.
61. Peter F. M. McLoughlin, 'Some aspects of Sukumaland's economic development problem', paper presented to the Sukumaland Research Conference, Philadelphia, Pa., October 1965.
62. Iliffe, *Agricultural Change*, op. cit., p. 36.

63. J. Gus Liebenow, 'Responses to planned political change in a Tanganyika tribal group', *American Political Science Review*, vol. 50 (June 1962), pp. 442–61.
64. Maguire, op. cit., pp. 253–6.
65. Ruthenberg, op. cit., p. 58.
66. Stuhlmann reported already in 1894 that 'the Wasukuma are interested in progress. They love European goods, in particular textiles.' Stuhlmann, op. cit., p. 187.
67. Suleman Sumra, 'A history of agriculture in Handeni District up to 1961', mimeo., Department of History, University of Dar es Salaam, 1974.
68. Crop statistics presented by Sumra show that cotton production between 1923 and 1973 varied considerably from one year to another with tops recorded in 1938/39 (1089 tons), in 1940/41 (1007 tons) and 1965 (1014 tons). For many years the production was below 100 tons, including all years after 1967.
69. Clyde R. Ingle, *From Village to State in Tanzania: The Politics of Rural Development* (Ithaca: Cornell University Press, 1972), p. 47.
70. Sumra, op. cit., p. 11.
71. Ruthenberg, op. cit., p. 52.
72. ibid., pp. 52–3.
73. Roland Young and Henry A. Fosbrooke, *Smoke in the Hills: Political Tension in the Morogoro District of Tanganyika* (Evanston: Northwestern University Press, 1960), pp. 141–7.
74. ibid., p. 150.
75. Ruthenberg, op. cit., pp. 53–4.
76. ibid., p. 54.
77. Alan Wood, *The Groundnut Affair* (Bodley Head, 1950).
78. Ruthenberg, op. cit.
79. Japhet and Seaton, op. cit.
80. Maguire, op. cit., p. 39.
81. Terence O. Ranger, 'Connections between "primary resistance" movements and modern mass nationalism in East and Central Africa', paper presented to the East African Institute of Social Research Conference, Kampala, December 1966.
82. Cliffe, 'Nationalism and the reaction', op. cit.
83. Pratt, op. cit., pp. 11–59.

CHAPTER 3

Big slips on small:
peasant agriculture after *uhuru*

In the struggle for independence – *uhuru* – in Tanganyika there had been general agreement that the colonial policies which were aimed at interfering with the local peasant economies were unacceptable. Opposition to these policies had provided much of the cement holding the nationalist movement together. As the struggle eventually turned into negotiations about the transition of power from the British to an independent government, signs of cracks in the unity became apparent. Some political leaders in TANU – and others outside it – saw some of Nyerere's proposals, notably his insistence on a multiracial Tanganyika after independence, as political sell-outs.[1] These leaders linked their general grievance to local issues and tried to mobilize opposition to TANU by manipulating grass-root suspicion of what the new government might do. Particularly in areas like Buhaya, Kilimanjaro and Sukumaland, where changes in the colonial period had intensified social cleavages, local opposition continued into the immediate post-independence years in spite of TANU's resounding victory at the polls in 1960.[2]

No issue was more important in keeping the opposition alive in those days than the decision by the new government in 1962 to nationalize all land, that is, to make the state the ultimate trustee of all land and rule out individual freeholding. Local opposition leaders, many of whom were petty-capitalist farmers, were not late to capitalize on peasant suspicion that their plots might eventually be taken over by the government and they themselves reduced to workers. This forced the new TANU Government on the defensive: government leaders had to tour the country in order to dispel the opposition charges and persuade the rural masses that TANU was really sincere about its promise of a new order. Some of the local opposition leaders were detained or deported from their home areas. By 1965, organized opposition in the rural areas had totally vanished.[3] In the meantime, rather than enforcing change within the existing farming systems, the new government concentrated its efforts on the establishment of new settlements.

The transformation approach

The transition to independence in Tanganyika coincided with a visit by a World Bank Mission entrusted to look into the future of the country's economy. For the agricultural sector the Mission recommended in its report, submitted in 1960, that more intensive use of the land on a sustainable basis was necessary. Promotion of that aim, however, could not be achieved solely by improving existing farming systems. To achieve more rapid progress, the report continued:

> something more is required, whether through intensive campaigns in settled areas, involving a variety of coordinated measures, or through planned and supervised settlement of areas which are at present uninhabited or thinly inhabited. In fact, the Mission judges that the second of these approaches is in general the more promising in the present conditions of Tanganyika.[4]

This recommendation reflected quite closely British thinking in Tanganyika at the time. We have seen that when faced with the Meru Land Case, the colonial authorities had thought of resettling landless Meru peasants rather than giving away land already used by European settlers in the area. Given their frustrating experience of modernizing existing peasant agriculture, there were strong reasons why the outgoing colonial officials should support the World Bank recommendation.

The final decision on the issue, however, was left to the new government which in 1962 approved the World Bank recommendation to 'transform' peasant agriculture through settlement schemes. A Village Settlement Agency was established to supervise the schemes and advise the government on matters relating to their implementation. Significantly, a number of ex-colonial administrators were appointed to occupy senior positions in the Agency.

The first few years of policy-making in Tanganyika, as in the other new states of Africa, was very much a trial-and-error affair. It is not always clear how far the new governments simply borrowed ideas, derived from the colonial experience, and how far they went ahead without any known precedent. On this issue, it seems, while the British had reason to support the World Bank proposal on grounds of previous experience, the new government certainly had a spontaneous interest in supporting the 'transformation' approach. It had a radical implication and promised better results than the conventional 'improvement' approach. It did not imply any controversial intervention in existing farming systems along the lines that the British had pursued. On the contrary, it meant setting up new farms and recruiting farmers willing to go there. By taking people out of their traditional social environment the belief was that they would be more open to change. Another reason for support of the World Bank proposal was the control that the government would be allowed to exercise over the settlements. They would be supervised by government-appointed managers and thus the authorities would have access to the farmers in a way that was impossible with smallholder producers scattered over a large area.

Some thirty government-planned settlements were set up in various parts of the country immediately after independence. Settlers were recruited from areas with land shortage, for example, the Kilimanjaro, Pare and Usambara Mountains and to a lesser extent from the urban unemployed. The new farm land was opened up with the assistance of mechanized equipment, and settlers invited to build houses and start farming on plots allocated to them. As long as the new settlers were unable to produce their own food the government provided them with food rations. Settling in was often a difficult process for the newcomers. Many were used to different soils and climates and found it hard to stand the new challenges. Illnesses were common. People who came together in the settlements did not know each other and their gradual accommodation and the establishment of a new social organization was fraught with tension.

The principal problems in these settlements, however, related to government supervision and aid. Agricultural production in the settlements was carried out with farm machinery of which the settlers themselves had no or little experience. The machinery was costly to buy and to operate and the settlers were expected eventually to repay the capital costs involved in establishing their farms. Government expectations were no lower than those of the German authorities at the turn of the century. The gain of political independence in Tanganyika created a 'new frontier' atmosphere. In fact, many political leaders held a *tabula rasa* conception of reality: independence gave Tanganyika an opportunity to start anew. The incoming political leaders had no sense of constraints. By contrast, they were anxious to seize on everything that looked like an untapped opportunity. This orientation created a rather uncritical approach to policy-making. In the case of the village settlements, shortcomings soon became apparent as a result of the absence of any real brakes on political ambition.

There was an over-capitalization in many of the settlements – more machinery than necessary in relation to land and available labour. Perhaps the most flagrant example of this was Upper Kitete in Arusha Region where a hundred settler families began their farm operation of 1600 acres of maize with ten tractors.[5] In economic terms, this meant an underutilization of labour in the settlement. Neighbouring capitalist farms, for instance, employed three times less people, although they had less equipment.

The settlement at Kabuku in Tanga Region was set up in collaboration with the Amboni Estates as a co-operative sisal plantation. Government did not take into account the possible differences between this form of production and that practised on the existing large-scale plantations nearby. A slavish imitation of the experience gained on the latter meant the introduction of expensive bulldozers for bush clearing. Other more labour-intensive equipment could have been used but the close links with the Amboni Estates dictated the use of the same equipment as theirs. As a result the settlers started off with very heavy debts – 2·5 million Tanzanian shillings. Part of the loan was eventually paid by the government but the peasants were still repaying it in 1975.[6]

Other studies of the settlements started under the aegis of the Village Settlement Agency reported similar problems.[7] Dumont's conclusion that the settlements created a group of semi-privileged people who were under little pressure to work because of an excessive degree of mechanization is valid. Still, it would be wrong to reduce the inadequacies of the settlements to purely a matter of over-mechanization. As becomes apparent when talking to the settlers, they have a very different conception of their situation.

The settlers at Kabuku flatly denied that the available equipment made them privileged. They all argued that the machinery made them work more. What seems true is that by being linked to the production demands of the adjacent Amboni factory, they were more like workers with limited control over their own time. When the supervisor from the Amboni Estates told them that they were producing far less sisal than the workers on their plantations and absenteeism was a rampant problem, the Kabuku settlers felt unfairly treated. They did not see themselves as workers but as peasants. Comparing themselves with peasants in other parts of the country they insisted they worked much more. They had less time to look after their own household needs and felt deprived of the autonomy that their relatives and friends outside the settlement enjoyed.[8] Particularly in the early years of the settlement when their livelihood was still fragile, tensions between the government staff at Kabuku and the settlers were very common. Efforts by the settlement manager to impose official regulations angered the peasant settlers and at one time some of them badly injured him. The settlers struggled for autonomy. Eventually, when the government decided to wind up the Village Settlement Agency, official supervision by government staff was terminated and managerial responsibilities shared between the settlers and Amboni. There is evidence that this increased settler autonomy and it gave the settlers a chance to diversify their production. Their commitment to produce sisal was more difficult to sustain and, given low world market prices on the commodity, Amboni supervision was becoming increasingly ineffective in the late 1960s.[9]

Generally the peasants in the village settlements were both unwilling and unable to support the costs of the over-mechanized and over-administered schemes. Many of them soon approached bankruptcy and could only survive with government willingness to relieve their financial plight. Few schemes produced sufficient returns to the farmers or to the nation as a whole to warrant their continuation. Both the Government

of Tanzania – Tanganyika became Tanzania after establishing a
political union with Zanzibar in April 1964 – and the World Bank
concluded the VSA interlude by blaming its lack of achievements on
premature mechanization.[10] In his major reassessment of the country's
rural development policy, the Second Vice President, Rashidi Kawawa,
declared in April 1966:

> In the future, it has been decided that, instead of establishing
> highly capitalized schemes and moving people to them emphasis
> shall be on modernizing existing traditional villages, by injecting
> capital in order to raise the standard of living of the villagers. It is
> envisaged that such improvement might take the form of pro-
> vision of water supply, better layout of villages, improved farming
> and production methods, and reorganization of land holdings.[11]

However, there is evidence to suggest that the failure of the settlement
schemes cannot be seen only in terms of wrong technology. The VSA
experience was not unique, but just another example of peasant
resistance to imposition of outside control over their life and work.
Over-capitalization was too obvious to ignore but it made policy-
makers insensitive to the possible influence of other factors.

The settlements sponsored by the VSA were not the only projects that
form part of the transformation approach. Members of TANU Youth
League began to take up farming after independence was gained. In the
spirit of 'building the nation' they opened their own settlements in
various parts of the country, recruiting young people from the urban
areas. These were conceived as co-operative farms and managerial
assistance to run these during their initial phase was obtained from the
Israelis. A follow-up to the early TYL settlements was the establishment
after 1963 of National Service farms. Both these efforts differed from
the VSA settlements in that they attracted young people, most of whom
had no family of their own. These people usually found it easier to
spend the necessary time to make the productive efforts on their farms
successful. The most successful of them all was Mbambara in Tanga
Region, which like Kabuku was started as a co-operative sisal plantation. An evaluation of twelve settlements carried out in 1967/68 places
Mbambara at the top both in terms of hard work, self-reliance (per
capita value of external aid) and socialist co-operation.[12] Not all the
TYL schemes were successful, but they were less capital-intensive and,
above all, they consisted of people who in addition to political
dedication required less time for their own reproduction than is true of
the average peasant household. The principal cause of their downfall
was not resistance to outside control – such control simply was not
considered necessary to the same extent – but mismanagement, notably
misuse of settlement funds.

The most explicit efforts to implement the transformation approach
generally ran into the most serious troubles. Projects which did not

receive political attention often did better. In fact, they seemed to prosper by being left relatively untouched by bureaucratic interventions. The most interesting of these was the villagization efforts pursued by the Ruvuma Development Association in Ruvuma Region. The RDA was the creation of local peasants who, with the promise of some outside help, were encouraged to form new co-operative villages in their area. They started in 1963 by adopting a constitution that stressed the principles of co-operation and self-development of the villages, but also allowed government representation on their committee. After a series of attempts by the officials to impose their will on the peasants, the peasants revised the constitution to allow for a management committee entirely chosen from themselves and under their control.[13]

This meant that their relationship with the local administrators remained cool, but since the development programme of the RDA villages called for very limited outside capital assistance, they could pretty much ignore what the officials had to say. They had access to limited financial and technical support from OXFAM; in addition, a number of American volunteers worked in the RDA villages for short periods of time. They all worked with the peasants without imposing their own ideas on the village leadership. The same was true of RDA's energetic chairman. They were all in agreement that the interest of the villagers came first. They had no vested interest in adopting a managerial approach to the village peasants. They were not politically dependent on them and could live and work with them on equal terms. Moreover, the RDA did not attempt a transformation of the existing farming systems. It wanted to 'hurry slowly' by improving existing practices and developing the social relations in the villages so that higher levels of co-operation could be attempted. These factors taken together explain why in the mid-1960s RDA, and particularly the village of Litowa, had proved successful in achieving agricultural development within communal forms of production. Cliffe and Cunningham conclude their review of the settlements in Tanzania at the time by quoting the experience of the Ruvuma villages to show what can be achieved in the way of hard work, commitment, self-reliance, returns with a minimum of investment – through another approach, where the schemes are voluntary and co-operative.[14]

Tanzania came out of its first post-independence experience of villagization with a belief that its shortcomings were due to having adopted the wrong approach. There was no real sense of the resilience of the peasant mode of production. The success of the RDA reinforced their belief. 'It can be done' – the slogan of the 1964–69 Development Plan – reflected quite closely the attitude among chief policy-makers towards agricultural development. Little notice was taken of the fact that the success of the RDA villages was achieved by accepting the premises of the peasant mode: autonomy and reciprocity within the context of an economy of affection.

The improvement approach

While the transformation approach acquired principal political attention in the first five years of independence in Tanzania, the efforts to
improve traditional peasant agriculture were not abandoned. They
encountered their own types of problem. TANU was anxious not to
take unpopular measures and this pretty much tied their hands, because
popular expectations were asking for the impossible: to do away with
the poll tax, to nullify ordinances prohibiting settlement on forest
reserves, to do away with all agricultural regulations, to raise producers
prices, etc. TANU took a 'soft' approach on these issues and relied
more on exhortation and persuasion than on compulsion.

The consequences of this situation were at least in part that people
felt free to ignore the regulations introduced in the previous era.
Settlement on state forest reserves became common and a general
clearing of forest areas for cultivation occurred in many of the more
densely populated parts of the country. Such tasks that had been
relatively well observed in the colonial period, for example, pulling up
and burning of cotton stalks to prevent diseases, were now carried out
in a much more careless manner. Enforcement of new regulations was
becoming a virtual impossibility. Government policies slipped as a
result of peasant indifference to their demands.

In areas where new crops were introduced and they signified a major
gain to the producers without disturbing their existing livelihoods, the
agricultural extension service was able to achieve some results.
Liebenow tells how the government successfully introduced the production of cashew nuts among Makonde peasants in Mtwara Region
during the early 1960s by applying the principle of persistent persuasion. The new crop did not impose any great demands for labour
the main task, apart from harvesting, was weeding the land.[15]

The same author refers to another problem facing Tanzania in those
days. It was difficult to get the educated people to engage in farming. In
the 1950s, TANU organizers in Mtwara had campaigned against the
agricultural bias of the middle-school curriculum. After independence
therefore, there was little response among the educated people from the
area to take up farming. A survey of cashew nut producers in Mtwara in
1967 proved that the vast majority of the peasant farmers were illiterate
and had never taken any courses at farming training centres.[16]

While the example of the Makonde peasants may not be typical of
Tanzania as a whole – the inclination to farm is stronger among
educated people in areas like Bukoba and Kilimanjaro – it demonstrates that it is relatively easy to introduce a new crop, but more
difficult to introduce new practices. Government efforts to encourage
Makonde peasants to grow rice in the Ruvuma River Valley with the
aid of mechanized equipment were met with a flat rejection. Liebenow

concludes that despite inducements, such as charging only half a shilling an acre for mechanical ploughing, Makonde farmers still preferred to use the customary hoes and digging sticks on the plateau.[17] This orientation has been explained to the author as being determined by the excessive demands for labour that mechanized rice cultivation imposed. Mechanized ploughing opened up new stretches of land, but it forced them to allocate more labour to planting and weeding than they considered desirable, particularly in view of recurrent flooding of the proposed area of cultivation and its exposure to vermin.[18] The peasants felt more secure with the existing arrangements and considered themselves to have obtained enough from hoe cultivation.

Agricultural training in the early 1960s was strongly emphasized, not within the formal school system, but in institutions established to cater for the farmers. A number of Farmers' Training Centres were built and courses organized for interested farmers. There is no evidence that these FTCs really reached the peasant farmers. Most participants were those showing an interest in modern techniques.

Agricultural education at the university level, as well as agricultural research, was expanded but essentially conceived in terms far removed from the concerns of the average peasant. University graduates in agriculture saw their future in bureaucratic careers, and research catered for the needs as conceived by policy-makers in the Ministry of Agriculture.[19]

The result of these policies was essentially to leave the peasants untouched while allowing those with interest in modern farming to benefit from government services and inputs. The discrepancy between petty-capitalist farmers and ordinary peasants, originally created in the colonial era, was reinforced. Distribution of benefits was becoming increasingly differential. A case in point was the tractor scheme in Sukumaland, introduced as part of government efforts to increase cotton production. Administered through the co-operative societies, it meant that 'progressive' farmers were able to increase their earnings while sharing the costs with all members even those who were uninterested or unable to make use of the tractor services.[20]

The progressive farmer occupied a privileged position in the rural development strategy practised in Tanzania in the first five years of independence. It was assumed, at least in the agricultural field, that the best farmers in each community would encourage their neighbours to improve. Their achievements would have a demonstration effect. The assumption underlying this approach was identical to much of the development thinking in the colonial era: only those who work deserve to become rich. Although oversimplifying the issue, the approach made a lot of sense to the people working with agricultural improvement in the rural area.

Thoden van Velzen has more thoroughly than anybody else tried to demonstrate this in a case-study of village development in Rungwe

District in south-western Tanzania.[21] His conclusion of this approach is essentially negative. He sees the agricultural staff and the progressive farmers, whom he prefers to call 'kulak' farmers, as forming a class alliance against the peasants. The extension staff have developed a symbiotic relationship with the rich farmers, involving the latter's provision of land, food and assistance on government projects to the staff. The latter, in turn, help the well-to-do farmers with access to government aid, support their dominance of local political institutions and assist in their conflicts with other peasants. While there is no doubt that this collaboration existed in the villages at the time, his analysis leaves a lot unexplained. It fails to do justice to the rich case material that he so generously presents to the readers.

The simplest explanation of why agricultural extension staff tend to be confined to interaction with the progressive farmers is that the ordinary peasants are not really seeking their co-operation. They know that getting involved with the extension staff is the beginning of a relationship that may lead to government intervention in their farming. At their level of farming it is preferable to stay outside the extension network rather than be absorbed by it. It is only when a peasant farmer finds his own knowledge irrelevant, or believes that he is capable of doing things differently, that he may turn to the agricultural extension officer. These choices are made essentially by considering factors within the unit of production, that is, the household. There is no evidence in Thoden van Velzen's study which shows that the peasants cannot benefit from the extension staff, if they want to. The point is that they do not wish to get entangled in a relationship with the government since it carries the strong probability of subjugation to demands over which they have no control.

Thoden van Velzen presents a considerable amount of evidence to prove the existence of an active economy of affection. Unfortunately, he makes very little out of this material. However, a colleague of his, J. H. Konter, has analysed the complex nature of this local economy.[22] He shows how in the Rungwe area, as in so many other parts of rural Africa, becoming rich is a process which entails a lot of non-economic considerations. Despite strong population pressures on the land in Rungwe, moving out to open up new land is not a step that people find easy to make. Everybody agrees that living alone in the bush enables a person to earn more because he gets a chance to work longer, and he has fewer distractions and temptations. Yet people still prefer the social life of the village. Of all those interviewed, 93 per cent claimed they preferred to live in the village. One of the respondents said: 'A man who likes to live apart is considered a fool or a bad man, more specifically a thief or a witch.'[23]

In some areas, becoming rich is considered bad and people are afraid of demonstrating wealth because it is seen as acquired through abnormal means. Such wealth may upset the social balance in the community and thus it is resented. A study of rural development in Njombe District, adjacent to Rungwe but inhabited by another tribal group, concludes that witchcraft plays quite an effective role in the life of the rural people.[24] In certain parts of that district people do not build houses for fear of being bewitched. Success is explained by people possessing supernatural powers. A progressive farmer is believed to have *mkwego* – the local word for such powers.

Local norms to enhance equality in the village community did not always take such expressions. In many areas, people retained the belief in everybody's right to subsistence by engaging in communal farming in addition to their cultivation of private plots. Ruthenberg reports the existence of some six hundred such communal farms in 1963, varying from one to fifteen acres in size.[25] This was the indigenous version of the German *Dorfschamba* – the village plot. There was one significant difference, however, in that the German version was imposed on the villagers as a source of surplus extraction while the post-independence village plot was a subsistence insurance.

Even when people become rich, the economy of affection makes its demands on them. Being rich implies status in those rural societies where it is not condemned outright as a product of witchcraft. Status, however, also implies growing obligations. Becoming rich, therefore, does not mean, as our paradigms take for granted, that such people estrange themselves from their local community. Instead they often get even more closely involved in it than before. This is true also of the well-to-do who migrate to work in the urban areas, but it applies particularly to the progressive, petty-capitalist farmers in the villages. To refer to them as 'kulak' farmers is strongly misleading. Still, this has been the most popular term used to discuss this group of people in East Africa.[26] The literal meaning of 'kulak' in Russian is 'fist' and refers to the harsh behaviour of the well-to-do farmers in pre-1917 rural Russia, particularly as it related to extraction of usury from the poor peasants. In that situation we are talking of a class of people who had wholly accepted the premises of capitalism and were prepared to impose their economic demands on other people at any cost. Even with a wide stretch of the imagination it is difficult to describe the rural African situation in those terms. Certainly in rural Tanzania, tenancy, as well as employment and money-lending, lack the attributes of capitalist class society.

The Household Budget Survey conducted in Tanzania in 1967/68 reveals that lending and borrowing is by no means confined to the better-off households, although it is relatively concentrated to those units.[27] Within the context of the economy of affection lending was also practised by the poorer households, who by virtue of good harvest or remittances from urban relatives had a small surplus. The same source also shows that in the rural households 80 per cent of all the loans were obtained from relatives and only 4·5 per cent from a public institution, usually a bank or co-operative society. The remaining balance was provided by employers, traders and moneylenders. If the rural households are divided into farm and non-farm units, it becomes clear that the latter are more strongly oriented to the commercial sources of credit. In the farm households, the purpose of borrowing is usually an emergency or to provide food and drink. It is difficult to conclude from this type of data that the peasants really operate within a capitalist mode. It may affect their comfort but to argue as if it were predominant amounts to self-deception.

Although the significance of subsistence production is always difficult to assess in absolute terms, because precise figures are difficult to arrive at, the official economic surveys in Tanzania have consistently recorded subsistence production as being well over half the total agricultural production, as Table 3.1 shows.[28] It amounts to almost a third of the total Gross Domestic Product. Even if we consider that Tanzania in 1966 began to include construction of owner-occupied dwellings in subsistence production, and this may account for close to a quarter of the total subsistence production figure for the last three years covered in the table, it is clear that agricultural production outside the monetary sector is substantial. Ruthenberg's survey of smallholder farming, moreover, concludes that the trend is in the direction of subsistence crops getting priority over cash-crop production in many densely populated areas of the country, for example, Bukoba, Usambara Mountains and Sukumaland.[29] Even in Kilimanjaro this tendency has become noticeable. Bananas and maize are given priority over coffee. Rather than modernizing agriculture which implies a heavier labour demand and the dependence on outside agencies, peasants have preferred to send their surplus labour in search of livelihood elsewhere.

As indicated in the first chapter, exploitation of peasant populations by rural landlords and 'gentry' has been the foundation on which modern class society has developed. Collection of rental incomes or rental tributes in kind have been the commonly applied methods. All available statistics show that money rental incomes in rural Tanzania are minimal. Even in areas in which capitalist farming has taken root, for example, Ismani in Iringa Region, less than 2 per cent of the cultivated land acreage is rented. Income from rents amounts to only 0·24 to 0·34 per cent of total proceeds in that area.[30] Use of land, or more specifically use of planted perennials, may in some of the more densely populated areas be paid in kind, that is, by labour. There are no reliable statistics to indicate the extent of this practice. What we do know is that even these exchanges take place within the premises of the economy of affection. Its consequences, therefore, are not those which we impute by thinking 'capitalistically'. The discussion of *nyarubanja* in Bukoba below will further illustrate this point.

Agricultural wage-labour outside the plantation sector in Tanzania has also been limited. Gottlieb has estimated, by using the

TABLE 3.1. Magnitude of subsistence production in relation to Gross Domestic Product (GDP) and total agricultural production in Tanzania 1960–68

Year	Total GDP (million T.shs)	Subsistence production (million T.shs)	Agricultural production (million T.shs)	Subsistence/ total GDP (%)	Subsistence/ agriculture (%)
1960	3701	1248	2256	33	55
1961	3870	1346	2282	34	58
1962	4189	1493	2485	35	60
1963	5547	1536	2787	27	55
1964	4837	1413	2805	29	50
1965	4894	1353	2651	27	51
1966	6592	2062	2952	31	69
1967	6935	2134	2954	30	72
1968	7326	2199	3062	30	71

Source: *The Economic Survey and Annual Plan 1970–71* (Dar es Salaam: Government Printer, 1970), p. 17.

1967 census and other available sources, that there were a little over 13 000 employers of labour in the smallholder sector. Those would presumably be the progressive, petty-capitalist farmers referred to above. They employed no more than 16 000 persons, involving altogether 0.6 per cent of the total farm labour force in Tanzanian agriculture (excluding Zanzibar).[31] Even if these figures exclude part-time labourers, used at peak periods, it does confirm the pygmy nature of the production units in rural Tanzania. In addition, it shows the limits of such concepts as 'proletarianization' in discussing the rural situation in Tanzania.

There is little evidence to suggest that the improvement approach practised by the Tanzanian government had much influence on agriculture in the 1960s. Agricultural production kept going up as a result of new acreage being laid under cultivation. This, however, was more in response to population growth than to the introduction of new technologies. The petty-capitalist farmers were the main beneficiaries of the improvement approach. They had a vested interest in exploiting the links with the government and the market. The peasants, on the other hand, were more careful. Their response to the calls for modernization was selective. Land was not treated as a capitalist commodity. Production tools remained simple, and reproduction, therefore, costly. No real transformation of the resource-based peasant agriculture was achieved. Although some marginal changes were recorded, the improvement approach failed to attract the peasants away from their conventional mode of production. Consequently, the principal instrument of extracting the peasant surplus product remained government taxation. As during the colonial days, in the 1960s rural households were required to pay poll tax to the local authorities. Rates varied from one district to another and they followed levels of income, if not in a progressive at least in a proportional manner. There is evidence that collection of this tax was uneven. Where people had very limited cash incomes, the local official, usually a man from the area, would not insist on collection. Even in areas where cash incomes were considerable, collection was never complete.[32] In addition to the tax, government used an indirect form of taxation by making a deduction, the produce cess, at the time of purchasing peasant produce. This was a more effective manner of surplus extraction, but still not as worrying to the peasants as the increasing deductions made to sustain the agricultural marketing system. Through membership of co-operatives peasants were generally conscious of these deductions. In the 1960s the government had given local co-operatives and state run marketing boards a monopoly to purchase and sell peasant produce. Due to a number of factors, including lack of managerial experience, misappropriation of funds, etc., the peasants witnessed a rapidly increasing inefficiency in the marketing system during the 1960s. The President appointed a special Enquiry Committee to look into these problems and its findings were given prominence.[33] Consequently, as the 1960s went on, peasants kept paying more to sell their produce than they had ever done in the colonial period.[34]

The nyarubanja issue

We noted in the previous chapter that the chiefs in Buhaya (Bukoba District) had by tradition claimed property rights over a portion of the land in their chiefdoms. The royal clans had thus been able to create a semi-feudal land tenure system, referred to as *nyarubanja*. It never became a predominant pattern among the Haya people, but was significant enough to become a major political issue in the post-independence period. Mutahaba estimates that when the Germans colonized Buhaya, the number of holdings, characterized as *nyarubanja* did not exceed one-tenth of the overall number of holdings in the area. The rest of the holdings were occupied by independent producers.[35] Being a freeholder in those days gave status but it also implied services for the chiefs in fields other than agricultural production. The *nyarubanja* tenants were looked down upon although in purely material terms they were not worse off than the others.

This changed, however, with the coming of colonial rule. As Austen suggests, the chiefs had a vested interest in expanding their *nyarubanja* holdings once the value of land rose as a result of the introduction of cash crops.[36] Thus, not only did the number of such holdings increase, out the burden of the tenants also grew. The *nyarubanja* landlords introduced minimum rent rates and in this way the foundation for a landlord-serf relationship was laid. While in earlier days the ownership question never featured explicitly in the relationship between lord and tenant, after the integration of agricultural production into the monetary economy, it became a more important concern. In an effort to systematize land registration in the District, the British formalized tenancy arrangements. In 1936, the *Nyarubanja* Register contained 9000 tenants, approximately one-eighth of all producers in the area.[37] A new tenancy system was developed in the 1940s and 1950s when large numbers of immigrants arrived from neighbouring districts in the country and from Rwanda and Burundi. They were all treated as *nyarubanja* tenants. By independence there were approximately 4000 such immigrant tenants. Even so, the *nyarubanja* system remained relatively marginal. One case-study of Haya land tenure shows that in one sub-county, an entity encompassing ten to fifteen villages, some two hundred *nyarubanja* tenants occupied approximately 10 per cent of all cultivated land.[38]

As long as the position of the royal clans in Bukoba was left unchallenged the *nyarubanja* system continued to grow, but in the 1950s political campaigns against the chiefs and their system of rule became strong enough to make the British consider laws to give every producer security of tenure. Foremost in the fight against the chiefs was the Kianja Labour Association, a political organization confined to the Kianja chiefdom.[39] The KLA made the life of the chiefs and their relatives difficult and they persuaded tenants to stop paying rents to them.

The chiefs, however, still controlled the local government authority and the British were not willing to impose their will on the chiefs. Although by-laws were passed in 1956, aimed at enfranchising some of the tenants, very little was achieved. Tenants in some areas formed their own organization to fight their case. Many people saw the chiefs as standing in the way of tenant rights. TANU leaders in the district were quick to seize on this and the years preceding *uhuru* saw a growing conflict between the chiefs trying to defend their rights, and TANU leaders taking a populist line. The latter tried to capitalize on the *nyarubanja* issue and became self-appointed spokesmen of the tenants. At the time of independence TANU was the only political organization on the district council.

The first post-independence elections to the council were held in 1963 and were a great shock to the incumbent TANU leadership. Many of the party's candidates lost to independent candidates, sponsored secretly by the Catholic Church. Those who had been instrumental in defeating the chiefs were now defeated by a group of people, mainly teachers, who were prepared to defend the old system. This paradox can only be fully explained by several factors. The abolition of the system of chiefly rule left a vacuum that was not adequately filled by the political promises and actions of TANU. Much had been said by its leaders about the need formally to abolish *nyarubanja* but independence did not bring it about. Most important, however, was the Land Tenure Amendment (1962) Act, which placed all land under state control and abolished individual freehold titles. Many of the independent peasants perceived the new law as a threat and the political candidates campaigning against TANU in the 1963 council election did not hesitate to exploit this issue. Since the independent peasants far exceeded the number of tenants in number, it is not surprising that the TANU candidates who continued to push the *nyarubanja* issue had difficulty in soliciting support.[40]

The election was declared null and void and TANU candidates nominated to the District Council. They were subsequently responsible for taking the *nyarubanja* issue to the national level where a Nyarubanja Enfranchisement Act was passed in 1965. The parliamentary debate, which was dominated by people from outside Bukoba District, portrayed the *nyarubanja* system in highly inflammatory and general terms, but Mutahaba has subsequently shown that they really attacked a 'strawman'. With the abolition of the chiefs and the coming of independence, *nyarubanja* had begun to resolve itself. The members of the royal clans found it difficult to uphold their rights. In particular, the collection of rents from the tenants appears to have come to a virtual standstill. Out of a total of 7117 people still affected by the *nyarubanja* system in 1965, two-thirds had their own land and tilled it without any interference from the original landlords. One-third, who had been given land by their landlords, the majority being immigrants from other places, were still paying rents.[41] One reason why the debate was so heated in the National Assembly may have been that *nyarubanja* was portrayed as largely disenfranchising members of other tribes than the Haya.

Certainly, the reaction in Bukoba was quite calm. Many people were pleased to hear that the *nyarubanja* issue had been resolved, but to the majority of the people it did not make any difference. Mutahaba, who interviewed a sample of local people shows that some tenants had already ceased paying rent prior to the Act.[42] Even if the Act did put an end to the material contributions demanded by the landlords, the *nyarubanja* issue was not totally resolved. The Act failed to address itself to many legal aspects of the system and consequently it became necessary in 1968 to pass new legislation in which these aspects were covered.

Thus, although the rent payments came to an end in the early 1960s, partly as a result of the abolition of the chiefs and hence independently of the 1965 Act, it remained an issue in the area because the social stigma of being a tenant did not disappear so quickly, and because the 1965 legislation was insufficient as a legal instrument.

The most important thing to note in the context of this book is that the resolution of the *nyarubanja* issue resulted in reversing the trend towards feudalism. The landlords lost their land and tenants became independent peasants, just like the majority of the Haya producers. Small was strengthened at the expense of the large. Semi-feudal dependence was eliminated in favour of smallholder autonomy.

The political economy literature does not readily admit the possibility of such historical reversals and it is thus not too surprising that Cliffe portrays the incorporation of the Haya peasantry into the capitalist system as if the *nyarubanja* holders have remained a privileged class. The semi-feudal landlords never really modernized their farms. They were under no pressure to do so, because they received enough remuneration from the traditional farming systems. Thus the petty-capitalist farmers in Bukoba are drawn from other backgrounds and even though they exist they are not too many, nor are they too large. A recent study of the agricultural system in West Lake Region, where Bukoba is the most important district, concludes:

> The overall distribution of land . . . shows the dominance of the farm-family-cycle adapted primarily to subsistence production and less to surplus production, by the lack of any class of markedly large landholdings that would indicate commercial production units. Few units have managed to break through the subsistence level and establish themselves with large plots. There is no division into qualitatively different classes and an absence of landlords controlling the major parts of the land, accompanied by any degree of landlessness.[43]

If this assessment is correct the problem is not capitalist penetration, but rather the fact that capitalism has failed to transform the agriculture in West Lake Region. The peasants have remained relatively unconcerned with the problem of raising agricultural productivity to meet increasing demands of the national economy. In some cases this has been due to an exclusive concern with the needs of the household; the family-farm-cycle has preoccupied the members at the expense of other demands. In other cases, however, there simply has not been any real pressure on the peasant to improve productivity or work more than necessary. A study of peasant households in Tanzania in the late 1960s makes the following quite relevant observation of the peasant:

> He [the head of the peasant household] is a man of considerable authority for whom the eternal economic problem has been satisfactorily solved. He eats well, he has a bed to sleep in, a chair to sit on. For recreation, he has his evenings of conversation round the *pombe* [beer] pot. There is no character in the economic textbooks who is more misinterpreted than he. He is conservative because he has a good deal to conserve and much more to lose than his chains. To suggest that he is 'underemployed' and imagines that one is bestowing a favour on him by providing more

work, is his *aim* to be as underemployed as possible
and to allow himself to be disturbed from his aim only by the need
to meet his austere objectives.[44]

The economy of affection serves as the guarantor of social reproduction. It offers collective security in a manner that the modern
economies do not. It does not necessarily mean that all are treated
equally. As the above account implies, the household head is always
sovereign in relations with other members of the same unit. Females,
when they themselves are not household heads, and children are
dependants in the most literal sense of the word. Still, without
romanticizing the nature of the economy of affection, there is little
doubt that to its members, particularly those who control it, there are
many intangible and invisible benefits offered.

Petty-bourgeois politics and the peasants

Because land is not generally treated as a commodity for sale and
because the peasants control the means of subsistence, petty-bourgeois
politics in Tanzania after independence has been characterized by this
structural determinant. Government has had great difficulties in getting
at the peasants in an effective manner. The many small have simply
slipped out of the controls imposed by government. The officials, when
dealing with the peasants, have often found them able to take as much
as they give in these transactions.

Tanzanian politics immediately after independence was very much
characterized by the notion of give-and-take. The official view of the
relationship between the government and the people was that of a two-
way process. People were expected to contribute in return for government services and assistance. TANU leaders were busy encouraging
self-help projects among the people, while at the same time trying to
steer social and economic amenities in the direction of those areas where
people were making active contributions. It is significant that the
political process in the first years of independence dealt very little with
agricultural production. While prior to independence, the principal
concern of the British had been to improve agriculture and consequently the political process was coloured by that issue, in the years
after independence, agricultural production was not allowed to feature
prominently. Peasants had no interest in raising production and the new
political leaders did not wish to undermine their popularity by imposing
this on the peasants.

It is true that the government tried to encourage village development
plans in which peasants were expected to include agricultural production targets, but given the laissez-faire nature of the political process,
peasants generally avoided such targets, knowing that they carried the
danger of government intervention. They were not interested in

obligatory production targets for which they might be held responsible. Bienen has shown that many regions in Tanzania failed to produce village plans and where they were produced they bore little relation to the objectives held by party and government officials. While the latter were interested in targets for cash crops, the peasants only set targets for food crops. The village development committees did not consider the range of economic activities with which the leaders were preoccupied.[45] My own examination of village plans in Bukoba and Karagwe Districts in 1965 also proved the same thing: peasants were giving priority to social and economic infrastructural projects, for example, schools, roads, and dispensaries. When channelled to the authorities, they were often scrapped. Certainly the West Lake Plan produced in 1964 took little notice of the contents of the village plans.[46]

While policy-makers, in order to produce a development plan that made sense in terms of the national objectives and demands, ignored the peasants' views on these matters, the peasants took their revenge by ignoring the policy-makers' demands. Politicians toured the country-side preaching the need for popular involvement in development efforts – kazi ya kujenga taifa. Landrovers would carry officials in and out of villages to allow them to preach the gospel of development. While people in the rural areas sometimes responded quite positively, because there was a tangible benefit to the local community, as for example in the case of contributions to the construction of a primary school, they remained quite indifferent to demands without obvious benefits to the local area.

It was not difficult for them to remain indifferent. They were usually not in need of the project under consideration. Those with a stake in it were the officials, who lacked the means to follow up responses in each village. Thus the peasants soon learned ways of inducing the officials to believe that they were enjoying widespread support. Most important was to appear for political meetings and generally applaud and support the development ethic of the officials. By proving their positive orientation, they would not be bothered again for some time to come. They could keep the officials at arm's length. Ingle reports how a high-level civil servant characterized the people in his home area: '[They] have learned how to say, Yes! Yes!, when they don't mean yes at all. They mean no!'[47]

Many politicians believed that they would be capable of doing what the colonial administrators had failed to achieve, because they claimed they had popular support among the people. While this may have been true to some extent, many of the politicians did not realize that the peasant orientation to outside intrusions into their local affairs did not really change with independence. Peasants retained an instrumental view of the politician. One study, for instance, shows that peasant farmers were inclined to see the politician's job as 'mere talking'.[48]

The peasants could afford a cynical attitude towards the officials because they knew that the officials had no economic base to their authority, such as controlling land usage, dictating job opportunities, allocating free transport, etc. Politics remained a superstructual phenomenon with little or no relationship to rural production. Although TANU in those days saw itself as the prime engine of development, there was not much it could do. The reason for this was not so much a scarcity of human and material resources, as Bienen claims.[49] More important was the fragmented nature of the political economy. The political organization had a natural tendency to break up into its smaller components. TANU – the rural African party – that Miller describes from research in the mid-60s, reveals itself as an organization of virtually self-contained units.[50] TANU tends to get dragged into every matter, large or small, at the village level. Its essential political function lies in authoritative conflict resolution at the village level. It has taken over the role of the defunct 'native authorities'. The fact that it also communicates policies from superior branches of the party to the villages seems to be more of a formality. Only when a party official plans to show up in person in a village are there signs of mobilizing resources to prove involvement in activities advocated by the superior organs of the party.

TANU with its network of Village Development Committees was a highly democratic organization in the 1960s. It offered opportunities for direct democracy to an extent that was probably unique in Africa. As an organization it struck a positive chord in the peasantry. It was because of its democratic nature, however, that it proved insufficient as an agency of change. The peasants were not willing to go all the way to meet the demands made by the leaders, and since they lacked resources really to change the orientation of the peasants, rural politics, despite overt expressions to the contrary, was largely a matter of what the peasants wanted.

Petty-bourgeois politics after independence differed from colonial politics in that it reflected much more closely the social formations of the peasant mode of production. While the government official often had to advocate policies that were derived from capitalist considerations, the politician was usually more inclined to start from peasant premises. The economic motive was not pursued in isolation from other considerations. The economy of affection was revived at the political level. What is suggested here is not that political leaders ceased to be acquisition-oriented, failed to calculate costs and benefits of their actions, etc. The petty-bourgeois leaders are as capable of economic reasoning as their bourgeois colleagues. Thus it is not the presence or absence of economic calculation that distinguishes post-independence from pre-independence politics. Most important is the redefinition of the parameters of political action that occurred after independence.

Petty-bourgeois politicians, like the peasants, were all interested in more wealth but perceived it differently from the British. In a society where the market had still had only a limited impact on social behaviour, there was no distinct economic motive, no reasoning without considering the effects of economic decisions on the social order.

This was widely manifested in the 1965 parliamentary elections, Tanzania's first after independence. The event followed the introduction of a one-party constitution earlier the same year which allowed for competitive elections within the single party framework. Two candidates were nominated by TANU district branches to stand in each constituency. These nominations from among several candidates who had submitted their nomination forms were completed through secret ballots. The two candidates were campaigning on the same platform, moving together from place to place.[51]

It is clear that the principal losers, including some ministers and junior ministers, were those who had forgotten to adhere to the principles of the economy of affection. George Kahama, a former cabinet minister, failed even to be nominated, ostensibly on the grounds that he had built a house and married outside his home constituency. Edward Barongo, a junior minister, reduced his chances of winning by insisting on the need for modern agriculture. Paul Bomani, a cabinet minister, lost because peasants in his home constituency held him responsible for the introduction of a levy on cotton sold to the co-operatives. I. Bhoke-Munanka, a junior minister, lost because his constituents believed he had done nothing for them. Other incumbents who had failed to deliver goods or benefits to their home area found themselves in trouble in the election. Those who still managed to win often had to resort to expensive patronage deals during the campaign. Most common was to 'hire' supporters who would buy beer for prospective voters, usually influential people in their respective communities. That way some of the incumbents were able to compensate for failure to live up to past promises.

The democratic nature of the elections gave free vent to peasant orientations and there is no doubt that the outcome was largely determined by these. Candidates who had devoted themselves to party or government work at the expense of their constituents could only save their skin by 'buying' votes in the campaign. Ideological differences between candidates did not really matter. The symbols assigned to each candidate – a 'house' or a 'hoe' – seem to have made some difference, the hoe being the more effective of the two.[52] Most important of all, however, was the performance of incumbent candidates. The rural voters took a highly utilitarian approach. Like the voters Barkan studied in Kenya, they gave proof of a highly rational interpretation of politics.[53] They proved themselves capable of a pure evaluation of political performance, something that is rare in Western elections, where so many institutional factors intervene in the evaluation process: party affiliation, religious denomination, and so forth.

The rather liberal framework of politics in Tanzania during the first years of independence, however, also gave rise to a form of patronage politics that pre-empted effective central control of the policy-making process. Political success was determined by access to resources and the willingness to distribute them, or at least part of them, to client-followers. Conspicuous display of wealth was not a liability to political leaders, provided they shared it with others. In fact to the majority of the peasants such display of wealth was the sign of status and leadership. Such people had achieved their wealth by being effective in their deals with the 'outside world'. As long as they worked within the economy of affection they had, in the eyes of the peasants, a greater leadership potential than any other person. Peasants expected a 'politics of largesse',[54] a phenomenon that according to Jowitt[55] is typical of all societies not yet overhauled by capitalism.

To sustain their position and influence with the followers, politicians in post-independence Tanzania engaged in the acquisition of private wealth, the income from which was often used to buy political support. By becoming economically more independent, they could more easily build up a power base of their own. This tendency became evident in Tanzania as elsewhere in post-colonial Africa.

Political leaders, however, were also inclined to use their public positions to serve the same end. Ability to influence the allocation of social and economic amenities was, in the eyes of the peasants, the most important sign of effective leadership. This was evident in the district councils whose authority included primary-school education, rural health and secondary roads. Stanley Dryden[56] has documented the same tendencies in Tanzanian district council politics as Colin Leys so vividly demonstrated in his case study of Acholi District politics in Uganda: the politics of location.[57] It centred more on the issue of *where* a project should be located than *what* that project ought to look like.

As nationally controlled resources often also had a bearing on local developments, this political arm-twisting by individuals with enough leverage extended to central government policy-making. This was particularly true of the educational sector. Despite government intention to allocate new primary schools to the more backward districts in the country, primary-school expansion continued faster in the already privileged districts. Very often, people from these districts occupied important positions in the ministry and could be used to secure funds for new schools, entries into secondary schools, access to scholarships, etc. Mutahaba has demonstrated how unofficial pressures exercised by influential people from Bukoba District secured a continuous expansion of primary-school education there, while Ngara District, which had been given priority in government policy, failed to meet its expansion targets.[58] Obviously the demand for education was much stronger in Bukoba than it was in Ngara, but this policy outcome can only be fully understood if account is taken of the economy of affection.

The government of Tanzania did take some steps soon after independence in order to control education more effectively. Much of it had been run by voluntary agencies, notably the Catholic and Lutheran Churches. In the colonial period schools had often been built to serve as incentives to join a particular religious denomination. This came to an end immediately after independence when the government took over control of these schools and insisted they be non-denominational. As Samoff shows in his study of local politics in Kilimanjaro, many of these control efforts were frustrated by pressures on ministry officials.[59] The importance of education to people in some areas, for example, Bukoba and Kilimanjaro, gave rise to unofficial political pressures that often ran contrary to government educational plans.[60] Given the shortage of land in these places, peasants realized that many of their children would be unable to survive on farming alone. Hence their desire to gain access to alternative channels of securing a livelihood. This orientation was not really the product of displacements by capitalism but of the resilience of the peasant mode of production which failed to accommodate more people without endangering its own existence. The peasant mode was trying to relieve itself of a difficult burden.

Conclusions

Peasant influence on politics in the days of colonial rule was not too difficult to distinguish because it was explicit. Colonial threats to the peasant economy led to active resistance and participation. Peasant influence on politics after independence is more difficult to recognize because it was more subtle. It was hidden behind the popular concept of African socialism. By abstaining from any systematic efforts at enforced agricultural change, the government did not force peasants into active participation. Where the government tried the 'transformation' approach, it had to admit defeat. Peasant power was manifested by their influence on the political process itself. They were not influential in the sense of shaping policies. They were influential, however, in terms of determining what issues the political system was likely to take up. Moreover, they were often able to divert the direction of government policies by frustrating their implementation. At the village level this was often achieved through direct democracy, where village development committees, in the absence of party of government officials, often decided to pursue activities which were in their interest but contrary to national policy objectives. Peasant influence was also exercised through patron–client relations. The patrons were by no means independent of the clients. Peasants had a hold on them because these relations were initiated by the bigger men who wanted to make some gains from them.

Given lack of economic control over their clients, they could only secure their support by offering something tangible in return. Thus patronage politics reflected peasant perceptions, cognitions and preferences. Certainly the political process took into account peasant interests in a way that colonial politics did not. Where post-independence politics failed to do so, it was because government itself often lacked the sensitivity necessary to attract peasant interest in matters related to the development of society at large.

Policies pursued by the petty-bourgeois government were becoming increasingly controversial. For President Nyerere, their costs were becoming only too readily apparent. Frustration with government policies and an incipient rivalry among political leaders with a growing autonomy within the party organization threatened the legitimacy of Nyerere's regime. Although he had condoned, even explicitly encouraged,[61] a peasant-based politics, it was now turning against him. With the capitalist sector already antagonized by some of his policies, there was a danger in 1966 that Nyerere would find himself in a political vacuum. The fate of many other African regimes, notably Nkrumah's, must have reinforced his belief that something drastic was needed to restore confidence in his government.

References and notes

1. The most comprehensive and detailed accounts of the transition period are Lady Listowel, *The Making of Tanganyika* (Chatto & Windus, 1965) and Cranford Pratt, *The Critical Phase in Tanzania 1945–1968* (Cambridge University Press, 1976).
2. See, for instance, William Tordoff, *Government and Politics in Tanzania* (Nairobi: East African Publishing House, 1967), Andrew Maguire, *Toward 'Uhuru' in Tanzania: The Politics of Participation* (Cambridge University Press, 1969) and Goran Hyden, *Political Development in Rural Tanzania: A West Lake Study* (Nairobi; East African Publishing House, 1969).
3. The suspicion that peasant farms might be taken over by government was still held by some people in Bukoba village in 1965 when the present author did field research there.
4. International Bank for Reconstruction and Development, *The Economic Development of Tanganyika* (Baltimore: Johns Hopkins Press, 1961), p. 129.
5. René Dumont, *Tanzanian Agriculture after the Arusha Declaration* (Dar es Salaam: Government Printer, 1969), p. 8.
6. Immanuel Bavu, 'Leadership and communication in the ujamaa process: a case study of Kabuku-Ndani Ujamaa Village Cooperative Society', unpublished MA thesis, Department of Sociology, University of Dar es Salaam, 1971. The present author stayed at Kabuku for three weeks in September 1975.
7. Clyde Ingle, *From Village to State in Tanzania: The Politics of Rural Development* (Ithaca: Cornell University Press, 1972), p. 51.

8. and 9. This was clearly revealed to the present author during interviews conducted in Kabuku in September 1975.
10. John de Wilde, *Experiences with Agricultural Development in Tropical Africa* (Baltimore: Johns Hopkins Press, 1967). In this volume the authors warn against premature mechanization.
11. Ministry of Information and Tourism, Information Services Division, 'Address by the Second Vice-President, Mr. R. M. Kawawa, at the Opening of the Rural Development Planning Seminar', at the University College, Dar es Salaam, 4 April 1966, p. 4.
12. R. W. Kates, J. McKay and L. Berry, 'Twelve new settlements in Tanzania: a comparative study of success', Bureau of Resource Assessment and Land Use Planning, University College, Dar es Salaam, 1969.
13. The present author visited the Ruvuma Development Association (RDA) villages in 1965 and the above information is taken from field notes. The RDA is discussed by Lionel Cliffe and Griffiths L. Cunningham in 'Ideology, organization and the settlement experience in Tanzania,' in Lionel Cliffe and John S. Saul, (eds), *Socialism in Tanzania*, vol. 2 (Nairobi: East African Publishing House, 1974), pp. 131–40.
14. ibid., p. 139.
15. J. Gus Liebenow, *Colonial Rule and Political Development in Tanzania: The Case of the Makonde* (Evanston: Northwestern University Press, 1971), pp. 296–300.
16. Poul Westergaard, 'Farm surveys of cashew producers in Mtwara Region: preliminary results', Economic Research Bureau Paper 68·3, University College, Dar es Salaam, 1968, p. 8.
17. Liebenow, op. cit., p. 299.
18. This was the information that the present author was given by local peasants when visiting villages in Mtwara District in 1972, in conjunction with a study of co-operative education and co-operative development.
19. Hans Ruthenberg, *Agricultural Development in Tanganyika* (Berlin: Springer–Verlag 1964), pp. 154–8.
20. Shem E. Migot-Adholla, 'The politics of a growers' cooperative Society', unpublished undergraduate dissertation, Department of Political Science, University College, Dar es Salaam, 1969.
21. H. U. E. Thoden van Velzen, 'Staff, kulaks and peasants', in Cliffe and Saul, op. cit., pp. 153–79.
22. J. H. Konter, 'Facts and factors in the rural economy of the Nyakyusa, Tanzania', mimeo., Afrika-Studiecentrum, Leiden, 1974.
23. ibid., p. 43.
24. Z. J. Mpogolo, 'The working and contribution of VDCs to rural development in Njombe District', unpublished undergraduate dissertation, Department of Political Science, University College, Dar es Salaam, 1969, pp. 26–7.
25. Ruthenberg, op. cit., p. 119.
26. It is consistently used by Marxist writers on the political economy of rural East Africa. See, for example, Mahmood Mamdani, *Politics and Class Formation in Uganda* (New York: Monthly Review Press, 1976) and Lionel Cliffe, 'Rural class formation in East Africa', *Journal of Peasant Studies*, vol. 4, no. 2 (January 1977), pp. 195–224.
27. This data is from Manuel Gottlieb, 'The process of differentiation in

Tanzanian agriculture and rural society', Economic Research Bureau, University of Dar es Salaam, 1972.

28. Kighoma A. Malima, 'Subsistence accounting and development planning in Africa', Economic Research Bureau, Paper 70·14 University of Dar es Salaam, 1970, discusses the problems of subsistence accounting in Africa.

29. Hans Ruthenberg (ed.), *Smallholder Farming Development in Tanzania* (München: Weltforum Verlag, 1968), p. 330.

30. Gottlieb, op. cit., p. 25.

31. ibid., p. 12.

32. In field work that the present author did in Bukoba District in 1965, records of tax collection in the five villages showed that the average rate did not exceed 75 per cent. The same records showed that the most common reason for non-payment was lack of cash money, that is, inability to pay.

33. *Report of the Presidential Special Committee of Enquiry into Cooperative Movement and Marketing Boards* (Dar es Salaam: Government Printer, 1966).

34. Herbert Kriesel, et al., *Agricultural Marketing in Tanzania: Background Research and Policy Proposals* (Michigan State University for the Ministry of Agriculture, Food and Cooperatives, Dar es Salaam), 1970.

35. Gelase Mutahaba, 'The importance of peasant consciousness for effective land tenure reform', unpublished undergraduate dissertation, Department of Political Science, University College, Dar es Salaam, 1969.

36. Ralph A. Austen, *Northwest Tanzania under German and British Rule: Colonial Policy and Tribal Politics, 1889–1939* (New Haven: Yale University Press, 1969), p. 96.

37. Mutahaba, op. cit., p. 12.

38. Priscilla Copeland Reining, 'Haya land tenure: landholding and tenancy', *Anthropological Quarterly,* vol. 35, no. 2 (April 1962), p. 69.

39. For a discussion of the Kianja Labour Association (KLA), see Hyden, op. cit., Ch. 3.

40. Field research that the present author conducted in Bukoba District in 1965 suggested that the *nyarubanja* issue was engaging some individuals (33 per cent) very seriously, but that the majority, albeit small (56 per cent), of the peasant respondents referred to the Land Tenure Act as the more important of the two issues.

41. Mutahaba, op. cit., p. 45.

42. ibid., p. 46.

43. Jannik Boesen Birgit Storgård Madsen and Tony Moody, *Ujamaa: Socialism from Above* (Uppsala: Scandinavian Institute of African Studies, 1977), p. 28.

44. Guy Routh, 'Mores and motivations of peasant and proletarian households in Tanzania', 6th Social Science Conference of the East African Universities, Dar es Salaam, 1969, pp. 17–18.

45. Henry Bienen, *Tanzania: Party Transformation and Economic Development* (Princeton: Princeton University Press, 1970), expanded edn., pp. 479–80.

46. Hyden, op. cit., Chapters 8 and 9.

47. Ingle, op. cit., p. 253.

48. Winston T. D. Makamba, 'Politics and agricultural development in Kilosa District: a case study of the cotton industry', unpublished undergraduate dissertation, Department of Political Science, University College, Dar es Salaam, 1969, p. 16.

49. Bienen, op. cit., p. 449.
50. Norman Miller, 'The rural African party: political participation in Tanzania', *American Political Science Review*, vol. 64, no. 2 (June 1970), pp. 548–71.
51. For a full account of the 1965 elections in Tanzania, see Lionel Cliffe (ed.), *One-Party Democracy* (Nairobi: East African Publishing House, 1967).
52. The present author completed an analysis of the role of symbols in that election; see Goran Hyden, 'The role of symbols in the Tanzania elections 1965', *Mawazo* (Kampala), vol. 1, no. 1 (1967), pp. 42–51.
53. Joel D. Barkan, 'Comment: further reassessment of "Conventional wisdom": political knowledge and voting behaviour in rural Kenya', *American Political Science Review*, vol. 70, no. 2 (June 1976), pp. 452–5.
54. The concept is borrowed from Norman Uphoff who has used it in his discussion of leadership strategies in Third World countries.
55. Kenneth Jowitt, 'The Leninist response to neocolonialism', Institute of International Studies Monograph Series, University of California, Berkeley, 1978. The notion of 'largesse' is similar to the 'big-man-small-boy' syndrome discussed by Robert Price; see his, 'Politics and culture in contemporary Ghana: the big-man-small-boy syndrome', *Journal of African Studies*, vol. 1, no. 2 (Summer 1974), pp. 112–34.
56. Stanley Dryden, *Local Administration in Tanzania* (Nairobi: East African Publishing House, 1968).
57. Colin Leys, *Politicians and Policies: An Essay on Politics in Acholi, Uganda, 1962–65* (Nairobi: East African Publishing House, 1967).
58. Gelase Mutahaba, 'Decentralized administration in Tanzania: Bukoba and Ngara District Councils 1962–69', unpublished Ph.D. dissertation, Department of Political Science, University of California, Berkeley, 1973.
59. Joel Samoff, *Tanzania: Local Politics and the Structure of Power* (Madison: University of Wisconsin Press, 1974), pp. 35–58.
60. David R. Morrison, *Education and Politics in Africa: The Tanzania Case* (Hurst, 1976).
61. See the earlier pamphlets Nyerere published on African politics, for example, Julius K. Nyerere, *Barriers to Democracy* (Dar es Salaam: Thakers Press, probably 1960) and Julius K. Nyerere, *Democracy and the Party System* (Dar es Salaam: Tanganyika Standard Press, 1963).

CHAPTER 4

Small goes into hiding: peasants and *ujamaa*

In the mid–1960s the inherent instability of the petty-bourgeois regimes in Africa had become only too apparent. One civilian regime after the other had been forced to give way to military rulers. Political divisions inside African countries as well as among them were on the increase, facilitating outside interference in the domestic affairs of these countries. The political morale among those who wanted to see a non-aligned and self-reliant approach to the solution of African problems was in danger of being undermined.

Julius K. Nyerere did not begin his career as leader of Tanzania with an explicit strategy of self-reliance or non-alignment, although the two concepts certainly were in the back of his mind. It was the political experience gained in the first five years of independence that enabled him to become more explicit about what he thought tomorrow's Tanzania should look like and how his conception of the future of the country could be realized.[1] His ideas became the ideology of TANU, when its national executive committee adopted the Arusha Declaration on the 5 February 1967.

The Arusha Declaration announced the nationalization of the 'commanding heights of the economy', that is, the principal financial, manufacturing, and trading institutions. It called for a complete stop to the accumulation of private wealth by leaders in party and government. It indicated the party's desire to give priority to rural development, thereby enabling a more effective utilization of domestic as opposed to foreign resources. In relation to the development, particularly of the rural areas, it launched the concept of *ujamaa* (literally: familyhood), implying the creation of communal village production units. In short, the Arusha Declaration with its key concept of *ujamaa* was rightly portrayed as the country's official blueprint for socialist development – a form of socialism that explicitly stressed the use of local ideas and resources.[2]

The timing of the Arusha Declaration is important. President Nyerere seized a strategic moment in the history of his own country and of Africa as a whole when announcing his socialist blueprint. It came at a time when the doors to neo-colonial penetration in Africa were wide open. His move hurt the agencies of international capital, although that aspect of it should not be exaggerated because, as Nyerere himself later said, there was not that much foreign capital to nationalize in the first place. The importance of the Arusha Declaration was particularly political. It demonstrated to the metropolitan bourgeoisie that Africa was not going to accept its presence unconditionally. It gave hope to all progressives who wanted to see the African countries pull off something of their own.

In the context of the domestic Tanzanian situation, it laid down specific rules guiding not only entry to the political arena but also the political game itself. The Arusha Declaration was a most intelligent political move. Above all, it gave Nyerere a chance to contain the influence of those who, by virtue of their private wealth, had been able to nurse the economy of affection. The main criterion of power was no longer the number of followers that an individual leader in the party could claim but his degree of loyalty to the new ideology and its chief architect. With the Arusha Declaration Nyerere had politically 'rounded up' the party leadership. It was becoming increasingly difficult to show disapproval of the new policies by remaining silent. The political leaders had to declare their stand on the issues affecting them. Nyerere achieved his objective in that some of the principal patrons in the party with considerable followings of their own, for example, Oscar Kambona, Bibi Titi Mohammed and Michael Kamaliza, all fell into the political traps laid by the new policies.[3]

The Arusha Declaration was not only a measure aimed at reducing capitalist influence in Tanzania. It was also directed against the economy of affection. It was possible to hit in both directions by reducing the private economic base of the political leaders which had been used to support the economy of affection, and by centralizing the control of societal resources to the state. The fact that many of the political leaders had lost in the 1965 election, or at least revealed that their local power base was weak, facilitated the rounding up exercise.

After 1967 Tanzania became a political Mecca for liberal and socialist progressives from all over the world, anxious to see a challenge to neo-capitalism. Praise of Nyerere and Tanzania was dished out almost unreservedly, particularly by socialist academics who exploited the new situation to prove the relevance of Marxist analysis to the African realities. While it is true that the Arusha Declaration brought to the fore social class relations, the attention among academics to this issue in the analysis of Tanzania has been somewhat exaggerated. The academic issues were all shrouded in a political euphoria, notably about the potential for socialist transformation created by the new strategy.[4] Given the enthusiasm generated by the Arusha Declaration, and the wide support for the new policies received both from within and outside Tanzania, it is easy to see why these and many other writers created the impression of *ujamaa* as having revolutionary implications.

This is an image which has been maintained ever since by many Tanzanians and non-Tanzanians alike. A recent evaluation of *ujamaa* states that in its conception 'the *ujamaa* ideology is clearly revolutionary.'[5] How valid is this assertion? By examining both the concept of *ujamaa* and the actual experience of the socialist policies in the rural areas, I hope to give an adequate answer to that question.

The concept of *ujamaa*

The concept of *ujamaa* in relation to rural development is spelled out by Nyerere in his pamphlet called 'Socialism and rural development'.[6] He traces three basic assumptions underlying what he calls 'traditional *ujamaa* living': (a) respect – each member of the family recognizing the place and rights of the other members; (b) common property – acceptance that whatever one person has in the way of basic necessities, they all have; and (c) obligation to work – every member of the family, and every guest who shares in the right to eat and have shelter, taking for granted the duty to join in whatever work needs to be done. On the other hand, the inadequacies of the old system included the acceptance of human inequality within the local community and poverty, stemming from ignorance and the limited scale of operations.

Nyerere's interpretation of colonialism was that it encouraged individualistic social attitudes. By becoming part of the monetary economy people had come to see money as having a value of its own. The urge for money often led to the employment of wage labour and thus social stratification. In short, colonialism generated more selfishness and less equality; a rejection of village life in favour of urban living. Fortunately, Nyerere maintains, Tanzania has not yet been irreversibly caught in this process. His country is still a predominantly peasant society in which farmers work for themselves and their families, and are helped and protected from exploitation by co-operative arrangements at the local level.

> It is this kind of development which would be consistent with the growth of a socialist Tanzania in which all citizens could be assured of human dignity and equality, and in which all were able to have a decent and constantly improving life for themselves and their children.[7]

Nyerere tries with his *ujamaa* ideology to develop the philosophical underpinnings of the economy of affection and formalize them into a nationwide strategy of development. He is trying to universalize the unwritten rules of living within rural households and apply them to larger social and economic forms of organization with modern objectives. Nobody has more aptly described this than Samuel Mushi, who calls it 'modernization by traditionalization'.[8] Nyerere turns away from the concepts associated with modern capitalist and socialist development and tries to find a formula which has its roots in peasant society – a strategy that is intelligible to the local peasantry.

There is no doubt that *ujamaa* struck a familiar chord in rural Tanzania but it is important to remember that it was a principle traditionally practised only within each household. The notions of rights and obligations only included the extended family living within that household, and its temporary guests. It did not address itself to the mutual responsibilities and rights of individual households in a given local community. For these, the rural Tanzanians use the concept of *ujima*. As Mushi notes in his article, *ujima* refers to the habitual practice of co-operation among villagers in certain peak seasons (cultivating, planting, harvesting, etc.) or in cases of emergency where someone needs to finish a certain job in a day or two with the help of his neighbours and relatives, instead of weeks or months by doing it alone.[9] This function was communal in the sense of implying mutual aid and reciprocity, but not in the sense of communal ownership. Those who assisted their neighbours did not expect a share in their harvest, only some entertainment at the completion of the task.

This way of looking at things still prevails in rural Tanzania. *Ujima* is often practised to secure the right of all to subsistence. What Nyerere was asking of the peasants, however, was to go beyond *ujima* and adopt *ujamaa* as the guiding principle of life and work, not only within the household but also in the relations between households in their community.

This was not the only challenge that *ujamaa* posed in its post-Arusha version. It also required the formalization of these customary principles into laws and regulations. A national strategy of *ujamaa* would only be possible with rules that could serve as implementation guides and criteria for the measurement of performance. Both party and government officials were quick to respond by devising rules that anticipated a three-stage, unilinear transformation of rural Tanzania from traditional village communities, via co-operative units to communal production villages. This created a contradiction that has been at the bottom of Tanzania's rural development efforts ever since. On the one hand, it is clear that such laws and regulations are necessary in order to make systematic party and government involvement possible. On the other hand, that move steals the principles of action from the peasantry. There is no longer much room for spontaneous application of values shared by people in the same community. The parameters of action are no longer local but imposed on the rural communities by the authorities.

The challenges of *ujamaa* were essentially confined to the peasant mode of production. First, they implied a transformation from individual to communal peasant production; secondly, the redirection of political and administrative efforts towards the peasant economy. Nyerere tried to avoid pitfalls of previous approaches by politicizing the state machinery, and thereby placing ideological commitment before technical expertise. There was a belief that TANU could achieve what the colonial administration and the foreign-aid agencies had failed to do, because its leaders were local men with ability to understand the peasant mind. By relieving the peasants from the colonial shackles and reducing their exposure to capitalist temptations, peasants would become more open to influence by the party and the government. In fact, Nyerere, and many with him, were of the opinion that the peasants would surge forward to produce more and transform the relations of production as a result of the anti-colonial and anti-capitalist stand taken by TANU. He did not anticipate the contradiction stemming from any major state intervention in the peasant economy. Certainly in the first years of socialist transformation. Nyerere believed *ujamaa* villages could be created by the people themselves and maintained by them. The role of government was to help the villagers make a success of their work and their decisions.[10]

There seem to have been at least two main sources of inspiration of *ujamaa* as it applies to rural development: one was domestic; the other foreign – the achievements of Mao's China. There the transformation of the rural areas into communal places of life and work was completed in a short period of time, using an approach in which the peasants were not alienated but strode forward on their own. Nyerere gained a first-hand knowledge of the Chinese experience when he paid an official visit to China in 1965. On his return, he did not hide his admiration for what the Chinese had achieved. His positive impressions opened up a close collaboration between the two countries.

The local source of inspiration were the achievements by peasants in various parts of Tanzania who in the first years after independence grouped themselves together for communal production purposes. Particularly important was the experience of the Ruvuma Development Association. This proved that the peasants had not forgotten their customary way of life and that it could be used as a starting-point. The RDA villages in the early 1960s had begun to practise the principles of *ujamaa* as we know them from Nyerere's writings, and subsequently Nyerere is quoted as having told the villagers in Litowa, the head-quarters of the RDA, that they should develop their village 'as a practical example of *ujamaa* where I can send people to see it in practice.'[11] The RDA experience, however, as Cliffe and Cunningham point out,[12] is primarily relevant to poor regions with empty cultivable land and with a limited exposure to the monetary economy. It was not so easy to replicate the success of RDA elsewhere.

Ujamaa in practice

The *ujamaa* policies were so far-reaching and complex that when it came to putting Nyerere's ideas into operation there inevitably arose conflicts between different policy goals that could not be reconciled at the stage of implementation. Maeda has identified eight major objectives which the new rural development strategy tried to accomplish: (1) establishment of self-governing communities; (2) better use of rural labour; (3) taking advantage of economy of scale to increase production; (4) dissemination of new values; (5) avoidance of exploitation; (6) increasing mobilization of people for military organizations; (8)

or together, these policy pretations. Nyerere had in his original essay on of action can be set out, take into account the is in different areas, and traditional structure.'[14] ism was ever extensively for reasons that will be to a discussion of the of the first few years of e useful.

aration saw a limited production by people bly to the new policies. itiated *ujamaa* villages ment into a communal o declared themselves, be *ujamaa* villages. In owards more socialist of Kabuku, where the d to move somewhere else.[15] effect on the existing ujamaa through sign- a reasonable amount es to complement the

Th systematic efforts by the regional party and government administration to promote *ujamaa* villages in some areas. In the parts bordering on Mozambique, people were grouped together in villages for national defence purposes. These villages were created and armed so as to prevent Portuguese infiltration into Tanzania in search of guerrilla fighters. Although many of these villages were started without systematic attention to the other principles of *ujamaa*, some did have a modest communal production. In West Lake Region, the local party officials also took an early initiative to promote communal villages, essentially by recruiting jobless individuals in the towns and people who could not find 'meaningful' employment in the existing traditional villages. This plan to create *makazi mapya* (new settlements) did not follow the principle enunciated by Nyerere: voluntary participation. Instead it was characterized by bureaucratic high-handedness.

With the exception of the 400 villages set up in Lindi and Mtwara Regions to strengthen the defence of the southern border, there were only another 400 villages registered as *ujamaa* villages in 1969.[17] Although the government adopted a much more explicit rural orientation in its welfare policies by initiating an ambitious rural water supply programme, expanding primary-school education and health facilities, as well as abolishing the poll-tax introduced by the colonial authorities to finance the local authorities, peasant response to calls for the creation of co-operative or communal production units in the villages was very limited. To the TANU leadership the growth of *ujamaa* villages appeared so slow that its promise to transform the rural areas was in danger of losing credibility.

It is in the light of this experience that in 1970 to 1971 TANU began to take a more active role in the creation of *ujamaa* villages. The President took a personal lead by initiating 'Operation Dodoma', a government-planned programme to move all people in that Region into villages with the hope of developing these into communal places of life and work. The people of Dodoma Region were moved into villages in two phases. To convince them, the President spent a long time living in Chamwino, one of the first *ujamaa* villages to be set up in the area. From there he visited other settlements and encouraged the peasants to comply with the new policies. As is evident from Table 4.1, between 1970 and 1971 the number of *ujamaa* villages in Dodoma Region rose rapidly from 75 to 246.

Operation Dodoma signalled the start of similar operations and campaigns elsewhere in the country to spread the policy of *ujamaa*. Regional party secretaries, the chief representatives of the President in the regions, made a point of taking a personal lead in these efforts. Particularly notable was the political work of the party secretary in Iringa Region, Wilbert Klerruu, who saw his aim as putting an end to capitalist and petty-capitalist farming in the region. He pitched his approach in class terms, setting the poor peasants against the well-to-do farmers. He eventually became a personal victim of the political tensions that he stirred up: on Christmas Day 1971 Klerruu was shot to death after an argument with one of the capitalist farmers in Ismani, an area known for its large maize farms. What Klerruu had not achieved before his assassination was achieved thereafter. By 1972 virtually all capitalist farming in Ismani had come to an end and the peasants were invited to farm this land on a communal basis. The campaign against capitalist farming grew so intense in 1971 to 1972 that European capitalist farmers in other parts of the country, notably Arusha and

TABLE 4.1. Number of *ujamaa* villages and total members by region*

Region	1970	1971	1972	1973	1974
Arusha	25	59	92	95	110
	5 200	14 018	19 818	20 112	25 356
Coast	56	121	185	188	236
	48 300	93 503	111 636	115 382	167 073
Dodoma	75	246	299	336	354
	26 400	239 366	400 330	378 915	504 952
Iringa	350	651	630	659	619
	11 600	216 200	207 502	243 527	244 709
Kigoma	34	132	129	132	123
	6 700	27 200	114 391	115 672	111 477
Kilimanjaro	9	11	24	24	14
	2 700	2 616	5 009	4 934	3 176
Mara	174	376	376	271	111
	84 700	127 371	127 370	108 068	233 632
Mbeya	91	493	713	715	534
	32 900	64 390	98 571	103 677	86 051
Morogoro	19	113	116	118	96
	6 000	10 513	23 951	19 732	25 509
Lindi	285	592	626	589	339
	70 673	203 128	175 082	169 073	218 888
Mtwara	465	748	1 088	1 103	1 052
	173 027	371 560	441 241	466 098	534 126
Mwanza	28	127	211	284	153
	4 600	18 641	32 099	49 846	40 864
Ruvuma	120	205	205	242	184
	9 000	29 433	29 430	42 385	62 736
Shinyanga	98	150	123	108	134
	12 600	12 265	15 292	12 052	18 425
Singida	16	201	263	263	317
	6 800	51 230	59 420	59 420	141 542
Tabora	52	81	148	174	156
	16 700	18 408	25 115	29 295	28 730
Tanga	37	132	245	245	255
	7 700	35 907	77 858	77 957	67 557
W. Lake	22	46	83	85	77
	5 600	9 491	16 747	13 280	15 968
Rukwa†	–	–	–	–	121
	–	–	–	–	24 988
Dar es Salaam†	–	–	–	–	25
	–	–	–	–	4 713
TOTAL	1 956	4 484	5 556	5 631	5 010
	531 200	1 545 240	1 980 862	2 028 144	2 560 472

* First figure refers to number of villages; second figure, to total members
† Regions created in 1973: Dar es Salaam out of Coast, and Rukwa out of Mbeya and Tabora Regions
Source: Prime Minister's Office, Planning and Research Division

Kilimanjaro Regions, began to leave the country. During these years of intensified *ujamaa* campaigns, most of Tanzania's capitalist farming came to an end. More than half of the country's sisal plantations were nationalized. Many of the large-scale grain farms were turned into state farms or given to *ujamaa* villagers to farm. The last capitalist enterprises in the agricultural sector to go were the coffee estates in Kilimanjaro which were handed over to local co-operative societies in 1974.

The number of *ujamaa* villages rose from 1956 to 4484 between 1970 and 1971. The following year the figure exceeded 5500, as Table 4.1 shows. By 1973 over two million Tanzanians were reported to live in such villages. The quantitative implications of the operations and campaigns to start *ujamaa* villages were quite impressive. It is important, however, to recognize that these figures conceal significant variations. First of all, *ujamaa* villages were registered even if their communal efforts were not successful; in some cases even villages without any communal cultivation were registered as *ujamaa* villages. Secondly, not all villages were new creations. People were simply told to move to the nearest existing village or trading centre and political efforts were made to create an *ujamaa* village out of that enlarged unit. Thirdly, the first years of *ujamaa* campaigns did not lead to more than a partial villagization. Although no precise figures exist, approximately only half of Tanzania's rural population in 1972 lived in villages, that is, places of residence with some concentration of people. The majority of these people lived in such villages even before the *ujamaa* campaigns and were not asked to move. Those who actually moved their residence during the *ujamaa* campaigns were a minority, except in Dodoma where large numbers of people were moved into new or existing villages. In Tanzania as a whole, at least some five million people continued to live outside villages. Fourthly, the figures in Table 4.1 do not reveal the fact that within each village some people depended much more on communal production than others. Communal production was introduced as a complement to individual production. Although many petty-capitalist farmers participated in communal production, their dependence on it was generally much smaller than that of other villagers. It would be wrong to assume, however, that the poorer farmers were dependent on communal production. In their case they reduced dependence on communal village production by simply staying out of it, or making a contribution only when they were forced to do so.

The policy of village settlements or concentrations was by no means new when it was launched as part of the Arusha Declaration. As shown in the previous two chapters such a policy had been followed by the colonial regimes and it had also been an integral part of TANU policy in the first post-independence years. The *ujamaa* approach, however, was unique in that it was conceived as part of a radical political transformation. It was meant to neutralize the powers of the petty-capitalist farmers and strangle the hold that they and other petty-bourgeois elements had on the economy of affection. Through such measures rural smallholder producers would get more opportunities to participate in the construction of a socialist economy. There are two reasons why this expectation has been difficult to realize. The first is the antithetical relationship of the state to the economy of affection; the second, the limited capacity of the peasant mode to support modern socialist development demands.

Bureaucrats and *ujamaa*

Ujamaa villages were not meant to be monuments of modernization in the way that the earlier village settlements had been. TANU wanted to avoid the folly of overcapitalization and premature mechanization. The *ujamaa* villages were to use existing technology, but it was asserted that economies of scale could be achieved through the organization of a larger labour force, even one using the simple techniques of hoe cultivation. The model picture of *ujamaa* production, as presented in Tanzanian mass media, contained large numbers of people engaged in hoe cultivation.

What has not been fully appreciated is the contradiction between this approach and the expectation that *ujamaa* could achieve a revolutionary transformation of the Tanzanian countryside. The first implied village autonomy, the second implied a directed effort by the state. In Tanzania's resource-based, essentially rain-fed agriculture, the state had never really had a meaningful role except as a protective mechanism. In Dodoma, for instance, people had grown used to the state as a dispenser of famine relief. Their response to Operation Dodoma was no doubt in part affected by this orientation. They went along with the government policy so as not to be punished, but their concern with production did not go beyond what they considered desirable and feasible within the context of their economy of affection. *Ujamaa*, because it was framed in revolutionary terms, inviting the state to play a major role in transforming the rural areas, carried its own seeds of contradiction. It asked the peasant farmers to accept a social relation that they did not conceive as necessary for their own reproduction. Neither the party officials nor the government servants were particularly welcome guests in the villages. To the peasants they were bureaucrats who, by virtue of being asked to work within their own set of rules, were likely to complicate rather than facilitate production. They had had enough experience of such contacts to draw such a conclusion.

The party or state bureaucrat always has very little to offer the peasant which he really needs for his own immediate reproduction. He does, however, have something to offer in the field of improving living conditions in the rural areas. The point is that TANU had already committed itself to supplying a number of social amenities free of charge to the rural population. Thus the bureaucrats could not easily use the offer of such amenities in exchange for increased production. The peasants had already been promised by the party that such amenities would be made available by the government. They saw their provision as government responsibility and were even reluctant to make some form of self-help contribution towards their realization. Government had abolished the taxation of rural households. Furthermore, there was a belief in official circles that the price incentive, that is, higher producer prices, would have a limited effect on the peasant producers and that it would essentially benefit the petty-capitalist farmers.[18] In short, the bureaucrat's hands were quite effectively tied and it was not easy for him to enter into a 'contract' with the peasant leading to his increasing his production. The new policies ruled out a market exchange from which the bureaucrat could walk away victorious.

In this situation, it is not surprising that the bureaucrats, virtually without exception, turned to an authoritarian, managerial approach. The new socialist strategy had forced the official to encounter the peasant face-to-face, but with few, if any, effective tools to influence him. The cushioning effect of the economy of affection on the relations between the petty-bourgeoisie and the peasantry had been reduced. The new policies forced upon the peasantry a growing bureaucratic bourgeoisie[19] whose primary loyalty lay with the President and TANU. Some of its most prominent members were political leaders who had lost the 1965 election and whom the President knew would have no power base of their own. The bureaucratic bourgeoisie was characterized by its orientation to party policies. Their career as state managers, either in a political or administrative capacity, depended on the ability to implement party policies. In the years after the Arusha Declaration it depended particularly on their ability to start *ujamaa* villages. Regional officials were particularly concerned that all activities were co-ordinated and managed at that level. There was little room for spontaneous and voluntary initiatives. The most drastic example of this was the dissolution of the Ruvuma Development Association and its subordination to the local TANU leadership.[20] Many political leaders resented having successful *ujamaa* villages in their area of operation over which they had no control. As bureaucratic managers they wished to be associated with these villages in such a way that they could reap political benefits from their success. Successful villages that did not succumb to bureaucratic control were often ostracized by the party leadership. Matendo in Kigoma Region, Mareu in Arusha Region, and Kabuku Ndani in Tanga Region are all examples of villages which at one time because of their relative autonomy and success ran into political conflicts with the district or regional officials.[21]

To justify their interaction with the peasantry, the party and government officials had to induce a political atmosphere which justified extraordinary action. One example is the Regional Party Secretary of West Lake Region who declared in April 1968, when announcing his plan for the implementation of the Arusha Declaration, that he had 'started a war' in the region. Anybody opposing it would himself be in trouble.[22] At this occasion, to which all party and government officials plus elected representatives of the people had been invited, only three people spoke. The question by the first speaker as to whether enough planning had been done was brushed aside as superfluous, because the whole plan had already been approved. The second speaker who asked how people in the proposed villages would be fed was told that it was the duty of relatives to feed them. The third speaker, a local MP, took the liberty of comparing the Regional Party Secretary to Hitler and reminded him that due to the harsh means applied by the latter he had lost although he was at one time close to total victory. The Party Secretary interrupted the speaker and accused him of ill-will.

The happenings at this meeting are not necessarily typical of what transpired elsewhere. Hidden in the frontal approaches of campaigns and operations, however, lay a definite antagonism between the bureaucratic bourgeoisie, on the one hand, and the petty-capitalist farmers and other local petty-bourgeois elements, on the other. By nursing the economy of affection, many of the latter had attained a certain measure of power of their own. This was now threatened by the new socialist strategy. The political efforts to reduce their influence in the rural areas continued into the 1970s when their most important institutional means, the district council and the co-operative union, were abolished.

The West Lake case is significant because later in 1968 it blew up into a national issue. Two local MPs made public their criticism of the Party Secretary. A committee of enquiry was set up to investigate the case and on its recommendation, the MPs were expelled from TANU and automatically lost their seats in the National Assembly. This incident and the simultaneous expulsion of a few other independent MPs of petty-bourgeois background, created the impression that the party leadership could not be officially criticized. Subsequently, elected leaders tended to be more careful in their public statements. As their political freedom was increasingly circumscribed within the party, they also became less effective rivals with the bureaucratic bourgeoisie. In fact some of them joined the ranks of the bureaucratic bourgeoisie by taking up salaried positions in the party or in the public sector.

This does not mean that the President condoned misbehaviour among his party and government officials, but he had less reason to worry about them, because they were all his *protégés,* if not his personal appointees. He could apply sanctions against them quite easily. The West Lake Party Secretary was eventually relieved of his duties, given the controversy he had stirred up in the process of implementing the *ujamaa* policies. Party officials who tried to take shortcuts to gain favours were also punished. Ingle quotes the example of the party official in Tanga Region who was relieved of his duties after he had literally created a *ujamaa* village from nothing solely for a pending visit by President Nyerere, after which it was to – and did – disappear.[23]

This example, while by no means typical, is still significant in the context of post-Arusha politics. Pressures had increased from the centre to produce solid development results, but it was difficult for the officials always to ensure quick results. Circumstances in rural Tanzania were such that the peasant mode did not lend itself to a revolutionary transformation. Consequently results were generally far short of expectation. To deal with this problem, party and government officials often resorted to passing false or inflated accounts of development results to superiors who were out of touch with local conditions.

There is no difficulty in finding proof of bureaucratic failures in Tanzania. The explanation offered by many observers, however, that officials deliberately bungled party policies because they had no interest in the success of *ujamaa* is far too simple.[24] It overlooks the fact that the *ujamaa* policies gave the officials few opportunities to relate to the peasants in a constructive and positive manner. In the absence of a real emergency, the nature of production and reproduction within the peasant mode did not call for state participation. Although officials tried to create an emergency atmosphere through artificial means, peasants remained unconvinced. The peasant mode simply appeared too strong for the officials to conquer. Rather than endangering their careers, therefore, most officials accommodated themselves to action based on the premises of the peasant mode. Their principal failure does not lie in having pursued their class interest in a naked fashion but in having failed to mobilize the peasants for alternative institutional forms of action by yielding to the inherent demands of the peasant mode.

The most common way out of their predicament was to develop patronage relations with individual *ujamaa* villages on the assumption that, in return for favours, village leaders would enforce party policies in their communities. The creation in 1967 of the regional development funds, devoted exclusively to the advancement of *ujamaa* villages, allowed the bureaucratic bourgeoisie to compete more effectively with the local petty-bourgeoisie who had previously monopolized patron–client relations in the rural areas.[25] The most important effect of this fund was to allow the party patron to strengthen his position at the expense of the local patron.

This shift of power, while not being unimportant for the Tanzanian political system at large, had very limited ramifications for the peasants. Patronage was essentially their language. It meant an official acceptance of the principles associated with their mode of reproduction. Patronage allowed the peasants to hold the officials at arm's length. Furthermore, it placed the officials in the trap of the economy of affection where one of the key principles is that if you give somebody a gift, that person gets a hold on you, because there is an ulterior motive to your engagement in such a practice in the first place. The ulterior motive of the officials was to make the peasants adopt the principles of *ujamaa*, but by appearing generous to the villagers, they did not increase their chances of realizing this objective. Instead, they reduced them, because the peasants did not feel obliged to give them more than a minimum in return. This 'minimum' usually consisted of a generalized support of the *ujamaa* policies and praise of their anti-capitalist implications. This was not really a sacrifice for the peasants because they had as little interest in the capitalist straitjacket as the policy-makers.

The rural development policies in Tanzania after the Arusha Declaration gave the officials opportunity to dispense a wide variety of goods and benefits to peasants appearing to support the party policies. Many of the villages were simply overwhelmed by gifts from the government. It was not always easy for the peasants to respond in a meaningful manner.

Many of the gifts extended to the *ujamaa* villages were such that they did not upset the economy of the villagers. They could be incorporated into it without too much trouble. For instance, this is true of poultry-keeping which was often started in *ujamaa* villages with the help of regional development funds. Such projects provided opportunities for a more nutritious diet, but few of them lasted very long because the villagers did not treat them as a priority. The chickens contracted diseases or died, or it was impossible to purchase chicken feed. Similar problems occurred in villages which were given cattle to keep. The village herd was neglected. Cows died or were simply slaughtered and eaten by the villagers.

The rules of the regional development funds prescribed that these could only be used for productive projects. This was meant to guarantee that these funds essentially supported the central government objective of higher production. In line with these rules, regional officials supplied *ujamaa* villages with fertilizers and mechanized equipment for the development of their communal farms. As it turned out, this was a double-edged instrument. Evidence from a large number of villages that I visited, shows that tractors were used to plough the land and make it ready for planting. The tractors generally allowed for the opening up of much larger areas of land than when villagers relied on their hoes alone. In these villages, it was found that a much smaller area was eventually planted and weeded, because the village labour force could not cope with all the land ploughed with the aid of the tractor. Most policy-makers assumed a peasant capacity far beyond what the peasants were really capable of. Mushi shows how in the case of Morogoro Region the official assumption was that *ujamaa* villagers would be able to cultivate three acres per person of the communal farm, while independent surveys showed that, in the absence of hired labour or harvesting machines, a target of two acres was more realistic.[26] Since the villager had to divide his time between his private plot and the communal village plot, the contribution he was really able to make to the latter would be even smaller.

The policy-makers sometimes assigned targets to villages which were far beyond their reach on the premise that the villagers would stretch themselves to produce more communally if they were aware of the high expectations of the government. This approach may have had some such effect, and is not totally invalid. For instance, in both Kilosa and Kigoma Districts I was told by government officials that it worked to their satisfaction.[27] On the other hand, it is true that the peasants had a very instrumental attitude towards the official approach, limiting its benefits. Von Freyhold shows how villagers in some parts of the Tanga Region turned against their district officials when they substituted tractor-farming for donkey-ploughing.[28] It did not make them more inclined to work on the communal village plot. Nor, however, was that automatically the result where tractors were used. Vail quotes one case where the villagers told him that the tractor did the work for them on the communal plot and gave them time to work on their own plots.[29] This is an attitude also adopted in many villages towards outside help by party and government officials, or groups of enthusiastic expatriates travelling to work in *ujamaa* villages.[30] While the villagers appreciate these gestures, they have a very limited effect on the village economy. It gives the peasants a temporary relief, and hopefully a larger overall harvest, but without the repetition of the same aid, production results will be back to a level commensurate with what the existing labour force in the village finds itself capable of.

Subsequent to their takeover, the capitalist farms in Iringa were subject to special treatment by the government, which wanted the new *ujamaa* farmers to make a success of their effort. The political leadership had a stake in proving the feasibility of communal farming. The regional authorities in Iringa planned an *ujamaa* development programme for twenty-nine maize-producing *ujamaa* villages at a total cost of 5 664 181 T. shs for the season 1972/73. Each village was expected to farm 240 hectares of maize communally with tractors and other mechanized equipment plus the use of fertilizers, all to be obtained through credit. The lending agency, the Tanzania Rural Development Bank, while approving the programme in general, insisted on phasing it and lowered the communal farm size to 120 hectares per village. The bank officials expected an average yield of 25 bags per hectare, or a total communal farm output of 3000 bags.[31]

This appears to be a highly inflated target, quite typical of policy-making officials who are not personally exposed to the structural constraints of peasant farming. A survey of fourteen *ujamaa* villages carried out by TRDB in 1974 showed that the average yield for the communal farms during the 1971/72 season had been 595 kilos per hectare, while the individual farms gave an average yield of 869 kilos per hectare despite the fact that *ujamaa* farms used fertilizers while individual farms did not.[32] What the TRDB, under pressure from the regional officials in Iringa, approved for the 1972/73 season was a programme expecting each village to produce 2350 kilos per hectare! Another paper, delivered in 1972 but obviously not considered by the policy-makers, showed that output per acre varied considerably according to availability of labour on a regular basis.[33] According to this survey, average yields per hectare among poor peasants were 899 kilos, among petty-capitalist farmers 900 kilos and among capitalist large-scale farmers 1800 kilos. Neglect of figures like these can only be explained by the fact that the maize credit programme was a form of political patronage. The authorities, after completing the takeover of the capitalist farms, had committed themselves to support the peasants. They believed that by giving them as much material aid as possible, the peasants would find it possible to succeed. The fulfilment of this political obligation, however, meant a diversion of the original *ujamaa* objectives, according to which mechanization should be at a minimum.

The outcome of the maize credit programme was a great disappointment because the officials had not considered the labour constraints in the peasant economy. Although villages using tractors to plough their land were able to achieve a higher output than those which did not, it was only a quarter of the official estimate. In the villages using tractors it was 716·8 bags per hectare instead of the target of 3000. In those not using tractors, it was as low as 343·8 bags. Even more distressing to the officials was the fact that villages using fertilizers did not have a greater output than those which did not. Average yields per hectare on individual farms, on which no fertilizers or manure were applied, were higher than on the communal farms.[34] The average gross income of the *ujamaa* villages using tractors was 16 558·45 T. shs, while their farm costs were 54 139 T. shs. The average gross income of *ujamaa* villages using fertilizers but not tractors, was 7942 T. shs, while their operational costs were 23 213 T. shs. These figures should be seen in the light of the official estimate of a gross income of 90 000 T. shs per village. The villagers were obviously not in a position to repay at the expected rate and agreed to pay only 16 per cent of the required repayment amount. The problem of repayment in maize-producing villages in Iringa has continued as another study shows. The maize crop *ujamaa* villages were costing the government on average 53 933 T. shs in 1973 and 11 977 T. shs in 1947, as well as having outstanding arrears of 148374 and 156 362 T. shs respectively.[35]

Because these amounts are so large that the peasants are in no position to repay their debts, these tend eventually to be written off as bad debts. Two predecessors of the TRDB, the National Development Credit Agency and the Co-operative Bank had collapsed as a result of the inability of peasants to repay their debts. Although it would be wrong to impute that there is no repayment at all, it has often been unsatisfactory when extended to food crop production. TRDB's experience of lending for export crops, coffee and tobacco, has not been discouraging. In fact, as Due shows in her study, repayment rates among such farmers have been commendable.[36] One major reason for this difference seems to be that in this case there was no political interference in the decisions made by the Bank. The deals with these farmers were strictly commercial.

The political pressures on lending agencies like the TRDB have remained strong, because the relationship between authorities and villages has usually been one of patronage. After 1967 when politics was elevated to a level of supremacy, wishes of political authorities in the regions and the districts have been allowed to prevail over technical considerations. Mushi shows how in Morogoro District the politicians argued that people in the villages wanted 'meat and milk' and would dismiss feasibility studies and insistence on technical decision criteria as delaying tactics on the part of the experts.[37]

Ujamaa politics was tantamount to a deliberate neglect by most party decision-makers of criteria such as efficiency, feasibility, and viability. Decision-making rules that guide policy-makers in modern capitalist and socialist societies were ignored so much that a Hungarian expert working with *ujamaa* development felt obliged to stress in a public speech:

> Very often can be heard declarations, that during the building of socialism we have to throw away every idea of capitalist origin, or every idea which does not derive from Africa. This is a grave mistake. Socialism doesn't reject capitalism in total. It takes useful ideas from it. The motive of the development of all societies is to preserve the useful ideas of the previous system, and to cast away only the unuseful ones.[38]

The political mobilization efforts by the party leaders did not uproot the peasants and make them socially available for new organizational alternatives, which *ujamaa* with its insistence on communal farming was trying to achieve. Because the premises of these policies were derived from the economy of affection, it tended to encourage approaches that in the guise of socialism achieved little but reinforcement of existing forms of social action in the rural areas. Sending officials to work with the villagers on their communal farm, while commendable as a strategy to make policy-makers more sensitive to rural needs and constraints, did not, as shown above, make Tanzania more socialist. Nor did the insistence of so many political leaders on giving gifts to exemplary *ujamaa* villages. These gestures of patronage bore little relation to village capacity. As both Bugengo[39] and Holmquist[40] show, villages were often saturated with aid in order to provide a semblance of *ujamaa* policy success. In modern economic terms such aid was wasteful and an example of how economics is asked to feed politics in pre-capitalist societies.

Peasant attitudes to *ujamaa*

Peasant conceptions of *ujamaa* differed from the official view in that by and large it was interpreted from the narrow angles of the peasant household. There was initially some apprehension in the same way as there was when the 1962 Land Tenure Act was passed and people believed that they would lose their land. The fear reappeared after the Arusha Declaration and rumours were spread that the peasants would lose not only their land but also their wives and children. *Ujamaa* meant communal living as well as communal work. Some people misconstrued Nyerere's message so as to scare the peasants. Through political education work by the party leadership, these misinterpretations were dispelled and a more relaxed atmosphere created. Even so, however, the peasant conception was far from the official one.

Many of Nyerere's political lieutenants talked of *ujamaa* in terms of class struggle. To the peasants this talk made little sense. That was seen to apply to the modern sector where contradictions had been created as a result of the establishment of capitalist relations of production. In the context of the economy of affection the notion of class war makes as little sense as the notion of purgatory does to the Marxist. This was particularly true in rural Tanzania, where the process of class formation had not really produced antagonistic relations between different groups of people. The petty-capitalist farmers who lived among the peasants were generally better-off than their neighbours, not because they had acquired their land and turned other people into farm labourers but because they had shown greater willingness to take risks and thereby modernize their farming. They may have used labour from outside the household on a temporary basis but hardly ever did such relations turn into permanent exploitation. The petty-capitalist farmers accepted, by and large, the premises of the economy of affection. They did not pose a threat to it. Peasants did not really see them as their exploiters, although the bureaucratic bourgeoisie tried to present them as such. Only in those exceptional cases when they appeared unwilling to accept the principles of the economy of affection was *ujamaa* used against the petty-capitalist farmers. On the whole, however, petty-capitalist farmers did not become political scapegoats in the efforts to build *ujamaa*. Since everybody was allowed to retain his private farm, and the main task, at least initially, was to build a communal farm to supplement activities on the private plots, the more successful farmers in the rural areas were left alone as long as they did not publicly work against *ujamaa*. Although there was an attempt by TANU to make ordinary peasants political leaders of the villages, the petty-capitalist farmers often ended up village leaders as a result of the democratic selection process. In other words, peasants very often chose petty-capitalists to head their villages on the assumption that they were best equipped to deal with the officials, including protecting them from government interventions that would threaten their livelihood. In places where there were no such petty-capitalists, villagers often chose individuals known *not* to be interested in change. Rather than choosing a dynamic person they deliberately elected to office somebody whose interest in interfering in their life was very small. Examples like this were frequent enough to make the party leadership increase its scrutiny of the local leadership process. In the early 1970s, the laissez-faire atmosphere that had characterized party elections before was giving way to closer supervision, in which definite criteria such as knowledge of party ideology and party policies, ability to work with and lead others, etc., were systematically considered.[41]

It would be wrong, however, to create the impression that peasants did not try to apply *ujamaa* in their villages. It was not laziness as much as a different set of priorities and limited capacity that explain *ujamaa* shortfalls in the rural areas. The peasants did not have a capitalist orientation and were thus unconcerned with the need for a surplus as an end in itself. This became particularly obvious in Iringa when peasants and ex-farm-labourers were invited to take over the capitalist maize farms. These farms which had previously supplied Tanzania with surplus grains were now turned into peasant farms, albeit communally operated. Although the peasants were interested in producing a surplus that would earn them a cash income, they had little interest, let alone capacity, to produce on the scale and at the level of productivity that characterized the capitalist farmers. The resurrection of the peasant mode on these capitalist farms had the inevitable effect of lowering production.

Peasants were doing what they considered a good job, but with the introduction of communal farming side by side with their private household plots, managerial complications inevitably arose. While the Arusha Declaration prescribed that Tanzanian leaders would not be allowed to hold two jobs at the same time, the introduction of communal farming in the villages was tantamount to asking the peasants to do exactly that: to work on their private plot and on the communal plot at the same time. Given the dependence of Tanzanian agriculture on rain, the timing of all farming activities is vital. Everything has to be done within the span of a few days. Usually there is a real limit, particularly to how much a peasant can plant. The insistence on communal farming heightened the problem. In trying to cope with it, peasants generally preferred to give first attention to their private farms, over which they had direct control, and only then devote their time to the communal farm. Although the poor peasants were expected to become the prime beneficiaries of the new policy, they had real difficulty in resolving the problem of doing individual and communal farming at the same time. As McHenry concludes in his survey of peasant participation in communal farming: the poorer members of the *ujamaa* villages had little room to gamble with their food supply.[42] The better-off households, and those which for one reason or another could spare labour, were the main contributors to communal farming. This explains why attendance on the communal farm was so irregular and why it differed drastically among members of the same village. It also explains why communal farming was given such limited attention and why, therefore, it ended up appearing so unprofitable to the peasants.

The dimensions of these problems are indicated in the figures contained in Table 4.2. The data presented there is incomplete for two main reasons. It was collected under different auspices and has been assembled by the present author only afterwards. It is included here because it is generally difficult to come by complete financial data from the *ujamaa* villages. The village leadership does not always keep records of these figures (although they are supposed to). When they have some financial data available, it usually differs from what can be collected in the next village. Even with these reservations, the figures in Table 4.2 give an indication of the limited income generated from communal farming, its changes up and down, and the uneven distribution of this income. Most villages applied a points system, whereby every villager was accorded one point for a full day's attendance on the communal farm. At the end of the season, the net income was distributed according to the number of points accumulated. Thus, in cases like Mareu and Igongole, the lowest paid member had only attended two full work days during the whole season while the highest paid had attended over one hundred days. Village leaders rarely enforced attendance when members stayed away, as in most cases their reason for non-attendance was, in the light of the economy of affection, fully comprehensible to them. To the peasants, work on the communal farm was never considered an end in itself. To them it remained a supplementary activity, to which attention was given when circumstances in the household permitted.

TABLE 4.2. Net income and payment to members in selected ujamaa villages in Tanzania, 1971/72 and 1972/73, in Tanzanian shillings

Ujamaa village by region	Net income		Average payment per member	1971/72 Highest payment to member	Lowest payment to member
	1971/72	1972/73			
Arusha					
Makiba	–	27 142	–	68/–	2/50
Mareu	20 000	–	–	587/–	3/20
Nkoanenkoli	–	77 594	–	–	–
Oljoro	–	4 000	–	–	–
Selela	–	15 947	–	–	–

Ujamaa village by region	Net income 1971/72	1972/73	Average payment per member	1971/72 Highest payment to member	Lowest payment to member
Coast					
Bwilingu	–	7 975	–	–	–
Kimbuga	–	1 804	–	–	–
Mfuru 'A'	3 189	2 500	70/–*	–	–
Msata	3 000	8 700	–	–	–
Nyambili	8 570	4 070	–	–	–
Iringa					
Igongole	–	–	13/20	49/75	–/35
Igosi	–	–	86/70	359/50	4/50
Kipengere	–	–	189/20	390/–	40/–
Lwanzali	–	–	8/–	12/–	3/–
Magoda	–	–	70/70	178/50	–/65
Mayale	–	–	111/50	785/–	2/50
Wanyama	–	–	159/90	468/30	8/60
Kilimanjaro					
Bendera	74 676	61 534	–	–	–
Chekereni	22 450	3 124	–	–	–
Iwami	–	288	–	–	–
Mtakuja	29 450	85	–	–	–
Shiri Matunda	9 000	25 670	–	–	–
Mbeya					
Mamba†	35 331	57 000	–	–	–
Morogoro					
Gairo‡	4 012	12 800	–	–	–
Kibedya	–	21 072	–	320/–	20/–
Kicharengani	–	1 440	26/60	–	–
Mkata	18 105	16 552	–	–	–
Mvumi	15 677	–	–	–	–
Tanga					
Kwamsisi	1 071	–	–	–	–
Magamba	–	131 257	–	–	–
Mawanga	7 468	24 120	–	–	–
Moa	50 147	46 172	–	–	–
West Lake					
Kyamyorwa	–	1 391	46/–	55/20	3/45

* 1972/73
† Gross income
‡ Gairo had a daily rate paid to all members 1971/72: 1/25; 1972/73: –/50
Sources· Student reports, University of Dar es Salaam and author's field data

McHenry, in his study referred to above, makes the low return from communal farming a principal reason for peasant reluctance to pursue it. In my view, it is rather the structural constraints of the peasant mode itself, notably the fact that communal farming complicated its management by adding to the labour demands during the critical peaks in the agricultural production cycle, that explain the shortfalls in *ujamaa* production. This is not to say that there were no individual differences in terms of readiness to work for *ujamaa*. Such factors as level of income from private farming and size of village did have some impact on performance, as McHenry and also Sumra[43] have shown. The point is, however, that these were variations contained by the structures of the peasant mode of production. These structures could accommodate obvious inequalities stemming from differences in income. Both the economy of affection and the *ujamaa* policies ensured that these never became gross and offensive. *Ujamaa,* as practised by the villagers, reinforced the humanitarian nature of the peasant mode.

Ujamaa was seen by Nyerere as an attempt to base development efforts on an indigenous base instead of borrowing models and ideas from outside. This objective had to be compromised, however, when it became clear that the peasant mode was not flexible enough to meet the modern development demands by party and government officials. Village egalitarianism in rural Tanzania has been essentially concerned with ensuring everybody's right to subsistence. Within the peasant mode social inequalities have been accommodated without tension by following the principles of the economy of affection. Few peasants, if any, were prepared to trade their own institutions for the modern concept of equality. Nor were they voluntarily going to work communally in order to support the demands of other classes when this in fact collided with their own needs. *Ujamaa* as a radical strategy of development at the national level could not be reconciled with its objective of promoting development from within the peasant mode. As a result of this conflict, party and government officials were inclined to discard traditional peasant institutions in favour of the official stereotype of *ujamaa*. This did not make their task of convincing peasants to adopt *ujamaa* easier. The peasants believed they were already practising it, and in those areas where there existed a rich network of social institutions, generated within the peasant mode, the official version of *ujamaa* remained a strange concept.

One case in point is Bukoba, where local village institutions, developed in response to peasant needs, have always been strong. Apart from the clan structure which still survives, there are, as Rugumisa has shown,[44] a number of special purpose organizations, *byama,* for example, cattle owner associations for the purpose of communal herding, masons' associations for house construction, and associations catering for needs in connection with funerals and emergencies. He lists a total of twelve *byama* in Bukoba villages, four for men and eight for women. The activities of the women's associations include cultivating the land of a sick member, gathering papyrus reeds (for traditional gift-making), accompanying a bereft member going to another village, and sowing beans for a bereft member. These associations which form an integral part of the economy of affection keep villagers busy. They are important in the context of the village economy and its development, but they do not concern themselves with the issues that preoccupy national policy-makers. The unwillingness that many policy-makers in Bukoba have found among peasants to support official government policies stems largely from their involvement in an active local economy that has a rationality of its own. For peasants to trade such a rationality for one derived from modern development demands would be seen as betrayal by the other villagers. Still, this is exactly what the party and government officials were asking of the peasants when requiring them to adopt their version of *ujamaa*.

There are other examples of how the lack of dynamics of the rural structures complicated the attainment of *ujamaa* objectives. One objective was to make rural living more attractive and stop the exodus of youth into the urban areas. By providing schools, dispensaries and water supplies, rural living, it was expected, would cease to be different from urban living. Although a great expansion of these social amenities in rural Tanzania was achieved in the years after the Arusha Declaration, there was little evidence that the younger generations were more inclined to stay in the villages. Many wanted education and a job in the urban areas, something that parents often supported because it gave them an opportunity to acquire extra cash in case of emergency. Even in those places where modern education was not highly valued, for example, in the Islamic coastal belt, other reasons determined the exodus of youth to the towns. Marja-Liisa Swantz has shown how migration of the youth from the villages is a consequence of the traditional social organization, in which it is expected that the youth would go for employment away from home as part of the test of their manhood.[45]

Because of the difficulty in penetrating existing social organizations in the rural areas, it is not surprising that government tried to invoke a sense of emergency in order to achieve its objectives. When nature contributed to creating such conditions, as for instance happened in 1968 when the Rufiji River overflowed its banks in the lowlands south of Dar es Salaam, the government immediately moved people *en masse* away from the delta basin on to higher grounds where they were resettled in *ujamaa* villages. Although this move was meant to spare people the problem of occasional flooding hazards, many of the resettled villagers returned to the lowlands for good reason. One study shows that income was uncertain on the higher grounds because of scanty rainfall and consequently, once the water had receded, people moved back to the river banks where agricultural conditions were far more favourable.[46] Another study of the same area shows how the whole ecological system carefully built up by the peasants was destroyed as a result of resettlement. On their new land crops were easily attacked by vermin, while in the river delta they had developed a system whereby the location of their residences prevented attacks from wild animals.[47] Thus the resettlement operation in Rufiji was a double-edged weapon, which left some villagers better off but many others ill-equipped to sustain their livelihood. That these people moved back to the river delta, even at the cost of occasional cursing by the forces of nature, was more rational than living on land where because of the uncertainty of the rains they were doomed to permanent frailty.

The effects of *ujamaa*

The first five years of *ujamaa* did not have any significant impact on agricultural production in the peasant sector. It remained resource-based and as exposed to the whims of weather as before. One peasant tells the story of how nature itself for two consecutive years upset the efforts of his village to comply with government policies:

> In the first year we cultivated paddy and cotton. We had used seven acres for paddy and twenty for cotton. All of the paddy was destroyed by *floods* and we got only 1,700 T. shs from the twenty acres of cotton. For this reason in the following year we decided to concentrate on paddy, since cotton was not paying for us here. We cultivated more than seventy acres of paddy communally. All of it was destroyed by the *drought*.[48]

Nor did the *ujamaa* policies improve productivity of the land. By initially stressing the primacy of hoe cultivation in the villages, the authorities left the productive forces untouched, with the exception of work organization. Since the principle of communal work was difficult to accommodate within the peasant mode, its demands were generally ignored. Virtually all studies of *ujamaa* production conclude that productivity on the communal farm was considerably below that on the private farms.[49]

Subsequent government efforts to offer *ujamaa* villages the assistance of mechanized equipment also failed to improve productivity. Peasants developed a parasitic relationship to the machines.[50] They allowed them to do the work which they would otherwise have done but they did not – or were not trained to – develop a capacity to service and maintain the machinery. When the tractor developed a mechanical fault it was often abandoned by the villagers. There are many rusty pieces of farm machinery in rural Tanzania which bear witness of the costs of its patronage politics, developed to induce peasants to achieve higher levels of production on their communal farms. The effect was often the opposite, as we have noted above: the machinery gave the peasants a

TABLE 4.3 Maize purchased by NAPB/NMC,* by branch, from 1970/71 to 1976/77† (1000 metric tons)

Branch	70/71	% total	71/72	% total	72/73	% total	73/74	% total	74/75	% total	75/76	% total	76/77	% total	1977/78 NMC estimate (May) – unofficial	% total
Arusha	45.1	24	7.6	18	17.1	16	7.0	10	2.9	12	10.1	11	11.8	10	19.5	14
Central/Dodoma	58.6	32	15.6	36	54.1	51	34.5	46	–	–	6.0	7	11.8	10	15.0	10
Coast	–	–	–	–	–	–	–	–	–	–	1.5	2	2.3	2	5.0	4
Iringa	36.5	20	7.7	18	8.2	8	11.2	15	4.1	17	10.5	12	14.7	13	14.0	10
Kigoma	0.2	0	–	–	–	–	–	–	–	–	0.2	0	0.6	1	0.6	0
Kilimanjaro	16.0	9	2.9	7	11.8	11	6.0	8	4.8	20	4.8	5	4.2	4	4.5	3
Lindi	–	–	–	–	–	–	–	–	–	–	1.2	1	2.7	2	2.0	1
Mara	10.0	5	1.6	4	3.6	3	6.2	9	1.7	7	1.1	1	3.7	3	7.0	5
Mbeya	2.5	1	0.2	1	0.1	0	1.4	2	0.7	3	2.2	2	6.1	5	5.0	4
Morogoro	6.7	3	3.9	9	9.6	9	5.4	7	1.0	4	10.5	12	9.2	8	16.2	11
Mtwara	–	–	–	–	–	–	–	–	–	–	2.7	3	3.9	3	1.0	1
Mwanza	1.3	1	0.1	0	0.2	0	0.4	1	–	–	2.9	3	0.9	1	4.5	3
Rukwa	–	–	–	–	–	–	–	–	0.7	3	3.0	3	6.4	6	10.6	7
Ruvuma	1.7	1	–	–	0.5	1	0.1	0	4.2	18	12.7	14	9.7	9	12.0	8
Shinyanga	0.2	0	1.4	3	–	–	–	–	–	–	0.7	1	–	–	neg	0
Singida	5.4	3	1.0	2	0.7	1	1.6	2	–	–	0.5	1	1.1	1	0.2	0
Tabora	1.3	1	0.9	2	0.5	1	–	–	–	–	0.1	0	3.1	3	10.0	7
Tanga	0.9	0	0.1	0	–	–	–	–	3.8	16	20.2	22	20.6	18	16.0	11
West Lake	–	–	–	–	–	–	–	–	–	–	0.2	0	0.7	1	1.1	1
Total	186.4	100	43.0	100	106.4	101	73.8	100	23.9	100	91.1	100	113.5	100	144.2	100

* NAPB started operations in 1963 harvest year and was dissolved in 1973 when NMC took over its responsibilities
† Year: 1 July to 30 June, except 1976/77 when NMC started buying 1st June 1976
Source: NAPB/NMC Procurement Department

greater opportunity to take care of their own private plots. While Mapolu and Phillipson may be correct in asserting that a certain political framework (presumably Marxist Leninist, although the authors do not make that explicit) is necessary if technical processes of various kinds are to bring about an overall development of the productive forces, they are overly optimistic in their judgement of the possibilities of introducing such a political framework in the African peasant society.[51] Tanzanian peasants remain largely uncaptured, and a revolutionary socialist starts from as difficult premises to achieve his ends as the capitalist does.

A major change in relations of production is difficult to achieve as long as the small producers remain owners of their means of production. *Ujamaa* proved itself capable of reversing the relations of production in the capitalist sector but failed to do so in the peasant sector. In other words, the socialist policies adopted in Tanzania after the Arusha Declaration did put an end to capitalist large-scale farming and replaced it with state farms or collective farms owned by small peasants. Although the number of capitalist farms in Tanzania never were large in the first place, their role as producers of surplus grains and export crops had been important in the context of the national economy.

Figures in Table 4.3 show the purchase of surplus grains by the parastatal bodies, the National Agricultural Produce Board (NAPB) and the National Milling Corporation (NMC). These organizations have enjoyed monopoly status and been the only official buying agents in the rural areas. Consequently it must be recognized that purchase of surplus grains is bound to vary inversely with national needs. When peasants are able to harvest a lot, they will be strongly inclined to sell to the official buying agent, while the opposite is true when the harvests are small. In such situations the peasant will retain most of the crop for use within the household and whatever he is likely to sell will be on the black market where his produce commands a higher price. Even if these variations are considered it is clear from the figures in Table 4.3 that surplus production in Arusha and Iringa Regions, where most of the large-scale grain farms are, has definitely gone down. Weather is a determinant of agriculture all over Tanzania and the dramatic shifts in quantities of maize purchased from each region can be explained accordingly. In the case of Arusha and Iringa, the takeover of the capitalist farms is also a factor to consider. Their transformation into peasant *ujamaa* farms meant a considerable drop in production. As Table 4.3 indicates, production in Arusha and Iringa has never recovered and reached the levels achieved before 1971/72. However, in other regions, where peasant agriculture is the exclusive source of supply, depending on weather conditions, they have been able to reach even higher levels of production in recent years than they did before 1972.

In the light of these figures it is difficult to accept Marjorie Mbilinyi's proposition that, in spite of *ujamaa*, Tanzanian agriculture was undergoing transition to capitalism.[52] Tanzania's socialist policies after 1967 definitely reduced capitalist forms of production in the rural areas. Failure to acknowledge this means overlooking one of the achievements of *ujamaa*. It is another matter that *ujamaa* farms could not reach the same production levels as their capitalist predecessors. This was not because of petty-capitalist opposition. The petty-capitalist farmers were not forced into active opposition as their role in the rural areas was not really threatened. In spite of political rhetoric denouncing this group of farmers, they were quite capable of retaining their influence by operating in the economy of affection. It should also be noted that many of them were elected to positions of leadership in their respective villages. These people were often forced to sacrifice the advancement of their own farms by devoting their extra time to village leadership matters and to working on the communal village farms where, contrary to most assertions, they usually played an important role as a result of their leadership positions.[53] Shortfalls in production on the communal farms of Tanzania's *ujamaa* villages cannot be blamed on opposition by petty-capitalist farmers but rather on structural constraints inherent in the peasant mode of production.

While the first years of *ujamaa* did not yield any improvement in agricultural production, rural living did not deteriorate. To be sure, the terms of trade of the peasant, that is, the relationship between the prices received by him for his produce and the prices of commodities he bought, declined between 1965 and 1974, as Amey and Leonard show.[54] Tanzania was by no means unique in this respect and the terms of trade of the peasantry declined less in Tanzania (30 per cent) than it did in neighbouring Kenya (42 per cent). In Kenya, peasants kept paying local taxes to the local authorities, while in Tanzania that tax was abolished. Moreover, Tanzania initiated generous programmes expanding the social infrastructure, notably rural water supplies, schools and health dispensaries, in the rural areas. After primary-school fees were totally abolished in 1973, peasants in Tanzania did not have to pay for any of these services. In Kenya, peasants still have to pay for them. Although regional inequities continued to be obvious in Tanzania, they were reduced as a result of a deliberate policy to extend the social infrastructure primarily to the more backward parts of the country. In all, it is fair to say that between 1968 and 1973 peasants in Tanzania did not experience a deterioration in their living markedly greater than that of other social classes. They were able to feed themselves comfortably and earn cash, although insistence on communal farming by the authorities complicated their work. In large part, because there was no crisis in production, there was only a limited response to the official calls for higher levels of production, intensified particularly after the party manifesto, *Siasa ni kilimo* (politics is agriculture) was adopted in 1972. Official calculations that peasants would produce more in response to government generosity with social welfare measures proved wrong. The Tanzanian experience essentially supported the Smocks' conclusion, drawn from their study of rural development in eastern Nigeria, that extending social amenities to the rural population without ties, inflates expectations and prohibits government from interacting effectively with the peasants.[55]

Conclusions

In virtually all preceding political economy analysis of Tanzania during this period the guiding premise has been that relations of production were capitalist.[56] Consequently it has been logical to blame the difficulties of realizing the *ujamaa* policies on the bureaucratic bourgeoisie, portrayed as deliberately sabotaging these policies because they threatened its class position. This view, apart from being too simplistic, is also misleading.

There is reason to question the assumption, so often made in the study of the African political economy, that the bureaucratic bourgeoisie is reluctant to pursue policies contrary to the interest of the agencies of international capital. There are not necessarily any 'hidden' bonds of class solidarity between them. The petty-bourgeoisie in Africa is clearly anxious, like any other class, to create a power base of its own and defend it. Tanzania's *ujamaa* policies must be seen as an effort in that direction. Discernible differences in the Tanzanian leadership as to how the effort should be realized are not easily derived from a priori assumptions about class positions. They are better understood as a consequence of the actual policy experience. After all, virtually the whole bureaucratic bourgeoisie jumped on the *ujamaa* bandwagon in 1967. That it later appears as if it has defected must be seen as a result of having faced the pre-capitalist barriers in the attempt to achieve a socialist transformation. The policy experience taught the officials the virtue of considering different approaches. This statement is not meant as a defence of the officials. Mistakes were made and clumsiness characterized many of the efforts to get at the peasants. The bureaucracy lacked the sensitivity that would attract peasants to join in the effort. It must also be pointed out that where capitalist relations of production were destroyed, as for instance in Ismani, it is attributed more to the work of party and government officials than it is to the peasants.

Most studies, in which class analysis has been used, have overlooked the fact that in Africa all regimes, irrespective of ideological orientation, are placed in an antagonistic relationship with the peasantry. The peasantry does not really need the other classes which, therefore, objectively must be exploitative. Even a Marxist–Leninist regime attempting a socialist transformation does not escape this predicament. As long as the peasants control the means of subsistence and no real transformation of the means of production in the direction of higher productivity is achieved, the African petty-bourgeoisie is bound to find itself in an uncomfortable relationship of dependence on the peasantry. That the African regimes try to mitigate this structural constraint by collaborating with the agencies of outside capital and expertise is quite comprehensible.

Bureaucracy in Tanzania, therefore, fails to be developmental or progressive not because it lacks links with workers and peasants, as for instance Coulson argues.[57] Such links do exist in the context of the economy of affection. The problem is rather that where the peasant mode still prevails, there is little room for a revolutionary potential in the relationship of the state to the peasantry. When the petty-bourgeoisie interacts with the peasants through the state, the outcome is not a 'bang', only a 'poof'!

This experience was reinforced in the first years of *ujamaa* in Tanzania by the fact that the government had relaxed its controls of the peasantry. It removed the poll tax and generally relaxed other administrative control measures, for example, by-laws regarding agricultural production, that had served to compel the peasants to meet demands imposed by the ruling classes. When government extended services to the rural areas free of charge, as was the case with both health, water, and later primary education, they had little opportunity to establish a 'contract' with the peasantry. The change of platform for interaction with the peasants – from the capitalist market to the pre-capitalist market-place – did not facilitate the government task. If anything, the shift away from the market helped the peasants. The officials 'gave away' some of the policy instruments that over the years had served to make the peasants more dependent on other social classes. In the political market-place, peasants and officials met as sovereign units, and here small could often walk away victorious.

This is not to suggest that the market forces always worked in the interest of the officials. Lofchie, for instance, has blamed insufficient response to *ujamaa* on lack of financial incentives, notably low producer prices.[58] Such incentives work no wonders in a situation where labour, as opposed to land, is the scarce resource. They may have a marginal impact on the peasant producers but are decisive only to the petty-capitalist producers, as Lofchie also notes. The low producer prices cannot really explain much of the difficulties encountered in realizing *ujamaa*.

The real problem of *ujamaa* is that the material base of the peasant mode was far too narrow for a rapid socialist transformation. In addition, the structural constraints of the peasant mode, encountered during efforts to bring the peasants to meet the demands of capitalism, operated also against a socialist transformation. The above account does not imply that the peasants in Tanzania are uninterested in or incapable of change. The problem is that they are unwilling, and usually unable, to achieve it at a pace and to an extent that other social classes demand of them. Socialist transformation is as taxing on the peasants as capitalist development. Such was the lesson learned in Tanzania between 1967 and 1973. During these years the peasants were spared the heaviest burdens by virtue of the fact that the officials could not easily get at them. The peasants could continue to hide away from the officials.

References and notes

1. This is particularly well documented in Cranford Pratt, *The Critical Phase in Tanzania 1945–1968* (Cambridge University Press, 1976).
2. Nyerere's own ideas on this subject are collected in his volume, *Freedom and Socialism* (Dar es Salaam: Oxford University Press, 1968).
3. While Oscar Kambona went into exile, Bibi Titi Mohammed and Michael Kamaliza, together with some other ex-leaders, were accused of plotting against Nyerere's government and after court hearing sentenced to imprisonment.
4. Although socialist academics have expressed their views on Tanzania in many articles and papers, a representative selection of their papers and those of other socialists with Marxist inclinations are contained in Lionel Cliffe and John S. Saul, eds, *Socialism in Tanzania*, 2 vols (Nairobi: East African Publishing House, 1972 and 1973).
5. Jannik Bosen, Birgit Storgård Madsen and Tony Moody, *Ujamaa: Socialism from Above* (Uppsala: Scandinavian Institute of African Studies, 1977), p. 164.
6. Nyerere, 'Socialism and rural development' (Government Printer, Dar es Salaam).
7. ibid., p. 10.
8. Samuel S. Mushi, 'Ujamaa: modernization by traditionalization', *Taamuli* (Dar es Salaam), vol. 1, no. 2 (March 1971), pp. 13–29.
9. ibid., p. 22.
10. Nyerere, 'Socialism and rural development', op. cit., p. 21.
11. Ralph Ibbot, 'The disbanding of the Ruvuma Development Association, Tanzania', unpublished manuscript, London, 1969.
12. Lionel Cliffe and Griffith Cunningham, 'Ideology, organization and the settlement experience in Tanzania', in Cliffe and Saul, op. cit., vol 2, pp. 131–40.
13. Justin H. J. Maeda, 'Popular participation, control and development: a study of the nature and role of popular participation in Tanzania's rural development', unpublished doctoral dissertation, Department of Political Science, Yale University, 1976, pp. 163–5.
14. Nyerere, 'Socialism and rural development', op. cit., p. 13.
15. Immanuel Bavu, 'Leadership and communication in the ujamaa process: a case study of Kabuku Ndani Ujamaa Village Cooperative Society', unpublished MA thesis, Department of Sociology, University of Dar es Salaam, 1971.

16. Philip Raikes, 'Ujamaa Vijijini and rural socialist development', paper presented to the Ninth Social Science Conference of the East African Universities, Dar es Salaam, December 1973, p. 15.
17. Prime Minister's Office, Planning and Research Division, *'Maendeleo ya Vijiji vya Ujamaa'*, Dar es Salaam, National Printing Co., 1974, p. 1.
18. This argument is made by Michael Lofchie, 'Collective villagization, agrarian crisis and economic liberalization', paper presented to the graduate seminar on African Agriculture, University of California, Los Angeles, spring quarter, 1978.
19. The term was originally coined by Issa Shivji to describe Tanzania's ruling class in the wake of the nationalizations of capitalist enterprises. See his *Class Struggles in Tanzania* (Heinemann Educational Books, 1976).
20. Ibbot, op. cit.
21. This has been confirmed through my own conversations with leaders of these villages.
22. I. K. S. Musoke, 'Building socialism in Bukoba: the establishment of Rugazi (Nyerere) Ujamaa Village', in J. H. Proctor, ed., *Building Ujamaa Villages in Tanzania,* Studies in Political Science No. 1 (Dar es Salaam: Tanzania Publishing House, 1971), p. 4.
23. Clyde R. Ingle, *From Village to State in Tanzania: The Politics of Rural Development* (Ithaca: Cornell University Press, 1972), pp. 253–4.
24. See Shivji, op cit., H. U. E. Thoden van Velzen, 'Staff, kulaks, peasants', in Cliffe and Saul, op. cit., volume two, pp. 153–79; Gerhard Tschannerl, 'Rural water supply in Tanzania: is politics or "techniques" in command?', paper presented for the Ninth Social Science Conference of the East African Universities Conference, Dar es Salaam, December 1973; Michaela von Freyhold, 'Government staff and ujamaa villages', paper presented to the same conference; and Andrew Coulson, 'The evolution of rural politics in Tanzania, or can a government bureaucracy bring about development?', Economic Research Bureau Seminar Paper, University of Dar es Salaam, January 1975. A non-Marxist who comes to the same conclusion is James R. Finucane, *Rural Development and Bureaucracy in Tanzania: The Case of Mwanza Region* (Uppsala: Scandinavian Institute of African Studies, 1974).
25. Finucane, op. cit.
26. This happened in Kibedya *ujamaa* village in Kilosa District, which I visited. Student reports indicate that it also happened in other villages in other parts of the country.
27. Interviews with officials in Kilosa, April 1976 and Kigoma, May 1976.
28. Von Freyhold, op. cit., p. 12.
29. David J. Vail, 'Technology for socialist development in rural Tanzania', paper presented to the 17th Annual Meeting of the African Studies Association, Chicago, November 1974, p. 11.
30. It has been quite common for groups of volunteers to travel to Tanzania and there visit and work in *ujamaa* villages. This has been organized through TANU or the government.
31. A. T. Mohele, 'The Ismani maize credit programme', Economic Research Bureau Seminar Paper, University of Dar es Salaam, February 1975.
32. Tanzania Rural Development Bank, 'Trends in maize production in Ismani and other parts of Iringa Region', mimeographed report, 1974.

33. Adhu Awiti, 'Economic differentiation in Ismani, Iringa Region', *The African Review* vol. 3, no. 3 (June 1973), p. 242.
34. Mohele, op. cit., p. 17.
35. Jean M. Due, 'The allocation of credit to *ujamaa* villages and to small private farmers in Tanzania', mimeo., Department of Agricultural Economics, University of Illinois at Champaign-Urbana, n.d., p. 28.
36. ibid., p. 26.
37. Samuel S. Mushi, '*Ujamaa* planning and the politics of allocation: the case of Morogoro District', mimeo., Department of Political Science, University of Dar es Salaam, 1977, pp. 18–19.
38. Frigyes Nagy, 'Effectiveness of aid to *ujamaa* villages', *The Standard* (Dar es Salaam), 31 December 1971.
39. James Bugengo, '*Ujamaa* in Mara Region', paper presented to the Ninth Social Science Conference of the East African Universities, Dar es Salaam, December 1973.
40. Frank Holmquist, 'Mechanisms of internal dependency: effects upon East African agricultural producers' associations', paper presented to the Joint Meeting of the African Studies and Latin American Studies Associations, Houston, November 1977.
41. For a review of the measures taken by TANU to supervise more closely the political process, see Election Study Committee, *Socialism and Participation* (Dar es Salaam: Tanzania Publishing House, 1975).
42. Dean McHenry, 'Peasant participation in communal farming: the Tanzanian experience', paper presented to the African Studies Association Conference, Boston, November 1976, p. 26.
43. Suleiman Sumra, 'Problems of agricultural production in *ujamaa* villages in Handeni District', Economic Research Bureau Seminar Paper, University of Dar es Salaam, March 1975.
44. S. M. Rugumisa, 'Mutual aid groups and their potential for agricultural development in Bukoba District with special reference to Bukabuye Village', paper presented to the Ninth Social Science Conference of the East African Universities, Dar es Salaam, December 1973.
45. Marja-Liisa Swantz, 'Youth and *ujamaa* development in the Coast Region of Tanzania', paper presented to the Ninth Social Science Conference of the East African Universities, Dar es Salaam, December 1973, p. 12.
46. Joseph Angwazi and Benno Ndulu, 'An evaluation of *ujamaa* villages in the Rufiji Area 1968–1972', paper presented to the Ninth Social Science Conference of the East African Universities, Dar es Salaam, December 1973.
47. Audun Sandberg, '*Ujamaa* and control of environment', paper presented to the Ninth Social Science Conference of the East African Universities, Dar es Salaam, December 1973.
48. Henry Mapolu, 'The social and economic organization of *ujamaa* villages', mimeo., Department of Sociology, University of Dar es Salaam, 1973, p. 83.
49. Henry Mapolu and Gerard Phillipson, 'Agricultural cooperation and the development of the productive forces: some lessons from Tanzania', *Africa Development* (Dakar) vol. 1, no. 1 (1976) discusses this problem with reference to several villages in Tanzania.
50. Von Freyhold, op. cit.
51. Mapolu and Phillipson, op. cit., p. 56.

52. Marjorie Mbilinyi, 'The transition to capitalism in rural Tanzania', Economic Research Bureau Seminar Paper, University of Dar es Salaam, February 1974.
53. Blame is placed on the bureaucrats by all the authors mentioned in note 24.
54. Alan B. Amey and David K. Leonard, 'Public policy, class and inequality in Kenya and Tanzania', mimeographed, Department of Political Science, University of California, Berkeley, September 1977.
55. David R. Smock and Audrey C. Smock, *Cultural and Political Aspects of Rural Transformation* (New York: Praeger, 1972).
56. For example, Shivji, op. cit., Mapolu and Phillipson, op. cit., Mbilinyi, op. cit.
57. Coulson, op. cit.
58. Lofchie, op. cit.

CHAPTER 5

Small the deceitful:
government versus peasants after 1973

November 1973 was important in the post-Arusha developments in
Tanzania for two reasons. It was the beginning of a drought that would
carry on throughout the agricultural season, reducing Tanzania's grain
harvest to less than half the normal. 6 November that same year was
also the date on which President Nyerere announced that all
Tanzanians would have to live in villages by the end of 1976. Although
the President made his announcement about compulsory villagization
at a time when the full dimensions of the drought were yet to be known,
the two events are interrelated. The drought illustrated the strong
dependence of Tanzanian agriculture on the whims of nature. It was
this type of dependence that was still decisive in rural Tanzania, not
peasant dependence on other social classes. President Nyerere's announcement confirmed this: the ruling classes had failed to capture the
peasants to serve their needs. In fact, as the two previous chapters have
tried to show, the peasants had continued to slip away from government
control after independence. Compulsory villagization was meant to
reverse that process. It was the strongest blow to peasant autonomy
after independence. Tanzania is still in the aftermath of this extensive
resettlement effort and the final outcome is not yet clear. What is
apparent, however, is the resilience of the peasant mode of production.
There is no evidence that the peasants are readily prepared to trade their
dependence on nature for a dependence on other social classes. While
nature causes only temporary humiliations (and these are often
alleviated by the authorities who for political reasons cannot afford
them), dependence on other social classes implies total and permanent
subjugation. Peasants, in spite of being forced into villages where
presumably official access is easier than in a situation of scattered
households, have continued in their reluctance to go all the way to meet
demands made on them by the bureaucratic bourgeoisie.

The villagization policy

President Nyerere first announced the compulsory villagization policy
when on an up-country tour inspecting the progress of the *ujamaa*

policies. As noted earlier it was not the first time that he had called for villagization. Such appeals go back as far as 1962. It was the first time, however, that he made it obligatory for all Tanzanians in the rural areas to live in villages. It is interesting that although his decree on villagization triggered off more far-reaching effects in the countryside than any other previous policy, unlike so many of his other public statements his speech never ended up as a published document bearing Nyerere's name.

His speech, broadcast on the government-controlled Radio Tanzania, reminded the audience about all the things that the TANU Government had done for the people after the Arusha Declaration: abolishing the poll tax, abolishing primary-school fees, building permanent, clean water supplies in the villages, expanding the number of health clinics and dispensaries in the rural areas, increasing primary-school facilities, etc. He then went on to ask what the peasants had done in return for these favours. In answering that question, President Nyerere suggested that they had done virtually nothing. They had remained idle and evaded their responsibility to make a contribution to the country's socialist development. He concluded his speech by saying that he knew he could not turn people into socialists by force, but what his government could do was to ensure that everybody lived in a village. He said he wanted that to be done before the end of 1976.[1]

President Nyerere's speech echoed sentiments that had been expressed earlier by both German and British colonial officials. They all sprang out of the same policy dilemma: what to do with an endless number of smallholder peasants whose concerns do not extend to the nation as a whole. In the same way as the Germans tried to instil in the peasant mind that they had a *Lebensaufgabe,* Nyerere stressed the moral obligation of the peasantry to contribute to the successful implementation of the *ujamaa* policies. His tone was sterner than usual, barely hiding his anger. He was talking as a teacher upset with the behaviour of his pupils.

The compulsory villagization in Tanzania between 1973 and 1976 is the largest resettlement effort in the history of Africa. Claims that as many as ten million Tanzanians were actually moved are exaggerated and derived from the number of people living in villages registered after the resettlement had been completed.[2] Not all these people had moved. In many villages there was already a nucleus settlement before villagization started. In these instances the policy required people living in scattered homesteads near such settlements to move there to set up permanent residence. In other words, not everywhere was it a matter of starting a completely new settlement. When account was taken in 1976 of what villagization had achieved such factors were not considered. Even so, there is no doubt that villagization was a gigantic effort, involving the movement of probably as many as five million rural Tanzanians.

Editorials in campaign

Villagization was organized on a regional or district basis as mass resettlement campaigns. Although people were not forced to move over long stretches of land, they had to agree to abandoning their previous residence and land. Where people refused to accept this condition, coercion was applied. Party and government authorities were anxious to prove their capacity to mobilize the people and consequently no resources were spared. Existing government programmes were abandoned in favour of villagization and army units were called in to supplement personnel and equipment. Although some campaigns were quite well planned, others were carried out in a great hurry, one region trying to prove that it was more capable than the other. Consequently, one cannot really talk of these efforts as planned programmes. They were more like mobilization campaigns, in which deliberately an element of coercion was used to achieve the objective.

People refusing to move into villages were portrayed as backward. The peasants in the Rufiji River valley, for example, who in 1974 again became the victims of floods, but still refused to move to higher grounds, were castigated in an editorial in *Daily News*, the English language daily of the Tanzanian Government, as 'selfish individuals' and people failing to know what was in their own interest. They were compared with Tanzanians living in villages where 'negative individualistic tendencies are already giving way to civilized communal feelings.'[3] The editorial concluded that the peasants in Rufiji must be made to 'hang their superstition' and be moved into villages compulsorily.

The individualism that concerned the party and government officials in these years was not really capitalist but one stemming from peasant autonomy and reluctance to co-operate with others for the development of the country as a whole. This was echoed in many public statements, for instance, the following editorial in the *Daily News*:

> Mwalimu [Nyerere] has frequently reiterated during the last ten years the importance of people congregating in villages. Such proximity is a necessity of development. For when people abandon their isolation and come together into well-planned and laid out villages, they can be reached by social services, and they can effectively operate in co-operation. Only then can they begin to develop.[4]

Villagization was the most important of a series of policy measures taken by TANU in the wake of the Arusha Declaration to replace the capitalist market with the political market-place as the principal forum for interaction with the peasants. This effort was accelerated after 1973 and comprised two sets of policies: (a) the removal of all middlemen, complicating the interaction between government and peasants; and (b) the reorganization of party and government structures to reach the peasants more effectively.

Removal of the middlemen

Apart from Asian and African private traders, co-operatives made up the most important middlemen in the rural areas. They controlled significant amounts of capital and thus provided a base for petty-bourgeois power independent of the state. Co-operative shops had been tried in Tanzania since the early 1960s when they began with extensive Israeli assistance. Apart from a number of such co-operative shops in Moshi, the regional headquarters of Kilimanjaro Region, these shops by and large fell victim to mismanagement and, even worse, in many cases to misappropriation of funds by office holders. In spite of an overwhelming evidence of dishonesty and inefficient management of these urban shops, the government decided in February 1976 to initiate a mass campaign – Operation *Maduka* (Shops) – to start communally owned shops in each village and close down all private retail outlets in the rural areas. Officials in many regions rushed headlong into this without awaiting policy guidelines from the Prime Minister's Office. Private shop-owners in the rural areas of Mwanza Region were given ten days to close down their shops.[5] The same rule was applied in Lindi Region, where, in addition, the Party Regional Working Committee declared that in future it would be supervising the distribution of essential commodities in the rural areas.[6] In Kyela District, Mbeya Region, the Regional Party Secretary ordered the immediate closure of forty private shops to be replaced by three *ujamaa* shops in the area.[7] A similar rush to close private shops was experienced in many other places.

The overall effect of this approach was to create shortages of goods in the rural areas, and so bitter were the sentiments in many places that the President had to call a stop to the practice of closing private shops two-and-a-half months after the policy was first initiated. Nyerere acknowledged that the peasants had been made to suffer unnecessarily by being forced to go without essential items such as sugar, salt, kerosene, soap and matchboxes, which all disappeared when the private shops were closed and there was not a sufficient number of village shops to take their place.[8]

The pace of implementation slowed down considerably after the Presidential statement. Private shop-owners who had lost their trading licences were given them back. The rule was that no private shop should be closed until a viable village shop had been established and its management proved competent. In spite of this stoppage, in March 1977 the Prime Minister's Office reported that there were 3284 *ujamaa* or co-operative shops in the villages, compared with 300 when Operation *Maduka* first began. Approximately 40 per cent of all villages had such shops, although it is not known how well they served the people. In some regions, like Dodoma, private retailers in the rural areas had completely disappeared.[9] More and more, distribution of commodities to the rural areas was handled through political and administrative channels.

Not all middlemen in the rural areas were operating in the guise of private shop-owners. The strongest middleman, from the viewpoint of the government, was the co-operative movement. This became increasingly clear in the 1970s, as TANU tried to replace the market mechanism with bureaucratic controls. The co-operative movement had originally been created in the context of a capitalist economy, where it was expected that these organizations would help to incorporate the peasant producers into the monetary economy. In those areas where viable co-operatives were started such was also the effect of their operation, although it is clear that the co-operatives never served members equally. The co-operatives were run by the petty-capitalist farmers, very often elected to leading positions by the peasants on the grounds that they were the most qualified to run these institutions. With a growing central direction of the national economy after the Arusha Declaration, co-operatives gradually became more closely tied to the state and its demands. The conflict between the notion of the co-operative as a voluntary association catering primarily for member needs, and of the co-operative as an agency of change responsive to central commands, grew increasingly tense. Co-operatives were asked to take on a wide range of responsibilities. They were unilaterally turned into multi-purpose institutions, although they clearly lacked the managerial capacity to handle all responsibilities. Technical assistance from the Nordic countries could do little to improve the situation. Operational costs increased as a result of inadequate management and members received less for their produce and had to pay more for their goods. Co-operatives lost their legitimacy in the eyes of the peasants.

This became the principal reason for a government decision to abolish all primary co-operatives in Tanzania in 1975. A subsequent step was taken in 1976 to close down all secondary co-operatives, the regional co-operative unions which had served as wholesale agencies of the primary co-operatives. There is little doubt, however, that the closure of all co-operatives was also determined by the fact that the bureaucratic bourgeoisie were unable effectively to control the co-operative organizations. The leadership of the co-operative movement often had divergent views from party and government officials on matters relating to rural development. By virtue of their position as leaders of organizations with a local power base, they could argue effectively with party and government leaders. Moreover, they could mitigate the pressures on the peasants by the party. Although the word 'middleman' was not officially used to describe the co-operatives,[10] this is how the bureaucratic bourgeoisie in party as well as government increasingly came to look at the co-operative leadership. Because they controlled a large share of the exchanges between government and peasants but were not fully incorporated into the party and government machineries, they were making policy implementation more difficult.

With the dissolution of all co-operatives, the parastatal companies dealing with the purchase and sale of agricultural crops were invited to deal directly with the peasants. According to the official view, this way peasants would be spared the extra costs of maintaining inefficient co-operative organizations and their deals with the government would be simplified.

Reorganization of party and government

Experience had shown in the 1960s that the political market-place was still a weak institution. Peasants could easily slip away or hide away from the policy-makers. Reorganization of both party and government, therefore, was necessary also as part of the effort to capture the peasants. A strong blow was directed against the local authorities, the district councils which, like the co-operatives, had served as instruments of petty-bourgeois power, largely independent of the state. The district councils were effectively crippled when in 1969 central government ministries were told to take over their most important functions: primary education, rural health and maintenance of secondary roads. The official reason for this intervention was the blatant inefficiency which had characterized the running of many district councils. It was also a way of breaking the power of local notables who had used the district councils to undermine party policies. With the growing emphasis on party discipline after 1968, district councils claiming autonomy were seen as outdated. With the sweeping decentralization reform of 1972, their legal autonomy was abolished. They were retained as 'development councils' within the policy-making set-up of the district.

The decentralization reform was essentially one of deconcentration, implying the delegation of authority from central government ministries to the regional administration. It was the first such reform in Africa that went far enough to include delegation of financial control to the regions. The regions were elevated to the same level as ministries with an annual budget of their own. While the Regional Party Secretary remained the political head of the regions, through the decentralization reform they were given as their administrative head a Development Director, whose responsibility would be equivalent to that of the Principal Secretary in government ministries but who, as the title suggests, was expected to deal particularly with development matters.[11]

The whole reform was conceived as a way of making government more development-oriented and better equipped to tackle local problems of development. Red tape had previously delayed decisions vital for rural development. By giving funds to the regions they were expected to plan and co-ordinate development more effectively than

the central government ministries had been able to. It was also assumed
that this attempt to bring the government closer to the people would
imply more extensive popular participation in decision-making.[12]

The most important aspect of decentralization has not been popular
participation, but the bringing under one single umbrella all development activities in the rural areas. Villages have been invited to
participate in the planning process by sending in their 'plans' – lists of
development priorities as conceived by the villagers – but the terms of
participation have been carefully controlled at district or regional levels.
Decentralization has been an effort to increase the intensity of the
interaction between authorities and the peasants and thus compel the
peasants to respond more frequently to government or party initiatives.
Regional Party Secretaries have tried to ensure that through the
administrative arm it has been possible to co-ordinate and control all
development activities and reduce the autonomy of any non-
governmental organizations. Where such organizations have been
important, they have usually been co-opted and invited to participate in
the development programmes conceived by the party and government
officials.

The principles of participation and efficiency which featured so
prominently in the original policy statements about decentralization
have gradually receded into secondary positions. Instead, 'operations'
and 'campaigns' to change the rural areas, in which all available
resources have been mobilized for a single cause, have developed into
the most important mode of policy-making. In those areas where
government has traditionally found it difficult to evoke response from
the peasants, this approach has been adopted quite frequently. They
have usually started from the assumption that the peasants are not
willing to meet government demands of their own free will and hence
have to be forced to accept them.

Since the government, however, has found it impossible to interact
with the peasants exclusively in terms of 'operations', the problem of
reaching the peasants has not been totally resolved, not even in the
context of the new villages. Non-availability of vehicles and impassable
roads have often limited the effectiveness of government services and
the follow-up of policies in the villages. This has been particularly true
with reference to the agricultural extension service which, after the
decentralization reform, got involved in more administration and lost
control of its own vehicles. Thus their effectiveness declined very
drastically. President Nyerere even went as far in 1976 as to claim in one
public speech that Tanzanian agriculture would do as well without the
extension service. This further lowered the morale of a group of officials
who already felt that decentralization had deprived them of their chief
responsibilities and turned them into assistants to a group of generalist
administrators with little feeling for the demands of extension work.[13]
Moreover the peasants, who in many places had never really fully

appreciated the work of these officials in the first place, were only too happy to use the words of the President to justify their indifference to them.

It was in the light of these shortcomings that the government in May 1977 tried to place its lower level officials in the villages. The first directive said that all technical field staff based in ward and division headquarters – the two levels between the district and the village – should move to live in villages by 1 June 1977. They were still to be paid by the government and live in the villages on their night allowance and, therefore, not be a financial burden to the village residents.[14] It was not clear to whom these officials would be responsible.

In the wake of the abolition of the primary co-operative societies in 1975, Tanzania had passed a new Act giving villages – whether *ujamaa* or not – status as legal entities, and thus authority to enter into contractual arrangements with other organizations.[15] The new legislation was also meant to encourage a certain amount of self-government in the villages, by institutionalizing the Village Assembly – consisting of all village members – as the ultimate authority, and the Village Council as its executive arm. Most villages are still financially too weak to take full advantage of this legislation but it is conceived as paving the way for more extensive popular participation in development in the rural areas. Many villages, when informed about the policy to make officials work in the villages, insisted that they become responsible to the Village Council.

Partly because of this political controversy and partly because the directive was implemented too hurriedly, its effect was very limited. The main constraints seem to have been lack of funds to pay night allowances and lack of vehicles to ensure transport of the staff to the villages.[16] The issue surfaced again in early 1978 when the government, this time wise from its previous mistakes, posted officials on a permanent basis to 4000 of Tanzania's approximately 8000 villages. There would be no question of night allowances and to boost the government work in the villages, not only lower level field staff were selected. The official title of these officers was to be 'village managers' but their exact role was left somewhat ambiguous, although officials in the Prime Minister's Office anticipated two major duties: to be a general manager of village affairs under the Village Council, and to be a production manager of the communal village farm that would be set up where it did not already exist. In short, the village manager is the extended arm of the government in the villages. It is an interesting example of how the government in the wake of villagization has tried to reach out and capture the peasants but it is also a comment on how difficult it is to achieve this objective within the framework of conventional administrative organization, particularly in a situation, like that of Tanzania, where an undeveloped infrastructure limits interaction between authorities and villages.

The creation on 5 February 1977 of the *Chama cha Mapinduzi*
Revolutionary Party) through the amalgamation of TANU and the
Afro-Shirazi Party – the ruling party on Zanzibar – crowned Nyerere's
effort to bring the two countries together not only in name but also in a
closer political union. The new party, however, also signified the end of
a series of efforts to regulate the political market-place that followed
after the Arusha Declaration and Tanzania's decision to go socialist.
Although due-paying TANU members automatically became founding
members of the CCM, it was stated clearly in the party constitution that
new members would only be accepted after having proved their grasp of
party principles and policies and sworn an oath of allegiance to them.
Although this did not automatically turn CCM into a vanguard party, it
did set definite conditions for membership. In its final years of existence
TANU tried to become a more disciplinary organization in which strict
leadership criteria were applied at all levels, including in the end the
villages. The new CCM is even more committed to getting at those who
nurse and support the economy of affection.

The importance of this can in part be seen as a result of the growing
tendency among leaders in Tanzania in the 1970s to engage in petty
corruption and favouritism. There were two types of unlawful practices,
one stemming from the extension of the economy of affection into the
party organization, the other resulting from a deliberate neglect of
fundamental party principles. The first was essentially practised by
party officials with a sufficiently strong power base of their own to get
away with it. For them it was important to prove to their local
constituents that they still possessed enough leverage to secure them
certain goods or services. The other type of corrupt practice was a more
direct abuse of office and usually adopted by members of the bureau-
ratic bourgeoisie to secure themselves favours in a situation of scarcity.
With the growth of the bureaucratic bourgeoisie in the 1970s and the
frequent shortages of goods in the economy, the second type of
corruption was on the increase.

In addition to enforcing stricter selection of leaders, the coming of
CCM also allowed for fresh election of new party leaders at all levels.
President Nyerere, at the time of the 1975 elections had hinted at the
possibility that he might resign as President of the country. One reason
for making that idea public was to make other leaders in the country
conceive the possibility of stepping down. In a way, his statement was a
polite hint to others that the time had come for them to retire from
politics. In the absence of a very wide response to this suggestion, he
reiterated it in a new form in connection with the formation of CCM.
Referring to the traditional principle in African societies that at a certain
point in time the elders give way to younger people, without necessarily
having to be told to do so, *kung'atuka* in Swahili, Nyerere appealed to
party leaders to accept that honourable principle.[17] This time, the
response was greater and a number of senior party officials, for

example, members of the Central Committee and Regional Chairmen, voluntarily stepped down.

Elections to leadership positions in the CCM were held throughout 1977 and it is clear that Nyerere to a large extent achieved his objective of leadership circulation. Although some of the old TANU hands were returned, a significant number of younger and more educated people were elected to senior leadership positions. These new leaders differ from the previous generation of party leaders in that they have no real mass base of their own, but occupy positions of leadership by virtue of their personal respectability. They are likely to be less susceptible to the pressures of the economy of affection and also better equipped to interpret and communicate party principles. They are all drawn from the 'respectable' section of the bureaucratic bourgeoisie; they are relatively well off (and presumably not in need of petty bribes); they are educated; and they are loyal to the demands of Nyerere. In the same way as cabinet positions have increasingly become occupied by technocrats, that is, people with a concern to get things done as efficiently as possible within the parameters determined by the ruling party, the party is turning to people who are believed to be able not only to talk, but also to do the things the party decides.

The creation of CCM gave Nyerere an opportunity to circulate leaders in such a way that people could not say that it was simply a matter of 'old wine in new bottles'. He was able to encourage leaders to retire in an honourable fashion, and by getting younger and more educated people into the leadership of the new party, he achieved in fact within the framework of the single-party system what would in multi-party systems be called a change of regime. His ability to orchestrate this change without any serious political disruptions bears witness of the enormous respect that Nyerere enjoys in Tanzania. It also made him unique in Africa in that this major circulation in leadership was achieved not by decree but by elections. The official mass media rightly heralded the coming of CCM as the 'fresh start of our revolution'.[18]

The reorganization of the political party in Tanzania was the climax of the efforts by Nyerere after the Arusha Declaration to replace the capitalist market with the political market-place, in which presumably a new contract of communal solidarity would take the place of the individualist, self-seeking orientations generated by the market. Ten years after the Arusha Declaration it is fair to say that Tanzania had created a society in which the principles of individualist acquisition of wealth, while still practised by some people, were generally condemned. The market may be an efficient system of allocating values in society, but it also introduces an uncomfortable element of ruthlessness into people's lives, by giving people a market value. Nyerere wanted to create a system in which the question: 'What are you worth in the market?' would not be asked. By the end of the 1970s, less than twenty ears after Tanzania's political independence, his country was well on its way to achieve that objective.

By reducing the influence of the market, Nyerere wants to achieve a more human society in which performance is assessed on the basis of other criteria than purely personal possessions and personal earnings. In trying to turn his country away from market criteria he has enjoyed spontaneous support by many since it is characteristic of all pre-capitalist societies that non-economic performance excites popular admiration. What Tanzania has achieved in the years after the Arusha Declaration is to replace an essentially capitalist-inspired superstructure with an institutional formation that more directly reflects the pre-apitalist realities of the country. Although Tanzania is imbued with a socialist development orientation, its social formations and institutional set-up can hardly be described as socialist, the main reason being that the pre-modern structures are still at work in the country. In this situation the bureaucracy which has grown as a result of the gradual removal of market influences is inevitably less efficient and faces particularly serious problems because of being maintained over a fragmented economy. Even after villagization, bureaucrats have had difficulty in relating to the peasants, because it is not the practice of the latter to use the 'voice', but instead the 'exit' option to demonstrate their will. In other words, participation by peasants in the policy-making process is often difficult to encourage because the peasants do not want to initiate demands, which later can be held against them and lead to their subjugation. They are therefore often more inclined to let government officials take the initiatives and give their support to these policies on their own terms rather than those set by the officials. That is why in political meetings in rural Tanzania, as elsewhere in Africa, the contributions by the peasants are usually in the form of questions or complaints about the performance by the officials but hardly ever in the form of major policy initiatives that are likely to bring them into collaboration with the authorities. In villages that I have visited in Tanzania there has been a difference between those which have already developed a relatively strong dependence on the market and those which have not. The former have taken initiatives of their own, which in some cases have gone contrary to policy preferences at regional or district levels. As the case of *ujamaa* villages such as Upper Kitete and Labuku Ndani shows, this has landed the villages in conflict with the authorities. By responding to the economic incentives on the market rather than the policy framework of the political market-place these villages are seen to violate the rules of the political game.

The vast majority of Tanzania's villages comply with these rules. If they do take initiatives, or are invited to do so, they are usually careful enough to choose projects which do not imply a long-term dependence. Above all, they are careful not to propose production targets for crops other than their subsistence crops. The fact that the peasants are reluctant to use their voice option is not because they are prevented from doing so by the officials but because they have a vested interest in not doing so. It is more rational for them to allow the officials to take the initiative. That way they can handle the bureaucrats more effectively. In the political market-place they have everything to gain from doing so. Although many observers of the Tanzania scene have seen this as peasant dependence on the government,[19] it is better understood the other way around. The bureaucrats are dependent on the peasants. By refusing to take initiatives, or only those which can be accommodated within the local economy, they exercise their 'exit' option vis-à-vis the political system at large. To the bureaucratic bourgeoisie the peasants become deceitful and they are forced to go in pursuit of them.

This tendency has clearly been more marked in recent years, as the market has receded in importance as a policy tool. The degradation of the market has reduced the basis of interaction between authorities and peasants. This has been one of the more obvious costs of the Tanzanian approach in which emphasis is laid on fundamental values such as human dignity and equality rather than the efficiency of various policy instruments. In practice, it means that the interaction between government and peasants is less diverse. The policy options in the political market-place are few and usually reduced to unilateral demands by the authorities that peasants do this or that. The arbitrary nature of government action becomes more apparent in the political market-place than on the economic market because it is personal. Although government interaction with the peasants in Tanzania always carries the danger of authoritarianism for the simple reason that the economic structures invite it, this element has taken on an increasing importance as the bureaucratic bourgeoisie has established its power at the expense of the petty-bourgeois groups outside the public sector. It also appears that peasant response has declined with growing authoritarianism. The peasants have become more inclined than ever before to use their exit option. This behaviour which in the eyes of the officials is deceitful because it reduces Tanzania's development potential has intensified their efforts to capture the peasants.

As a result, they find themselves in a difficult policy dilemma: in order to expand the domestic base for development, the peasant mode of production needs to be transcended, yet with the degradation of the market Tanzanian officials have reduced the range of policy tools available to achieve that objective. The bureaucratic bourgeoisie, therefore, is left with a more intensified use of the few tools at their disposal. Most of these are political and administrative rather than economic. They belong to the political market-place rather than the capitalist market. The former is not particularly sensitive to cost-benefit considerations. It is quite possible, therefore, that both costs and benefits take time to realize. Although planning is stressed in Tanzania, it is difficult to apply effectively in the inorganic environment of rural

production and development. These policy-making realities are important to bear in mind as we return to government interaction with the
peasantry in the post-villagization period.

The bureaucrats' approach to agriculture

The approach by the bureaucratic bourgeoisie towards agriculture after
1973 has been twofold. It has aimed at reducing state dependence on
peasant agriculture, but it has also tried to achieve greater control over
that same peasant agriculture.

Both party and government officials have been particularly concerned with food production in Tanzania after the serious drought that
forced the country to import large quantities of food after 1973.
Although the import of maize began on a significant scale in 1971 after
the takeover of the capitalist farms, the most dramatic increase in grain
imports took place in 1974. As Table 5.1 shows, for the 1974/75 season
Tanzania was forced to import more grain than it had done in all
previous years after the Arusha Declaration.

The government was aware of the difficulties in purchasing grain
from the peasants in times of emergency. In spite of appeals by both
party and government to sell their surplus grain to the official buying
agencies,[20] the response was limited throughout 1974 and 1975 when
weather conditions remained adverse in many parts of Tanzania and
peasants were inclined to build up their food reserves on the farm.

TABLE 5.1. Official grain imports to Tanzania, 1966–75* (in metric tons)

Crop	66/67	67/68	68/69	69/70	70/71	72/73	73/74	74/75
Maize	14 322	–	–	46 921	–	92 283	78 944	294 100
Paddy-rice	7 586	5 753	–	–	–	–	–	72 600
Wheat	–	13 600	36 700	35 700	11 600	45 500	8 200	46 500
Total	21 908	19 353	36 700	82 621	11 600	137 783	87 144	413 200

Source: Ministry of Agriculture, Dar es Salaam
* no figures available for 1971–2

To cope with this problem, the government of Tanzania has taken a
variety of measures. It is considering the expansion of large-scale maize
production on state farms in various parts of the country. A proposal
for six such farms to be run by parastatal companies was laid before the
government in 1976 and later approved. The objective was to increase
the total maize production by 20 000 to 30 000 tons of maize annually
through semi-mechanized farming, the basic operations to be executed
by tractors but other activities, such as clearing, weeding, picking, etc.,

to be done by hired labour. Farm management, at least initially, would be in the hands of expatriates.[21] Although the effects of these farms on maize production were unknown at the time of writing, it is clear that they were justified in government circles as ways of ensuring alternative channels for the production of surplus grain. After the 1973/74 drought there was a legitimate concern to set up a strategic grain reserve in the country. For this reason new storage facilities were needed. In addition to three main grain elevators, built soon after the Arusha Declaration when there was hope of major strides forward in agricultural production, the official view in Tanzania stressed the need for expanded grain storage in major regional and district capitals. Although the proposal had been made by certain aid donors that it would be more effective to improve farm and village storage, the attitude of the government officials was that the peasants knew how to store their own crops; the main problem was to have sufficient storage capacity to meet the demands of the non-farming population.[22]

As a result of their difficulty in making the peasant respond sufficiently to their demands, government officials have been forced to turn more to international aid agencies. Fortunately, Tanzania enjoys an excellent reputation in the international aid community, both because of its interest in alternative strategies of development and its satisfactory foreign debt service.[23] It was not hard to obtain extensive foreign aid to boost Tanzania's own development resources after 1974. Apart from major donor involvement in regional planning efforts with a view to identifying projects that could be financed by these donors, the aid donors got more extensively involved in a whole range of other projects. In agriculture, the American International Development Agency (A.I.D.), and later the World Bank, approved financial support for the National Maize Project, a government effort to increase maize production through the use of better varieties and more effective techniques. Although, according to the original agreement, the NMP would be confined to a limited number of regions, essentially those with the greater prospects for good maize harvests, the programme was extended to cover two-thirds of all regions in the country. There were political pressures in this direction, leaders arguing that the need for food grains was equally strong all over the country. Feasibility was sacrificed in the interest of more equal access to the resources provided by the NMP. The technical package of that programme has been used by the government to try to link the peasants more closely to the demands of the other sectors of the economy. Although the government had originally agreed to subsidize fertilizers sold to the peasants to the tune of 75 per cent of the market value, it later unilaterally lowered that subsidy to 50 per cent, in part to increase the pressures on the peasants to produce more. The belief was that if the peasants knew that they had to pay back half the value of their fertilizers, they would use it more carefully to increase their production.[24] Government leaders were now increasingly aware that giving away resources free did not have the effect of making the peasants more interested in production.

The government also raised producer prices on all major grain crops in Tanzania, including sorghum and cassava for which there had been a growing demand during the drought period. The price of maize was increased in three stages between 1973 and 1976, as shown in Figure 5.1. These were the first such increases after independence and they were addressed less to the smallholder peasants than to those petty-capitalist and remaining capitalist farmers whose production of maize had declined in the absence of price incentives. In the heyday of *ujamaa,* the official attitude towards these farmers had been cool and even hostile, as shown in the previous chapter. In 1974, they were unofficially encouraged to play a greater role in the efforts to overcome the agricultural crisis. The party stand was now that production had to be increased at any cost; the form of production was relegated to secondary importance.

FIG 5.1. Producer prices for maize, in Tanzanian shillings per metric ton, from 1961 to 1977. (Source: Marketing Development Bureau, Ministry of Agriculture, Dar es Salaam)

Tanzanian Shillings	1961	1962	1963	1964	1965	1966	1967	1968	1969	1970	1970 -71	1971 -72	1972 -73	1973 -74	1974 -75	1975 -76	1976 -77
1000																	
900																	
800																	x
700																x	
600																	
500															x		
400	x	x															
300			x											x			
200				x	x	x	x	x	x	x	x	x					
100																	

Such was the attitude also towards the small peasants. There was no longer insistence on communal farming. Production on private holdings or privately within village block-farms was given priority. Significantly enough, new villages were not referred to as *ujamaa* villages, but as 'planned' or 'development' villages. Although confusion has remained about the appropriate terminology for Tanzania's villages, the predominant view after 1974 has seemed to be that *ujamaa* villages are only those where activities are carried out communally.[25]

Official supervision and control of the peasant sector was intensified with and after villagization. Intimidation and coercion were frequently used in moving people into the villages on the (correct) assumption that peasants would move back to their old land and into their old houses if they were not effectively blocked from doing so. The dry weather conditions prevailing in certain parts of Tanzania at the time played into the hands of the officials: many peasants had no harvest to return to. Knowledge of what happened in various parts of the country is limited. Little was reported in Tanzanian news media, although rumours certainly hinted at the hardship that some peasants were forced to undergo. Virtually the only published eye-witness account confirmed this:

> Many peasants in inchugu (Mara Region) were taken by surprise to see armed militiamen, climbing on top of their houses, taking away the thatch; in some cases the iron-sheets were torn off, doors smashed into pieces and houses pulled down. Many people, especially polygamists who had several wives, children and many houses, were faced with the problem of accommodation. Their homes having been destroyed, people received orders to move with all their property to the village building sites that same day; they moved with chicken, children, wives, cattle, goats and sheep, with beds and beddings. Some of them settled under the trees for shelter provided they were within the village site.[26]

It is difficult to know how representative this account is about the implementation of villagization. Official mass media were not critical of leaders for using coercive means. The ends of villagization justified the means. Military discipline and military organization were often invoked and it is no coincidence that after 1974 there has been a conscious policy to send all senior party and government leaders for several months of military training as part of the preparation of their political task. Exhortation was not only seen as insufficient; it was actually condemned outright.[27] Militarization was yet another means to cut out the economy of affection.

When the effects of villagization began to become apparent, criticism in the mass media increased. Special attention was paid to the haphazard manner in which people had been moved. 'Some enthusiasts', the *Daily News* wrote in its editorial, 'sacrificed permanence of the villages for quick results.'[28] They brought together more people than the land of the village could hold. Their houses were built as if in a township and consequently many peasants had to walk miles to obtain plots of cultivation. The most important criterion for location of the villages was convenient access. There was a tendency to create villages near the roads or in conjunction with existing trading centres or old mission stations. Although it would be wrong to claim that all villagization moves were badly planned, the policy was often imple-

-mented, as Coulson points out, irrespective of the consequences for agriculture.[29]

TANU Central Committee members were sent to the regions to inspect for themselves the impact of the campaigns to move people into villages, and in at least two regions, Mwanza and Shinyanga, peasants had to be moved a second time as a result of the blunders in connection with the first efforts to villagize. This 'Operation *Masahihisho*' (Rectification) was necessary because villages had been sited on low lands, and were therefore subject to flooding, or had too little land to support the population.[30]

Another way of intimidating the peasants to accept party calls for expansion of agricultural production was to revive the old by-laws that were invoked by the authorities concerning minimum acreage or weeding requirements. Several peasants in the coastal belt, as many as 200 in one single ward, were taken to court to answer charges of failing to weed their cashew-nut and coconut farms. In most of these cases, the peasants were fined.[31]

Both TANU and the government also tried to influence village leadership more directly by ensuring the election of people whose commitment to the party policies could be counted upon. This was not always easy to achieve. The economy of affection has often stood in the way of effective party influence on village development. One account tells how the village leaders in Mtwara District are unable to carry out development policies because they see themselves as being in the same predicament as the rest of the villagers. Given their dependence on nature in carrying out agricultural production, the existence rationality of each individual household that its own needs come first is so strong that village leaders find it impossible to impose party directives that go contrary to this orientation.[32]

In these villages, leaders minimize conflicts by refusing to perform their role as conceived by the party. In other places, tension may stem from the difficulty of getting rid of a village leader within the new system that requires approval by superior organs of the party. Maeda quotes the case of Oljoro *ujamaa* village in Arusha Region, where the villagers were demoralized as a result of bureaucratic red tape delaying the removal of their chairman who allegedly abused his office.[33]

Whereas it is wrong to create the impression that these are necessarily typical cases, there is little doubt that the pressure on the village leadership by higher party organs has increased. They are told to put the communal welfare of the village above that of individual households. This issue has grown more important in the rural areas as a result of the decision by the National Milling Corporation to pay commission to villages which sell their produce to the NMC before a particular date. By giving this commission to the village, the hope is that the leadership will use it to develop the community as a whole. The leaders, however, are under strong pressure from the villagers who maintain that the commission should be shared equally among all members. Many of them are less interested in a village fund, which they believe leaders may use for their own benefit and instead insist on immediate distribution.

Peasants and villagization

Villagization coincided with the drought that hit large parts of Tanzania in 1973/74. It is fair to say that from the viewpoint of the objectives of villagization, the drought was a blessing in disguise in that in many areas it facilitated the movement of people. There was little they left behind on the land and consequently it was easier for them to accept living in the new villages. It is one of the reasons why some people did not object to moving but did so without government pressure.

While the movement of people in itself caused disruptions in agricultural production, those were essentially of a temporary nature. The argument that villagization was the principal cause of Tanzania's decline in agricultural production in the mid-1970s does not hold water.[34] Some temporary dislocations did inevitably occur as peasant farmers concentrated on production of food crops to meet their most immediate needs in the new settlements. Peasants had little time for cash crops, something that was noticeable particularly in the cotton, tobacco and cashew-nut growing areas of the country.

TABLE 5.2 Indices of export volume of six major agricultural crops in Tanzania, 1965–75 (1966 = 100)

Crop	1965	1966	1967	1968	1969	1970	1971	1972	1973	1974	1975
Cotton	65	100	71	73	66	70	64	75	70	57	44
Coffee	56	100	88	97	98	89	70	108	119	81	108
Sisal	107	100	103	95	86	109	81	77	57	47	51
Cashew-nuts*	89	100	98	110	114	107	133	156	152	158	135
Tea	68	100	97	106	121	110	132	146	151	152	165
Tobacco†	97	100	144	153	147	226	194	209	209	356	253
Total	75	100	88	92	88	93	82	99	95	82	82

* raw; † unmanufactured
Sources: Annual Trade Reports of Tanzania, Uganda and Kenya of the East African Customs and Excise Department, and various issues of the *Economic Survey*, published by the Government of Tanzania.

The production in subsistence agriculture (mostly food) is reported to have gone up by 10·5 per cent while production in monetary agriculture (mostly cash crops for export) in 1975 increased by only 1·9 per cent over the figures of the previous year.[35] Figures for subsistence production are always unreliable. Moreover, production figures for 1974 were unusually low in some areas. Thus one cannot rule out the possibility that in spite of the recorded increase in production by 1975, it suffered from the fact that many peasant farmers were forced to farm in new and sometimes unfavourable conditions.

This is not to suggest that the peasants were slow to respond to the challenges of the new situation.[36] Production to meet the needs of his household was so important to the the peasant that, villagization or not, he would produce. Though weather continued to play havoc with agricultural production in some areas during 1974/75 and there was clearly a limit to what the peasants could produce before having settled in properly, the fact of the matter is that subsistence crop production went up during that year.

It is difficult to know how much this should be attributed to spontaneous peasant efforts. Still it is likely to be more the result of such efforts than government pressures. A peasant does not need to be told to grow food crops. He often believes that such production is his sole prerogative. One of the few studies of villagization confirms this attitude:

> The villagers have the view that they should be left on their own in agricultural production. We should however remember that despite its scarce rainfall the district and the region (Mtwara) as a whole has never experienced food shortages (crop failures) for a very long time. One factor behind this is the growing of such drought resistant crops as cassava and millet. Confidence has been built among the people that if they have survived through all these generations without food shortages, they can and will survive in future without someone telling them what to grow, how to grow, where to grow and at what quantity.[37]

Figures presented in Table 4.3 (page 120) also indicate that, to judge from sales to the National Milling Corporation, production of maize picked up quite quickly in the villages, once weather conditions turned more favourable. Particularly interesting is the fact that maize production increased after people had settled down, especially in those regions which had been most heavily villagized, for example, Morogoro, Rukwa, Ruvuma and Tanga. Smallholder producers in these regions were making a large contribution to the production of surplus grain in a manner which had not happened before. There is no doubt that weather conditions were largely responsible for the increases in grain production in Tanzania between 1975/76 and 1977/78, but there were also other factors at play. Peasants themselves were certainly inclined to produce more to ensure that they would not again fall victim to famine. There was a desire to create a safety valve in the form of more production. This view was held by people in several villages visited during 1976.[38] The fact that the government gave the peasants carte blanche to produce more food crops only reinforced this orientation. Producer prices on all grain crops had been raised in Tanzania in the wake of the drought. In the last few years (1976–78) of good harvests peasants have sold large quantities of not only maize but also millet and cassava to the National Milling Corporation. It is difficult to assess how far the new prices served as incentives and how far increased sale was the product of inflation: peasants simply needed more cash to buy their necessities. Certainly, peasants were far from displaying capitalist behaviour when they responded by selling more. It is always a probable inclination at times of large surplus harvests. Tanzania benefited from the new situation. By 1978 NMC had purchased far more food crops than it could dispose of on the domestic market. Less than five years after the big crisis in Tanzanian agriculture the country found itself exporting grain to neighbouring African countries. Such is the predicament of Africa's rain-fed and resource-based agriculture.

Although production of cotton, which fell considerably during the period of villagization, was still short of official targets, and still far below the levels of production reached before 1973, it did increase significantly in 1976/77 in both Mwanza and Shinyanga Regions, the main cotton-producing area. In Mwanza it rose from 78 000 bales in 1975/76 to 148 196 bales the following year.[39] In Shinyanga the increase during that same period was from 76 936 to 112 703 bales.[40]

Whereas these achievements should temper the most gloomy accounts of the effects of villagization in Tanzania, there is still reason to ask whether this upward curve can be maintained. Although increased pressures by the authorities have been exercised vis-à-vis the peasants, there is little evidence of any transformation of the peasant mode. Production still remains essentially resource-based, and hence dependent on local endowments. It also depends on peasant ability to manage these resources. The know-how that peasants had prior to villagization has often been rendered invalid in the new settlements, where soil conditions and other factors of production are different. At least in Singida Region reports indicate that peasants became victims of famine after having planted their crops in the new villages at the wrong time.[41] With increasing concentration of people on the land, there is also a question of how far present, simple technologies suffice to allow peasants to reproduce themselves. Kjekshus, who has studied the consequences of such concentrations in the colonial days, warns in an article on villagization:

> Unless villagization can be coupled with infrastructural inputs to create a novel technology to master the environment, the nucleated settlement pattern may, by itself, be counterproductive in economic terms and destructive of the ecological balance maintained under the traditional settlement pattern. Nucleated settlement will mean overcrowding of restricted areas with people and

domestic animals and the accompanying soil erosion, gulley formations and dust bowls which are all common features in situations where human initiative has suddenly overtaxed the carrying capacity of land without compensatory inputs to increase the quality of cultivation.[42]

Villagization does militate against a number of time-tested peasant answers to advantageous man–land relationships, as Kjekshus notes. There are also unconfirmed reports of peasants trying to move out of the new settlements in order to find a more satisfactory solution to their existential predicament. Official policy, however, has been to insist on nucleated settlements and instead encourage peasant farmers to improve their production on the village land through the use of better seeds, and inputs such as fertilizers. The conflict between peasant rationality, as determined by the production structures in the villages, and government rationality as determined by macro-economic demands, is still apparent in the context of the National Maize Project.

Government, with initially A.I.D. and later World Bank support, has tried to modernize maize production by insisting on the use of better seeds and fertilizers. In areas, where villagers have experience of commerce and the use of inputs, the management of the project has not been too difficult, but since for political reasons it has been extended to

TABLE 5.3 Village credit and repayment for inputs supplied by the National Maize Project during the 1976/77 season, by regions (T. shs)

Region	Total credit	Repaid to date	Percentage	Balance
Arusha	1 263 765/–	270 622·85	21·4	993 142·15
Kilimanjaro	1 099 225/–	804 200·15	73·2	295 024·85
Tanga	728 500/–	75 648·45	10·4	652 851·55
Morogoro	553 375/–	325 655·20	58·8	227 719·80
Dodoma	764 863/–	413 855·45	54·1	351 007·55
Tabora	1 810 550/–	260 300·00	14·4	1 550 250·00
Iringa	3 155 755/–	1 544 419·30	48·4	1 611 336·70
Mbeya	2 741 130/–	1 281 084·00	46·7	1 460 046·00
Lindi	530 082/–	104 836·55	19·8	425 245·45
Mtwara	348 940/–	26 557·35	7·6	322 382·65
Ruvuma	354 500/–	133 063·00	37·5	221 437·00
Rukwa	1 469 123/–	357 722·30	24·3	1 111 400·70
Mara	531 430/–	7 402·20	1·4	524 027·80
Shinyanga*	52 325/–	5 196·25	9·9	47 128·75
West Lake*	35 000/–	–	–	35 000·00
Total	15 438 563/–	5 610 563·05	36·3	9 831 009·95

* included in NMP in 1976
Source: National Maize Project Servicing Unit, Ministry of Agriculture, Dar es Salaam.

cover many regions in which modern maize cultivation has never been practised, the overall performance of the NMP has been less satisfactory. As figures in Table 5.3 indicate, it has been difficult to retrieve the costs of the 'political maize', that is, such maize that was essentially introduced as a result of political pressures on the NMP management. In some cases, modern maize production on credit was introduced against the will of the peasants, who were reluctant to enter into such financial obligations.

In spite of favourable weather conditions, production in NMP sponsored villages has been considerably below official estimates. Five out of six villages show a gross output per hectare of less than one-third of the appraisal estimate. In the light of such shortfalls in production, it is no surprise that repayment in many areas has also been slow. The repayment rate for the 1976/77 season was 36·3 per cent. By October 1977, this had gone up to 62 per cent.[43] While by that time some regions had completed their repayment altogether, others were trailing far behind and their ability to improve repayment would be largely dependent on favourable weather conditions allowing sufficient surplus grain.

There is also evidence that peasants have become increasingly reluctant to use fertilizers. As NMP has continued, peasants have refused to use fertilizers in many areas, because they have proved to have little effect on production and have only landed the villagers in debt. By the end of the 1976/77 season 15 000 tons of fertilizers were lying unused in village stores in various parts of rural Tanzania.[44]

While there is no doubt that the NMP may have taught some peasants better production techniques, there is evidence to suggest that the main beneficiaries were already market-oriented farmers, producing in a petty-capitalist fashion. For the majority of the peasants, to whom maize is a food rather than a cash-crop, there was understandable reluctance to accept the NMP package, an attitude which in some areas was reinforced by inadequacies in the marketing system. Some peasants were not sure they could sell surplus maize, even if they produced it. One evaluation of the NMP showed that when peasants were asked about what the government could do to increase maize production, the vast majority replied in terms of what the government could *give* them– a tractor, free inputs, transport.[45] While the author of that report sees this as an illustration of village dependence on the government, it can be argued that it is more proof of peasant desire *not* to increase their dependence on government. By having the government give them resources free of charge they feel under no obligation to reciprocate and thus they can retain their autonomy.

Increases in grain production in the peasant sector seem to be more the result of enlarged acreages than improved practices. While villagization and stronger government pressures may have yielded results with respect to land use, these factors have been far less influential in re-

lation to modernization. Tanzania today has more land under cultivation than ever before, but its agricultural practices still remain simple
and traditional. Exceptions are the petty-capitalist farmers in various
parts of the country, who have adopted more modern cultivation
methods. Government measures, such as the NMP, have helped them to
become more effective producers. Whether these policies indicate a
temporary change in tactics, as during the New Economic Policy (NEP)
period in the Soviet Union, or whether they represent a more definite support for petty-capitalist farming, along the lines suggested by Dumont,[46]
is too early to judge. Yet one thing seems clear. The main reason why
Tanzania, despite its socialist commitment, has been obliged to
encourage petty-capitalist farming is because of the resilience of the
peasant mode of production. Attempts to transform or transcend it
have so far yielded only modest results.

   While we have some idea of the economic effects of villagization, little
work has been done on the social effects of villagization. How traumatic
was this experience? Did it make peasants more or less open to outside
influences? Are new institutional forms taking shape in the villages?
These are only a few of the many questions that can be raised in relation
to the effects of the resettlement campaigns. Some degree of social
dislocation was inevitable given the scope of the exercise. Examples of
this were given in the mass media at the time. In Singida Region fighting
broke out between members of the Nyaturu and the Barabaig tribes
over land rights that were upset in conjunction with the enforced
movement of people into villages.[47] In certain areas, for example,
Nachingwea District in Lindi Region, incidences of witchcraft showed a
definite increase.[48] In Hanang District in Arusha Region, a self-styled
'Jesus' found himself with a considerable following in areas where
villagization had increased uncertainty and insecurity among people.[49]

   These social disturbances were eventually all brought under control.
The benefits of living in villages have also become more apparent to
people, once they have settled in. More social interaction with other
people has been particularly important for the rural women. Access to
schools and clinics, and increasingly clean water, is also a factor that
most villagers have appreciated. From a welfare point of view, living
together in villages is an advantage. As President Nyerere stresses in his
assessment of Tanzania's first ten years after the Arusha Declaration,
the opportunities for social reproduction in the rural areas have greatly
improved for this generation as well as for future ones.[50]

Conclusions

The period covered in this chapter was primarily characterized by the
intensified efforts of the ruling classes to get at the peasantry. Although
some attempts were made to revive the capitalist market, the main

achievement was the further refinement of the political market-place. New laws and regulations were introduced to allow the petty-bourgeoisie a better deal in their interactions with the peasant producers. The party as well as the government tightened its grip so as to prevent peasants from going into hiding. A second effort of importance was directed against the leading figures of the economy of affection. By introducing new party rules, by 'militarizing' the leadership and by placing government officials in the villages as managers, it was hoped to limit the impact of the economy of affection. Thirdly, by villagizing the peasant producers, it was assumed that they would be more easily accessible to political and administrative interventions.

There is little doubt that in spite of bureaucratic high-handedness and other excesses, the new policy measures were successful in some respects. People have by and large accepted their new locations of domicile and production. Production has also increased in many villages, although it is too early to say how far this can be attributed to villagization and the other policy measures taken during this period. Agriculture still remains largely unaffected by the efforts to introduce new production techniques and achieve a rise in productivity on the land. The constraints of the peasant mode are still in operation. The material base is still too narrow to support a major breakthrough in the efforts to build modern socialism. This is shown in a number of recent documents. The NMP evaluation report, for instance, quotes labour as a definite constraint in many peasant households.[51] Peasants are simply unable to produce more because the available labour is exhausted. A similar remark is made in an evaluation of the World Bank sponsored Kigoma Rural Development Project: '.... many households continue to spend an important part of their active hours in non-productive but still essential activities.'[52]

Virtually everything in which the peasant engages is essential to him. He starts from such low levels of health standards, education and other aspects of what we consider 'development' that he takes for granted that once the government offers him the opportunity to share the benefits of modern development his own needs should have exclusive priority. This has been very evident in Kigoma Region, which started from particularly typical conditions of underdevelopment: people had lost faith in their own ability to do something in their home region; instead, they migrated elsewhere in search of income.

The various policy measures pursued since 1973 have facilitated the articulation of class relations. Conflicts which were previously mitigated by the economy of affection are now displayed more openly. This is likely to be an important step, not only towards development but also towards socialist transformation. This transformation is inconceivable without a situation in which people have no other option but to obey the demands of the ruling classes. Where small retains his exit option, socialism at least in its modern form, is impossible.

The regime in Tanzania has closed many of the doors that used to be open for such exit options. Yet they have by no means closed them all. In the political market-place, the peasants retain a certain measure of sovereignty. This enables them to deceive the petty-bourgeoisie. Whether the latter decide to use the political market-place or the capitalist market to capture the peasants more effectively, peasants will continue to appear deceitful as long as the social logic of the peasant mode is sustained by economic structures. It is easy to understand that in the contemporary situation, with a strong socialist development orientation prevailing, despair comes easily to the Tanzanian policy-makers. Desperate measures, however, can be avoided. How far this is possible is at least in part likely to be determined by the performance of the public sector, the topic of the next chapter.

References and notes

1. The summary of his speech is based on my personal notes at the time of its broadcasting. The newspaper coverage the following day stressed some of the same points, but not all those mentioned here.
2. In his major review of the achievements and problems after the Arusha Declaration, President Nyerere mentions that 9·1 million people were moved between November 1973 and June 1975. See his, *The Arusha Declaration Ten Years After* (Dar es Salaam: Government Printer, 1977), p. 41.
3. *Daily News* (Dar es Salaam), 23 August 1974.
4. ibid., 15 November 1975.
5. ibid., 20 February 1976.
6. ibid., 22 March and 9 April 1976.
7. ibid., 19 May 1976.
8. *Sunday News* (Dar es Salaam), 23 May 1976.
9. *Daily News,* 24 March 1977.
10. The then Minister of Agriculture, Derek Bryceson, had made a reference to the co-operative unions as 'middlemen' in October 1971. His statement stirred up such a political controversy that it became necessary for the President authoritatively to resolve the dispute.
11. The decentralization reform, while requested by the President and TANU, was designed with the assistance of the American management consultancy firm, McKinsey & Co. Their work was appreciated by the Tanzania authorities at the time, but it is clear in retrospect that much of their work was based on assumptions which had little to do with the policy-making realities in Tanzania. Eventually many of the cornerstones of their design were abandoned.
12. See, for instance, President Nyerere's policy statement on the subject, *Decentralization* (Dar es Salaam: Government Printer, 1972).
13. This was a very common sentiment recorded in conversations with the present author while completing a study on 'Decentralization and the

government staff', a working paper submitted to the University Research Project on Decentralization, Faculty of Arts and Social Science, University of Dar es Salaam, November 1976.

14. *Sunday News,* 15 May 1977.
15. United Republic of Tanzania, The Villages and Ujamaa Villages (Registration, Designation and Administration) Act, 1975, Government Notice No. 162, published on 22 August 1975.
16. *Daily News,* 18 May 1977.
17. ibid., 16 April 1977.
18. *Sunday News,* 6 February 1977.
19. See, for instance, Philip Raikes, 'Ujamaa and socialism', *Review of African Political Economy,* vol. 3 (May–October 1975) and Michaela von Freyhold, 'Government staff and ujamaa villages: the Tanga experience', mimeo., Department of Sociology, University of Dar es Salaam, n.d.
20. See, for example, *Daily News,* 25 October 1974.
21. Marketing Development Bureau, Ministry of Agriculture, 'Large–scale maize production: a preliminary economic analysis', Dar es Salaam, December 1976.
22. This view was stressed in interviews with officials in both the Ministry of Agriculture and the Prime Minister's Office during April 1977.
23. The concept of 'debt service' refers to the ability of the debtor countries to repay interests and amortizations.
24. This view was expressed in interviews with government officials both in the regions and in the Ministry of Agriculture during the months of April and May 1976.
25. This view is certainly predominant in the 1975 Villages and Ujamaa Villages Act, op. cit.
26. Reuben R. Matango, 'Operation Mara: the paradox of democracy', *Maji Maji,* vol. 20 (1975), Dar es Salaam, p. 21.
27. See editorial in *Daily News,* 16 October 1975.
28. ibid., 17 October 1975.
29. Andrew Coulson, 'Peasants and bureaucrats', *Review of African Political Economy,* vol. 3 (May–October 1975), pp. 53–8.
30. *Daily News,* 23 January 1976.
31. See, for instance, *Sunday News,* 8 September 1974.
32. Mussa S. Mdidi, 'The leadership factor in planning for local development after decentralization: a case of Kitere Ward, Mtwara District', unpublished undergraduate dissertation, Department of Political Science, University of Dar es Salaam, March 1977, pp. 29–31.
33. Justin H. J. Maeda, 'Popular participation, control and development: a study of the nature and role of popular participation in Tanzania's rural development', unpublished Ph.D. dissertation, Department of Political Science, Yale University, p. 196.
34. Coulson, op. cit. and Michael Lofchie, 'Collective villagization, agrarian crisis and economic liberalization in Tanzania', paper presented to the Graduate Seminar on African Agriculture, Department of Political Science, University of California, Los Angeles, spring quarter, 1978, mimeo.
35. United Republic of Tanzania, *The Economic Survey 1975–76* (Dar es Salaam: Printpak, 1976), p. 3.
36. Juma Volter Mwapachu, 'Operation planned villages in rural Tanzania: a

revolutionary strategy of development', *African Review*, vol. 6, no. 1 (1976) pp. 1–16.
37. Abillah Omari, 'Decentralization and development: the case of Madimba Ward, Mtwara District', unpublished undergraduate dissertation, Department of Political Science, University of Dar es Salaam, March 1977, p. 23.
38. This view was expressed in villages in Kilosa, Kigoma, Dodoma and Songea districts, visited in connection with fieldwork for the Decentralization Research Project in April and May 1976.
39. *Daily News*, 28 February 1977.
40. ibid., 17 February 1977.
41. ibid., 1 April 1977.
42. Helge Kjekshus, 'The Tanzania villagization policy: implementational lessons and ecological dimensions', *Canadian Journal of African Studies*, vol. 11, no. 2 (1977), p. 282.
43. Figures obtained from the National Maize Project Servicing Unit, Ministry of Agriculture, Dar es Salaam.
44. 'National Maize Project mid-term Review', Project Servicing Unit, Ministry of Agriculture, Dar es Salaam.
45. Louise P. Fortmann, 'An evaluation of the progress of the National Maize Project at the end of the cropping season in Morogoro and Arusha Regions', U.S.A.I.D. Dar es Salaam, November 1976, p. 20.
46. René Dumont, *Tanzanian Agriculture after the Arusha Declaration* (Dar es Salaam: Government Printer, 1969).
47. See editorial in *Daily News*, 9 January 1976.
48. ibid., 7 May 1974.
49. *Daily News*, 5 March 1977.
50. Nyerere, *The Arusha Declaration Ten Years After*, op. cit., p. 15.
51. Fortmann, op. cit., p. 19.
52. R. B. Mabele and M. Schultheis, 'Evaluation of the Kigoma Rural Development Project', Economic Research Bureau, University of Dar es Salaam, March 1977, p. 59.

CHAPTER 6

Small as infiltrator:
problems of developing the public sector

Previous chapters have noted the limited impact capitalism had on the relations of production in rural Tanzania. Its impact in other sectors of the economy was not much stronger. Foreign capital penetrated East Africa mainly through its headquarters in Nairobi. What reached Tanzania was usually the spill over of capitalist progress in Kenya. With the perpetuation of this situation after independence, it is understandable that Tanzania found itself confined by prevailing economic structures. Efforts were made in the context of the East African Community, comprising Kenya, Uganda and Tanzania, to alter the nature of economic relations in favour of the latter two. These policies, however, were not very effective and it was only after the nationalizations in 1967 that Tanzania gained an increasing control of its economy. Foreign capital was either taken over outright, bought out, or in some cases invited to continue in partnership with the Tanzanian state.

After 1967 the public sector took the place of the private sector as the principal vehicle of modern development. With more direct control over the most important instruments of development the petty-bourgeoisie was, at least theoretically, in a position to reduce its dependence, not only on foreign capital but also on the small peasant producers. The political leadership had achieved a stronger position by obtaining access to new resources. The debate about Tanzania has generally overlooked the importance of this point in a situation where the dependence of the petty-bourgeoisie was both on foreign capital and peasant producers. Instead, it had focused very much on the question of how far these measures were socialist.[1]

Capitalist principles of operation were retained in the companies for a few years before measures were taken to involve the workers in the management of public enterprises. Particularly important were *Mwongozo* – the Party Guidelines – issued in 1971. This initiative signalled the end of capitalist forms of management in Tanzania. While efforts were made to replace these with more participatory, presumably socialist, forms of management, the most interesting thing that happened in the wake of *Mwongozo* was the pre-capitalist takeover of the public sector. The frailty of capitalism, and its failure to transform the economic structures of Tanzania, was no better illustrated than by the weakness of the base for a modern socialist development. After 1971 that base was almost immediately undermined by the forces of pre-capitalism. The principle of small comes first, which characterized Tanzania's peasant mode, began to infiltrate also the public sector, the shelter of the bureaucratic bourgeoisie. The debate about Tanzania has completely overlooked this point.

Background to *Mwongozo*

Virtually all nationalized enterprises in the manufacturing sector were placed under the control of the National Development Corporation (NDC), which had been set up in 1964 as a holding company for state-owned industries. There were quick gains from the acquisition of the capitalist property. In the case of the NDC the annual surpluses earned rose from roughly 10 million T. shs in 1966 to almost 40 million by the end of 1967.[2] As Packard notes in his review of the parastatal enterprises, the gains were even greater in the banking and financial institutions that had been nationalized.[3]

In the first few years after the Arusha Declaration there were no real changes in the organization and management of these enterprises. In fact foreign management was retained. Capitalist work customs remained in the NDC subsidiaries as well as in other parastatal enterprises. Foreign management consultancy firms, notably McKinsey & Co., played an important role in streamlining NDC operations and in setting up the State Trading Corporation. In some cases, management agreements were signed with former owners or new partners willing to take managerial responsibility of the state-owned companies. Given the lack of experience of the NDC leadership to negotiate such deals there is no doubt that the management agreements often gave the foreign partner unusually large benefits. That such mistakes had been committed was also admitted by the NDC General Manager at a later point.[4]

The public sector took on the nature of a state capitalist enclave in which operations continued without much interference from government. There was a growing criticism of TANU for not having taken their policies one step further so as to root out capitalist management practices altogether. Nationalization, it was argued, was no more than a half-measure. This relative isolation of the public sector stands in sharp contrast with what happened in other sectors in society where TANU after the Arusha Declaration had established control over existing institutions. In schools, for instance, youth league branches had been set up to strengthen political education. While the party was trying to bring teachers and students closer into the mainstream of Tanzania's socialist thinking, workers in parastatal enterprises were left untouched until February 1970 when the President took a first step in that direction by issuing a directive on workers' participation in the management of public enterprises. Public enterprises were instructed to reorganize their executive boards to allow representation by workers and also to establish workers' councils with an advisory function in management.

The directive was not in response to active workers' restlessness. On the whole, the workers had continued operating within the existing capitalist framework. Strikes had been prohibited in the country since 1964, and although unofficial strikes did take place occasionally, there had really been only one such incident in 1969. That took place in a private company where workers felt mistreated by a member of the management. The Second Vice-President who visited the company unilaterally ordered the dismissal of the manager and insisted that workers must be treated with equality and dignity.[5]

It is not known how far tacit workers' disenchantment with capitalist management had been simmering under the surface prior to the Presidential Directive on Workers' Participation. Officially, however, workers' councils were certainly introduced with a view to reducing the influence of capitalist practices in parastatal management:

> When we first began to own industrial and agricultural enterprises as a community, and especially after the Arusha Declaration, we inevitably – and rightly – concentrated first on the sheer mechanics of setting up, or taking over, economic concerns. We therefore followed in our public enterprises the same work customs as we had learned from the traditional capitalist enterprises.[6]

The reaction to the Presidential directive was modest in the course of 1970, although it was expected that every parastatal enterprise would have completed the reform by the end of that year. Most managers were reluctant to comply with the directive, mainly because it appeared as an unnecessary complication of the management task. This reluctance on the part of the managers to go ahead with workers' participation may at least in part be responsible for some of the unofficial strikes that took place in 1970. Three such incidents were reported, two in parastatal enterprises. Unsatisfactory working conditions and favouritism appear to have been the main causes behind these incidents of workers' unrest. Party leaders tried to arbitrate in these disputes but with only limited effect. They lacked the instruments to do so.

This changed with the *Mwongozo* which was launched by the party soon after the military coup in Uganda that ousted Nyerere's close friend, Milton Obote. There is no doubt that this event, plus the unsuccessful invasion of Guinea by mercenary troops in November 1970, triggered off this statement by the party. It addressed itself to many issues, but stressed in particular Africa's continuous vulnerability to neo-colonialist manœuvres. As a way of strengthening Tanzania's vigilance, the Guidelines ordered the establishment of a people's militia and party branches in all national institutions, including the parastatal companies. Being still influenced by capitalist thinking these companies became the main target of the renewed efforts to reduce the capitalist hold of the country. *Mwongozo* stressed:

> For a people who have been slaves or have been oppressed, exploited and humiliated by colonialism and capitalism, 'development' means 'liberation'. Any action that gives them more control of their own affairs is an action for development even if it does not offer them better health or more bread. Any action which reduces their say in determining their own affairs or running their own lives is not development and retards them even if the action brings them a little better health and a little more bread.[7]

The Guidelines emphasized the importance of involving people in solving their own problems and warned that no Tanzanian leader should be allowed to be arrogant, extravagant, contemptuous or oppressive. It went one step further in arguing that nobody should any longer be forced to accept orders from superiors simply because they had the authority to give such orders.

The reasons for *Mwongozo* are many and complex but it seems clear that at least one of them was to undercut the influence of those members of the bureaucratic bourgeoisie who took too easily for granted the authority systems established under capitalist auspices in the para-statals. The Guidelines were to ensure greater control of a faction of the petty-bourgeoisie that in other African countries had proved disloyal to leaders with progressive orientations. Nyerere and his followers were trying to prevent the kind of political instability that had followed in the wake of struggles between various petty-bourgeois factions in African countries.

The *Mwongozo* tried to get at the parastatal managers through the workers. By claiming to be on the side of the workers, the party leadership were in the position of forcing the managers to obey political instructions or otherwise be exposed and forced to quit. Without using any obvious coercion to achieve his ends, Nyerere had, with *Mwongozo*, almost completed the task of creating a unified superstructure that could serve as a bulwark against capitalist penetration of his country. He had limited opportunities for competition within the political system to the parameters set by the top leadership of TANU. No leader could any longer claim autonomy from the party control. All were part of a large 'fraternity' guided by the party principles. Although there were attempts to break the rules of the game, the consolidation of the bureaucratic bourgeoisie into a homogeneous leadership group has been achieved without much use of coercion. All state institutions are today subordinated to the party, which has branches in all such organizations. In addition, virtually all senior officers in the public sector are personal appointees of the President, who has the prerogative of punishing or rewarding these people in accordance with how well they implement policies on which the legitimacy of the regime rests. Company performance on the market is no longer the exclusive concern for parastatal managers. More important even are such criteria as belief in Tanzania's ability to pursue a socialist development and an austere life-style.

Workers, managers, and *Mwongozo*

Mwongozo was to the workers what *ujamaa* was to the peasants: a promise of a better life, with no specific conditions attached. The belief was here, as in the case of the peasantry, that workers would come forward and make a greater contribution to Tanzania's socialist development. By relieving them of the bonds imposed under capitalism, the political leadership believed that workers would turn to socialism. They overlooked the fact that capitalism had not yet transformed them into individuals who would be readily available for alternative social action. The labour force was still held captive in pre-capitalist bonds.

For most wage-earners work was the price you paid for urban residence and access to its amenities. It was not something honoured in itself. Only the sanctions imposed by capitalist management had made many workers accept their obligations. When *Mwongozo* undermined the rationale of this system, and the party promised a better life without adherence to strict rules imposed by people with authority, workers were not slow to respond. They began to pay more attention to other matters that were important to them. Most of these were part of the pre-capitalist baggage they carried with them in the urban areas.

Some matters coincided with the party policies as originally announced, for instance, workers' protest against poor working conditions, abuse of office, etc. One common target was the right of managers to personal use of official cars. Workers were very vocal on this issue and received support from party leaders and mass media. Since the use of official cars could not be completely dispensed with on the grounds that such vehicles were important to ensure easy movement to and from work, the issue was eventually resolved by giving the workers buses to take them to and from work. The investment in such buses was justified because the public transport system in Dar es Salaam had deteriorated so badly after the nationalization of the city's privately-owned bus company. The company buses increased workers' convenience but it did not necessarily make them work harder. The point is that while the workers generally agreed with the official view of reducing the capitalist influence over the economy, they were not necessarily going to accept

the new socialist demands. Above all, they were not individuals who in
the name of socialism would sacrifice themselves when their families
were not being adequately looked after, because they had to work eight
hours a day. People were still oriented primarily to the needs of their
extended families. In the wake of *Mwongozo* requests for time off to
visit sick relatives, or loans for emergency needs in the family, were
made with less constraint, because many workers expected such favours
to be granted now that the capitalist concern for profit had been
officially condemned. The impersonal organization of the capitalist
enterprise had been a real straitjacket to most workers and they were
not very anxious to trade it for another organization demanding that
they give up part of themselves for an abstract cause, the implications of
which they understood little. Their sense of socialism was that they
would have more time for themselves and their families. In a society
where the features of pre-capitalist society still survived this was the
most rational option to take. The workers were recruited from the heart
of pre-capitalist society and they were only too happy to return to it, or
at least give it more attention, now that the bonds of capitalism had
been weakened.

How much the pre-capitalist, familial forms of organization still
remained in Tanzania has been documented by Michaela von
Freyhold.[8] While these never became politically important in the urban
areas in Tanzania as in many other African countries, these forms have
survived as important social organizations. She shows in her study of
attitudes among workers and members of the bureaucratic bourgeoisie
that both these categories retain strong links with their homes in the
rural areas. Almost half of the casual workers, about two-thirds of the
lower paid blue- and white-collar workers in permanent work and
around three-quarters of all the better paid occupational groups in Dar
es Salaam, send regular remittances to relatives up-country. About every
tenth casual worker, every second permanently employed worker, and
about three out of four of those people earning more than 1000 T. shs
a month take a sum of money with them to distribute among people
when they go home. One-tenth of the casual workers send money home
on special occasions such as marriages, funerals, sickness or famine.
About one-third of the lower-paid blue- and white-collar workers, and
abet half of the higher-paid blu -collar workers and the highly-paid
senior staff, also donate in emergencies or on special occasions. What
all this suggests is that both common workers and members of the
bureaucratic bourgeoisie do not place personal economic achievement
above family solidarity. Social security is seen to rest more within the
parameters of the economy of affection than within the modern
economy. The Tanzanian data, as presented by von Freyhold, refutes
the assumption that the petty-bourgeoisie have cut their ties with the
rural areas. It also questions the general validity of the point made by
Marris that the petty-bourgeois traders give little to their rural relatives,

because they are always asked to give but get nothing in return.[9]

The von Freyhold survey shows that urban members of the petty-bourgeoisie in Tanzania visit their rural homes more often, have more concrete plans concerning their next visit and remit more money and provide other kinds of assistance to rural relatives than poorer urban residents. The majority of the petty-bourgeoisie see themselves as retiring back to their home areas, and even among those who claim they will remain in Dar es Salaam there is a strong willingness to remit money to relatives up-country.

It is increasingly true as Gutkind,[10] among others have noted, that African labour today is much less migratory than it was during the colonial days. Workers are in urban areas on a more permanent basis. While this is likely to lead in the long run to the emergence of a genuine proletariat, this process will take its time, at least to judge from von Freyhold's data on Tanzania. Not only are the majority of workers and the petty-bourgeoisie integral parts of the economy of affection, but many are also landowners in their own right. Four out of five casual workers, and low-wage blue- and white-collar workers, said they had access to land which they could cultivate. About two-thirds of the higher-paid blue-collar workers and three-quarters of the middle- and top-salaried officials also reported they had land available to them. Thus, although not everybody says he has a *shamba* (farm), the vast majority of all von Freyhold's respondents are confident that they can retire to the rural areas and cultivate land for their own use. In this respect they all have an option of exiting out of the system in which they are employed. Retirement, or even dismissal, is not such a heavy blow to them as it is for somebody in modern capitalist and socialist societies where workers and officials lack the option of returning to the land. In the context of Africa, however, Tanzania is not unique. A survey of industrial workers in Kenya and Uganda conducted in 1965, concluded that about three-quarters of all respondents in Kenya and four-fifths in Uganda had their own *shamba*.[11]

In understanding the position of the workers and the petty-bourgeoisie in Africa it may be useful to take note of an observation, made originally with reference to other non-industrialized countries, that while in Western Europe

> the proletariat ... participated in the industrial revolution not only by their effort but by their inventions [and] shared the cultural background, skills and languages of their masters, [in] Romania, as in Algeria and Peru, master and worker belonged figuratively and sometimes literally to different nations.[12]

While it is important to note that industrialization has been carried out by Europeans, and to that extent the demands of the industrial sector are regarded as alien by many Africans, the most significant thing is not the nationality or the ràce of the modernizers, but the fact that they work with people emerging out of a totally different mode of production. To the latter, by and large, the industrial sector was a foreign plant. Von Freyhold's data suggest that the workers – and the petty-bourgeoisie – are more dependent on capitalism than the peasants only as a matter of degree. All of them still labour under a strong influence of pre-capitalist forces. They all belong to corporate family units and unlike societies where capitalism has really penetrated relations of production, the basic units of social identification, organization, and action are not the individual and the nuclear family.

In these circumstances in which not only workers, but also the petty-bourgeoisie, are still strongly oriented towards the demands of pre-capitalist social formations, it is unrealistic to expect their spontaneous loyalty to be towards the public sector. By contrast, they are more likely to act so as to maximize the benefits for themselves and their relatives. Having been squeezed by capitalism, many workers – and officials – saw the changes heralded by *Mwongozo* as a move away from the strict discipline imposed by modern organization. This was the trap of the small into which Tanzania's socialist policies for the public sector quickly fell. The base for a socialist transformation was too narrow to harbour the new policies and they soon disappeared into the pre-capitalist abyss.

Effects of *Mwongozo*

In the pre-*Mwongozo* days managers and workers had accepted a set of impersonal rules that were part and parcel of the capitalist management outlook. There were organizational blueprints and disciplinary codes that bore the mark of bourgeois thinking. Although not necessarily internalized by the employees, these features of the working scene were not questioned. *Mwongozo* blew up this myth. The new situation invited the employees to relate to each other not only as cogs in a wheel but as full personalities. What this meant was that managers and workers in the wake of *Mwongozo* would come to work carrying all their pre-capitalist baggage. They would bring into the organization all those concerns they had been prevented from taking up before. This, however, did not facilitate the management process. On the contrary, it made organizational management virtually impossible because demands were often raised that could not possibly be accommodated within the principle of productivity. Workers demanded rights to autonomy that in many cases made them immune to any use of organizational authority. Managers, in response to demands made through the economy of affection, often made decisions that satisfied such demands but which went contrary to the interest of the organization. In short, both workers and managers acted in such a way that the public institutions were the prime victims.

Before 1971 workers' interests, to the extent that these had been at all catered for, had been channelled through the workers' committees. Their role, however, had been essentially to serve as a disciplinary organ within the organization. Hence, it did not carry too much legitimacy in the eyes of the rank-and-file workers. The new workers' councils were expected to provide the opportunity for them to participate in management. Even these organs, however, failed, in most companies, to acquire much credibility among the workers. Management tended to dominate their sessions and workers' lack of experience and know-how was often used as an excuse not to discuss technical issues. Although workers in some parastatals tried to bring up welfare issues in the workers' councils, the main organ for workers' demands became the new party branches. The authority of the party was used to undercut the lines of managerial authority. In fact, in many cases workers used party authority to intimidate the managers. Since few managers were prepared to challenge the supremacy of the party, short of giving in to the workers (which often happened), they could only go for a deadlock situation. They could prevent the workers from realizing their demands but they could not easily engage in a constructive dialogue with them. Many managers felt as if they were handcuffed by the new setup.

The effects of the new situation became obvious quite soon. Articles began to appear in Tanzanian newspapers less than a year after *Mwongozo*, asking which way workers were going.[13] A little later the articles carried headlines such as 'The price of workers' awakening'[14] and 'Who should discipline whom?'[15] Eventually the concerns became even more serious: 'We need to tighten our parastatals'[16] and 'Can we afford labour unrest?'[17]

Marxist writers have interpreted the work stoppages as manifestations of revolutionary class struggle.[18] While there is no difficulty in accepting their claim that workers' dissatsifaction was genuine, and that *Mwongozo* created an unprecedented occasion for expressing this dissatisfaction, there is doubt whether these incidents should really be seen as part of a revolutionary struggle for socialism. Such an interpretation ignores the possible impact of pre-capitalist structures also on industrial production. It presupposes devotion to work, discipline and a definite measure of subordination to the demands of a large-scale organization. These features are the same, whether industrial production is carried out on capitalist or socialist premises. In modern societies, where the ruling classes control the workers by virtue of having alienated them from the means of production, and reduced their ability to subsist on their own, a conflict between management and workers is inevitably articulated as a class contradiction. Workers in these societies have no alternative but to accept or fight the system. Where, however, the system is not 'waterproof', and the producers can exit by ignoring the demands of those who are in charge of the system, conflicts have other dimensions too.

The work stoppages in Tanzania were hardly class conflicts in the conventional sense of the phrase. What facilitated them, and what made it so difficult to contain them, was the relative autonomy of the workers vis-à-vis management. Most Tanzanian workers still have alternative sources of outcome, notably in the form of farms in the rural areas, as shown above. Work in a modern organization is not an absolute necessity for most of them. They can always retreat to their own piece of land and secure their reproduction within the context of the economy of affection. The work stoppages were neither evidence of a revolutionary struggle for socialism nor of parochialism or cultural traditionalism. They were fully rational acts, induced by the pre-capitalist structures of the Tanzanian economy.

To the workers *Mwongozo* was an instrument of liberation from a mode of production in which man is reduced to being merely a producer. The Party Guidelines gave him a chance of regaining his *utu* – humanhood – as interpreted in the context of the economy of affection. The Tanzanian workers can hardly be said to have struggled for the objectives of modern socialism. Certainly, there is little reason to believe that they were primarily interested in creating a new morality of labour built on self-discipline. This presupposes an individual freed from his pre-capitalist obligations. Von Freyhold's data on the workers, as well as their actual behaviour, demonstrated that they still laboured under these obligations. *Mwongozo* gave the workers an opportunity to free themselves from the shackles of modern production. The struggle between management and workers in Tanzania after 1971 centred more on the contradiction between capitalist and pre-capitalist structures than it did on the conflict between capitalism and socialism. It is a manifestation of our 'false consciousness' that this was not discovered earlier.

Those Tanzanian managers who were committed to building a modern socialist society grew increasingly disappointed with the behaviour of the workers. The more unscrupulous members of the bureaucratic bourgeoisie, on the other hand, did not hesitate to take advantage of the new situation. The frequency with which accusations of nepotism and favouritism were made against managers, is evidence that the economy of affection was at least as well nursed after *Mwongozo* as it was before. A third category of managers reacted by keeping a low profile. They did not take management decisions that could land them in political trouble. Management of the public sector was, if not para-lysed, at least considerably weakened after *Mwongozo*. The managers found themselves in a position similar to that of the bureaucrats vis-à-vis the peasants: they could not really get at the workers easily and the workers only showed contempt for management. The poor state of management affairs in the State Trading Corporation led to a serious shortage of essential consumer goods. The National Housing Cor-poration also found itself in deep trouble. The pressures on housing in the urban areas kept growing in the 1970s, both because of an increased influx of people to the towns and because of an exodus of private contractors. As Stren has shown with reference to Dar es Salaam, finding a house or an apartment is virtually impossible for the majority, who instead take to squatting.[19] Those who tried to go for a regular house or apartment found the waiting-list so long that the only possible way of obtaining a place of residence would be through the use of the economy of affection or bribery.[20]

The dismantling of the pre-*Mwongozo* management system in Tanzania's public enterprises was not only a blow against capitalism but also against modern organization as such. *Mwongozo* effectively destroyed the flimsy fabric of modern organization that had been institutionalized in Tanzania. That modern production requires a system of authority to resolve its conflicting demands and thus, as Dahrendorff tells us,[21] inevitably carries the seeds of class conflict, was generally ignored in Tanzania in the first years after *Mwongozo*. The gains in pre-capitalist equality and dignity that *Mwongozo* was bringing to the workers were prematurely interpreted as part of a socialist transition. The false nature of such an interpretation gradually became apparent to Tanzanians. The following quotation from a feature article cannot be dismissed as merely an expression of management ideology. It reflects the dilemma in building socialism on pre-modern foundations:

> We have dismantled and demoralised the disciplinary machinery and the terminal focus of loyalty in institutions, offices and other work-places. Management no longer has control over labour and workers' misinterpretation of political speeches and documents.... As a result in some work-places there is technically no management, no foreman, no leaders of operations, no organization. Workers have neither motivation nor incentive because management has crumbled down and is not in a position to reprimand and reward.... In effect, these days no government officer in a ministry, no manager in a para-statal organisation, no foreman in a work unit and no person technically responsible to direct public operations or a piece of work dare insist on work standards or better job performance of his colleagues without risking to be disastrously unpopular or appear eccentric. In most cases he will be stigmatized as a 'colonialist' by both his co-workers and the immediate associates (before his expulsion is demanded).[22]

Another local correspondent stated in May 1972 that 'the best thing to do these days is to shut one's mouth even at the expense of the nation, that is if one wants to be on the safe side. "Why bother" is a general saying these days.'[23] This attitude of 'no man's property' and 'no man's work' was becoming very widespread in Tanzania after 1971. A common expression that could often be heard in the streets of Dar es

Salaam was: '*Mali ya umma haiumi*' – public property does not hurt. The assumption of the many workers who made themselves the arrogant advocates of this view was that the demands of parastatal management could pretty much be ignored.

In short, *Mwongozo* had the effect of undermining the moral underpinnings of the public realm. Many workers – and also some managers – interpreted the new political directive as an invitation to ignore the obligations to the public realm. *Mwongozo* stressed workers' rights but said nothing specific about their duties. The public realm was still associated with capitalism and colonialism and it lacked legitimacy, as Ekeh so rightly points out.[24] The events in Tanzania immediately after the *Mwongozo* definitely proved the accuracy of his argument. The obligations of the economy of affection (the 'primordial realm') were taking precedence over those of public institutions to such an extent that less and less capital was generated domestically for use in socialist development tasks. Action to reverse this trend became inevitable particularly in 1973 and 1974 when the performance of the agricultural sector was very sluggish.

Revival of discipline

The efforts to save the socialist policies of Tanzania from the pre-capitalist abyss have been a long and often frustrating experience. Tanzania has worked on all fronts and around the clock. While it had been reasonably easy to erase *kasumba* – the remnants of capitalist or colonial thinking in the midst of Tanzanian society – it was a totally different matter to reintroduce *nidhamu* – discipline. *Mwongozo* had advanced political consciousness in Tanzania to new levels. Tanzanian workers had become aware of the historical roots of their predicament in a way that few other African workers had. This new consciousness, however, was not immediately supportive of productive demands in a society where pre-capitalist social formations spilled over into the urban areas and created barriers to socialist transformation. *Mwongozo* had created a situation in which the new political relations were non-congruent with the relations of production, as conceived in either capitalist or socialist blueprints. Party efforts after 1974 have been directed primarily to the task of bringing about greater congruence between the political relations and the production relations; to subordinate again the former to the latter.

A major means to achieve this end has been the political education of both managers and workers. The turning-point was the May Day address by President Nyerere in 1974, when he stressed that discipline in work was essential for socialist development. The new target was *uzembe* – laziness – which, according to Nyerere, now characterized most work-places in Tanzania. He appealed to his fellow-countrymen to promise themselves: *uhuru ni kazi:* freedom is work! Nyerere continued:

> The peasant who does not go to the fields and work hard at the right time is damaging the country's total production. But at least he will not receive money for the crops which are destroyed by his laziness. Wage-earners are not disciplined in that way; they get their wages at the end of the month. But in return for the assurance of his monthly wages, a wage-earner is expected to observe the discipline of group work. If he does not like that discipline he can go back to working as an individual peasant.[25]

President Nyerere concluded his speech by claiming that those who talked of socialism as if it meant avoiding work were cheating and should be considered enemies of the country. This theme was reiterated virtually every time Nyerere and other leaders addressed the public. Wage-earners, like peasants, were now considered as exploiters of other people, if they did not make their rightful contribution to production. Examples of this form of exploitation began to circulate in the mass media. In September 1974, the *Daily News* summarized the trend that had gone on virtually unchecked before:

> We have many examples of people who regularly report late for duty, and quite often the excuse is that the transportation system was to blame. We have many others who come into their offices, as it were, to register their presence and then go on doing nothing all day. They make large numbers of phone calls to their friends and acquaintances, just to pass the day. We have others who report for duty, albeit on time, only to quietly sneak out of their offices to conduct other business, unrelated to work. Examples of people queuing at offices to get services only to find the person at the counter is busy making a friendly telephone call, or worse, has disappeared from sight, are not wanting.[26]

These habits became the target of political education in government and parastatal offices. There was discussion over whether these political meetings should be conducted during or after office hours. Although many felt it proper to do it outside office hours, the only way to secure satisfactory attendance at these meetings was to hold them during office hours. They were seen as part of the staff or workers' development programme.

Party and government officials hardened their stand vis-à-vis the workers. They tried to prevent the outbreak of 'unnecessary conflicts' at work. 'Laying down the tools', as the illegal work stoppages had been referred to, was no longer to be permitted. In those cases, where such incidents still continued to take place, the workers were dismissed.[27] Workers' committees and TANU branch committees were no longer permitted to echo only the workers' voice. Instead, they were expected to educate workers, discipline them, and where necessary, serve as conciliatory organs. NUTA – Tanzania's labour union – pledged itself to stamp out idleness among workers.[28] The laissez-faire atmosphere that had characterized Tanzania's work-places after *Mwongozo*, however, could not be erased by focusing on the workers only.

The attitude among managers was not very different from that of the workers. Most of them seemed unwilling to stick their neck out and preferred to do what was minimally required of them. This definitely contributed to the slackness of performance that became increasingly apparent in Tanzania's parastatals after 1971. It would be wrong to claim that the managers were always to blame. They had often been placed in situations over which they had little control. Political decisions took precedence over management decisions that had already been made and the parameters of action often changed so drastically that planning for the development of the parastatal companies was becoming an almost impossible task. With the reduced importance of the market and the growing bureaucratization of the public sector, there was a tendency to produce commodities with little knowledge of existing demands. One case in point is Tanganyika Packers, which in 1974, after having lost its overseas sales agent, still continued to produce canned meat with no assurance of market outlet. The end result was a huge pile-up of meat that was in danger of being destroyed.[29]

Even if account is taken of the complications brought about by bureaucratization it seems fair to say that the managers of parastatal companies were unwilling or unable to perform at pre-*Mwongozo* levels. Particularly disappointing was the trend among managers to 'pass the buck'. Blames and counter-blames were becoming the order of the day. In some cases, it may have been true that the root of the problem was beyond management's reach, but only too often managers were inclined to blame others to escape attention to shortcomings within their own organization. One such example is the severe pile-up of sugar that took place in November 1974, making it virtually impossible to obtain sugar anywhere in the country. This was particularly embarrassing because one of the few crops that Tanzania produced in sufficient quantities within its own borders could not reach the local consumers. In this case, sugar company officials blamed railway officials and they blamed ministry officials for lack of planning, and so forth. This pile-up took place, although the President a few weeks earlier had made an unexpected personal inspection of sugar distribution.[30]

These examples occurred over and over again and on one occasion in his home village, Butiama, the President found it necessary to dismiss fifty-eight workers who had delayed the construction of cattle sheds in his village for three years, although the village had a loan of 200 000 T. shs from Tanzania's Rural Development Bank for that purpose.[31] In announcing the dismissal of these workers the President said that a worker who, through his laziness or negligence, retarded the country's development but received his monthly salary was a thief just like any other gangster.

Employment in the public sector had shot up very quickly in the 1970s, particularly following the decentralization reform of the government. At the same time revenue collection had deteriorated. Government agents were less effective in collecting dues, and parastatal companies, while paying their taxes to government, found overhead costs rising quickly and profits declining, in some cases turning into deficits. In the light of the national economic crisis in 1974/75, following the drought, government had to retire no less than 9500 officials in 1976. The interesting thing about this mass retirement was the relative ease with which it was carried out. The vast majority of the workers returned to their land and got absorbed into peasant farming. Although the exercise at least in part was treated as a punishment, since the majority affected were the least 'desirable', it was a rather ineffective disciplinary instrument. Since the vast majority of all workers and petty-bourgeoisie already have land, or could easily gain access to it, effective state action is difficult. If the Tanzanian state displays features of 'softness', it has structural explanations. It is not merely a matter of cultural traditionalism. It is not only the peasant producers who can ignore the state. Even the petty-bourgeoisie can, although with greater difficulty. Within the economy of affection, however, they are capable of organizing alternative means of sustaining their livelihood. They are capable of a social livelihood; they are capable of a social elasticity that is impossible in societies where the ruling classes have cut their ties with production on the land. Thus, not only are the peasants in Tanzania capable of ignoring state demands but so are the state's own employees. By virtue of having an alternative livelihood and by being involved in the economy of affection, most public sector employees can remain indifferent to demands for devoted service to the nation. Small has infiltrated large.

It is in the light of these factors that Nyerere has placed such great importance on building up a leadership cadre who do not fall prey to the traps laid by the small. The dilemma in which he finds himself in pursuing this exercise is that, while committed to popular participation and democracy, he can only succeed in building up such a cadre if they are prepared to cut their ties with the economy of affection. In other words, it is difficult to conceive of Tanzania continuing in a socialist direction without a rupture of those social ties that more effectively than anything else have reduced the tensions between the state and the rural producer.

This is implied in the regulations of the new party, Chama cha Mapinduzi (CCM), in which people will be allowed to serve as leaders only if they fulfil the qualifying conditions of being selfless and incorrupt individuals, willing to lead the people in a mobilizing and not in arrogant fashion. The increased militarization of the leadership is another case in point. By exposing party and government leaders to military discipline and organization, the belief is that they will grow more immune to the demands of the economy of affection. There is also a growing tendency to appoint political commissars, usually trusted members of Nyerere's leadership cadre, as watchdogs of public institutions. The experience of using the party branches in these institutions for such a purpose was not very encouraging, for reasons discussed above. The overall effect of these measures is likely to be less room for views from below, at least in the sense that the party leadership will become more insistent on determining the premises on which development efforts will be allowed to take place. The mobilization potential of this approach cannot be denied; after all, this is how major social transformations have been carried out elsewhere. On the other hand, nor can the potential hazards of this approach be denied. There is the danger that leaders will ride roughshod over local views in a situation where the latter carry weight with the people. Samoff offers one illustration of this danger: the regional development officer who, after consultations in the capital on the region's annual development plan, categorically insists that 'our job is to bring the thinking of Dar es Salaam even down to the village level.'[32] Finucane's warning of the pitfalls of this approach cannot be ignored: 'the difficulty in mobilizing support from those who have not participated in decisions, and the inaccuracy of bureaucratic estimates of the "price" people will demand to be induced into producing differently and more.'[33]

This insistence on greater regulation of the development process from above also implies more bureaucratization in the sense of a greater number of rules tying the hands of the decision-makers. The public sector becomes less flexible. In such a situation the advantages of devotion and self-sacrifice will be minimal. The machinery becomes too complex for effective management and a lot of waste is the main outcome. The producers get less in return for their efforts. This has been true of the various parastatal bodies serving the peasants. Table 6.1 illustrates the division of income from the sale of cotton between the different bodies involved.

The figures show that in the case of the Tanzania Cotton Authority, the parastatal company in charge of marketing cotton, direct as well as indirect marketing costs, both in absolute terms and expressed in cents per kilo of seed cotton produced, increased markedly in the first five years of the 1970s. It has been difficult to stem this trend even more recently because the TCA, like other such companies, have been required to engage in providing additional services and facilities for the producers. For instance, in May 1976, when government announced that all fertilizer prices would be subsidized by 50 per cent, the agricultural parastatal companies were instructed to contribute 68 million T. shs to the Fertilizer Subsidy Fund, while the Treasury would

TABLE 6.1. Cotton price and marketing cost structure, 1970/71 to 1974/75 (Tanzanian cents per kilo seed cotton)

| | 1970/71 | | 1971/72 | | 1972/73 | | 1973/74 | | 1974/75 | |
	cts	%	cts	%	cts	%	cts	%	cts	%
Sales price	161·4	100	192·0	100	194·7	100	298·4	100	345·0	100
Export tax	6·8	4·2	6·8	3·5	6·8	3·5	6·8	2·3	24·4	9·1
Parastatal margin	24·6	15·2	55·2	28·7	55·0	28·2	151·0	50·6	139·6	40·5
Co-operative margin	26·6	16·5	26·6	13·9	26·3	13·5	34·0	11·4	41·2	11·9
Producer return	103·4	64·1	103·4	53·9	106·6	54·8	106·6	35·7	139·8	40·5

Source: Ministry of Agriculture, *Price Policy Recommendations for the 1977/78 Agricultural Price Review*, Vol. II: Parastatal Marketing Costs, Part B Export Crops. p. 127.

supply 61 million T. shs. The cost of subsidizing fertilizers has remained one of the largest items of all agricultural parastatals and the payment of this subsidy has been met by restricting price increases paid to producers. De facto, therefore, the producers have been required to pay much more for the fertilizers than the nominal price offered them. In general, it is true to say that the costs of non-marketing involvement by parastatals have been met by keeping the producer price at a low level. Although many of these services are seen as essential for the producers, their willingness to engage in the relatively labour-intensive production of cotton seed will become increasingly difficult to sustain, if marketing costs cannot be reduced.

The review of other parastatal companies concerned with agricultural production and marketing revealed additional serious shortcomings.[34] One is the lack of up-to-date accounts that facilitate cost control and planning. In most cases managers do not follow cost estimates and expenditure budgets as approved at the beginning of the financial year. The preparation of these takes on the character of being merely a pro-forma exercise in many parastatals.

A second shortcoming of many parastatals are the high costs incurred in conjunction with the payment of interest on overdrafts and loans. Overdrafts have often been necessary to provide finance for activities such as fertilizer distribution, provision of crop purchase funds, investments, and even for meeting deficits in the overall expenditure of the parastatal. Interest payment also figures prominently in the accounts of some companies, for example, the Tobacco Authority of Tanzania which in 1975/76 had bank charges and interest payments amounting to 45 per cent of total head-office expenses. The National Milling Corporation, which is the principal buying agent of surplus

grain for the government, in 1976 had a bank overdraft of 400 million
T. shs and were thus liable to interest payments to the tune of 2·5
million T. shs per month.[35]

A third problem relates to the capital accumulation capacity of the
public sector. While its share in capital formation in the monetary
economy increased from 40 per cent in 1965 to 78 per cent in 1974, this
impressive record of investment effort was matched by a strong savings
performance only up to 1970. After that, savings in the parastatal
sector, as well as in the private sector, have declined considerably as a
result, in the case of the public sector, of low levels of operational
efficiency, and in the case of the private sector, as a result of the
uncertain climate for investment opportunities and of increased
taxation.[36]

A fourth shortcoming of the parastatal sector has been faltering
production caused by growing difficulties in obtaining raw materials,
poor maintenance, etc. The Tanzania Cashewnut Authority found itself
unable to purchase nuts from the peasants during the 1976/77 season
until the government gave it extra funds, and lorries belonging to other
public institutions and private individuals were commandeered for
transportation.[37] Tanzania's only cement factory ran into serious
maintenance problems during 1976 causing a large fall in production.
Needless to say this caused a severe shortage and a flourishing black
market.[38] Table 6.2 illustrates trends in production in selected industries in Tanzania. In addition to showing downward trends in many
industries, it demonstrates the difficulty of keeping upward trends going
in the light of such factors as shortages of power, water or insufficient
supply of raw materials.

The situation has improved in some respects since 1975 with the
completion of the Kidatu hydro-electric power plant and the expansion
of the water supply for Dar es Salaam in 1976. As Table 6.3 shows, there
have also been shifts in government development expenditure towards
more directly productive ventures. Although the figures for 1975/76 and
1976/77 are not confirmed, the trend indicated by the budgetary
estimates has been upheld. Whether more investments in directly
productive ventures, as opposed to economic and social infrastructure,
will reduce the problems experienced in the public sector, it is too early
to assess.

It can be argued that Tanzania's principal economic problem is not a
reallocation of capital but its generation. Many expatriate observers are
inclined to blame this problem on the system of public ownership. They
argue that public enterprises cannot be as productive as those privately
owned. It has been shown here that private farming is more productive
than communal farming for essentially non-economic reasons, that the
production for household needs is so vital that even if modern inputs
are provided for the communal farm, the peasant sticks to his private
plot. In the modern economic sector, private business is only likely to be

TABLE 6.2. Production in selected industries in Tanzania, 1972–75

Commodity	Unit	PRODUCTION VOLUME					
		Full year 1972	Full year* 1973	Full year 1974	First half 1974	First half 1975	1974/75
Textiles	000' sq. m.	74 136	80 763	81 100	44 700	40 428	-9·6
Cement	000' metric tons	237	314	296	195	165	-15·0
Fertilizers	metric tons	not available	32 594	58 778	29 300	26 134	-10·8
Shoes†	000' pairs	2457	2320	2800	974	1853	90·3
Petroleum	000' metric tons	763	731	753	416	367	-11·8
Vegetable oils‡	000' litres	n.a.	n.a.	n.a.	1964	843	-57·1
Canned meat	metric tons	5125	2044	5425	3050	2900	-4·0
Tyres and tubes	metric tons	n.a.	3752	4788	1498	2350	56·8
Sisal ropes and twine	metric tons	22 575	25 354	29 496	14 760	11 459	-22·4
Rolled steel	metric tons	4308	4776	8591	3820	5387	41·0
Blankets	000' sq. m.	4533	5476	2686	1975	1944	-1·0
Enamelware	000' pieces	4267	4150	1378	760	1017	60·1
Fishnets	metric tons	237	292	161	98	98	–
Batteries	000' pieces	36 552	45 049	48 001	30 000	22 105	-26·3
Iron sheets	metric tons	20 800	22 300	26 000	15 600	15 800	1·3
Aluminium	metric tons	3602	3332	3660	1674	1767	5·6
Pyrethrum extract	metric tons	207	156	116	68	108	58·8
Beer	000' litres	64 826	69 323	63 659	43 232	30 025	-30·5
Cigarettes	000'000	2729	2890	4649	1064	1526	43·4

* Data for 1972 to 1974 has been revised
† Only production by the Tanzania Shoe Company (Bora Shoes) which accounts for nearly 75 per cent of total production in the country
‡ The figure for the first half of 1975 represents production by Vegetable Oil Industry (VOIL) only
Source: Central Statistical Bureau and Bank of Tanzania

TABLE 8.3. Government development expenditures in Tanzania, 1970–77 (in Tanzanian currency)

	1970/71 to 1973/74 Average annual		1974/75 Budget		1974/75 Provisional actuals		1975/76 Budget		1976/77 Budget	
	shs million	%	shs million	%	shs million	%	shs million	%	shs million	%
Directly productive	210	22·9	688	35·7	527	28·1	1098	38·5	1317	43·2
Agriculture	145	15·8	499	25·9	334	17·8	778	27·3	710	23·3
Commerce, industry and mining	65	7·1	189	9·8	193	10·3	320	11·2	607	19·9
Economic infrastructure	439	47·9	718	37·2	833	44·6	1039	36·4	900	29·5
Water	85	9·3	215	11·1	215	11·5	387	13·5	296	9·7
Power	97	10·6	216	11·2	216	11·6	162	5·7	117	3·8
Communication	183	19·9	214	11·1	303	16·2	328	11·5	348	11·4
Other*	74	8·1	73	3·8	99	5·3	162	5·7	139	4·6
Social infrastructure	73	7·9	195	10·1	164	8·8	275	9·6	370	12·2
Education	49	5·3	112	5·8	95	5·1	198	6·9	264	8·7
Health	21	2·3	80	4·2	66	3·5	75	2·6	95	3·1
Other	3	0·3	3	0·1	3	0·2	2	0·1	11	0·4
Other	196	21·4	326	16·9	347	18·6	443	15·5	458	15·0
Total	917	100·0	1928	100·0	1871	100·0	2855	100·0	3045	100·0

* Housing and urban development; natural resources and tourism; Dodoma Capital Development; and other regional infrastructure
† Regional and central administration and planning; information and broadcasting; and security
Sources: Auditor-General's Reports, Annual Plans 1974/75 to 1975/76 and estimates of the Ministry of Finance and Planning

more productive if there is a capitalist system to offer incentives in such a direction. Such is not unequivocally the case in Tanzania. Private business is not likely to show great productivity gains over the public enterprise as long as the economic system remains only marginally capitalist. The main problem with the public enterprises in Tanzania is twofold. On the one hand, they are often falling prey to pressures by pre-capitalist forces. On the other, they are held in shackles by a bureaucracy set up to contain the influences of these forces. This situation carries the dangers of a vicious circle. While it is possible for bureaucracy to serve a developmental role in modern capitalist and socialist economies, such a role is virtually precluded in a society where pre-capitalist formations prevail or linger on as important social forces. Tanzania definitely belongs to the latter category. She is stuck with a bureaucracy of her own making that will pose a limit to any productivity gains as long as the pre-capitalist forces are capable of holding capitalist and socialist penetration at bay.

Towards a socialist managerial elite

The gravest mistake committed by many Marxist analysts of the Tanzanian situation is to reduce her development equation to a choice between capitalism or socialism without realizing her predicament: of not being easily accessible to either of them. To argue that if Tanzania does not follow socialist policies (whatever the meaning of socialism, she must automatically be going capitalist is extremely superficial. There is no reason to doubt Tanzania's commitment to socialism. Capitalism has already proved itself incapable of transforming her economy and, therefore, there are no strong forces to reverse the socialist policies. It is true that Tanzania may have initiated policies that do not meet the socialist expectations of the Marxists, but these policies are best interpreted as tactical and not strategic shifts.

Tanzania's greatest problem in building a socialist society is to create a machinery that can dutifully serve such an end. It is no coincidence therefore, that President Nyerere has placed such importance on good leadership. We have already mentioned the qualifications attached to being a leader in the new party, CCM. Another important feature of the same orientation is the President's desire to replace the old party leader with new, more educated and technically competent men. While the former were quite firmly rooted in the pre-capitalist formations that have developed out of the peasant mode of production, the latter are seen as more easily accessible to the demands of modern socialism. The President has also increased his personal control of appointments in the public sector so that he can more effectively reward and punish those who occupy senior positions of leadership in the system. Nyerere' expectation is that a growing number of people below him will be able to modernize the society and develop the economy along the socialist lines adopted by the ruling party. In short, Nyerere is committed to achieve for his country what capitalism and colonialism have failed to achieve. However, this is both a complicated and an expensive affair.

To grasp fully its dimensions it is necessary to remember the unfavourable circumstances in which he begins this exercise. In pre-capitalist Tanzania, very few individuals are really dependent on the state; even its own employees are not. In modern society loyalty to and compliance with state demands are taken for granted. Society is sufficiently differentiated to have produced people for whom working independently on the land is no longer possible or desirable. Although such individuals do exist also in Tanzania, their number is limited and experience has shown that creating the conditions for the emergence of such people is a prerequisite of socialist development. It can be said in favour of those Tanzanians who have served dutifully in the party or the government that they have done so with often limited rewards. Employment as an official has not been an absolute necessity in most cases. Many could probably have remained in farming but in the context of the economy of affection it fell upon them to be its 'extended arm' in the modern sector of society. They were educated by members of the economy of affection with the specific purpose of offering some-thing in return once they had reached a position of importance in society. Many public servants have naturally remained loyal to these expectations. The structural pressures to nurse the economy of affection have been at least as strong as those working in favour of the modern capitalist or socialist economy. After the Arusha Declaration, when public officials were disallowed more than one income and also the right to own property for rent, many used the economy of affection to mitigate the sacrifices that this policy implied. For instance, it was not uncommon for property to be registered in the names of relatives. Others, however, accepted the new policy and ended up far less well-equipped to support the economy of affection. They now form the embryo of a socialist managerial elite, expected to remain loyal to party policies and directives and ignore the unofficial demands placed on them within the context of the economy of affection.

It falls on their shoulders to complete the construction of an economic system with no loopholes, with no opportunities for the peasants and workers to ignore the demands placed on them by the rulers. To ensure their loyalty to this task, official remunerations have been raised over the years, particularly for party officials. While in the 1960s, party leaders had meagre salaries and lived off allowances they could accumulate from meetings, today's party leader in Tanzania is at every level in the hierarchy receiving a salary, fixed at least one step above the highest paid state official at equivalent rank. This has been one way of maintaining party supremacy and of attracting to the party ranks officials from various public institutions. The effect of this salary reform paid out of government funds has been to allow easier mobility between party and government. It has increased the opportunities to transfer and promote manpower resources to organizations or positions where they are urgently or badly needed.

The whole matter of manpower utilization has been tackled in Tanzania from the point of view of the system at large. Nyerere has ignored the micro-efficiencies of individual organizations in favour of the macro-efficiency of the policy-making system as a whole. Transfers of individuals have often caused disruptions in the management of single public organizations but this has been justified in the name of a stronger development management system. Thus, to achieve socialism in the context of a pre-capitalist economy it has been necessary to invest in strengthening the political machinery. Economics, as we noted in the introductory chapter, has been called upon to 'feed' politics.

This build-up of a machinery for socialist development management is likely to be inevitable in a pre-capitalist society which does not want to depend on the market forces for allocation of its values. It does, however, carry its own dangers. One of them is that the officials become more upward than downward oriented. They will look at the solution of problems only in terms of what the ideology prescribes and forget the fact that, particularly in agricultural production, success is still highly dependent on sensitivity to local variables. Even more serious is the reluctance to accept mistakes and the opportunity of learning from mistakes. Officials find it embarrassing to admit failures or mistakes and instead of learning from them try to cover them up. This tendency which exists at all levels in Tanzania is, perhaps more than any other factor, likely to reduce the gains of the development machinery under construction. Unwillingness or inability to learn from past experience, even when negative, is a serious shortcoming that will prevent the generation of a local body of knowledge for use in tackling development problems. Without such a body of knowledge there is danger that Tanzanian policy-makers will keep plunging into darkness forever. Yet another danger with this system is that in trying to 'run while others walk', officials may be blind to the many constraints that exist along the road of socialist construction. Not only may individual officials run so fast as to stumble (and thus ruin their career); even more serious is the danger that the officials run away from those who are unable to move fast, notably the peasants. In such a situation the losers will not be the peasants but the officials.[39]

Conclusions

The enlarged public sector was conceived by the Tanzanian leadership as the principal instrument for generation of surplus capital. It was also seen as being in a position to serve better the smallholder peasant farmers. Although it is far too early to come to categorical conclusions about the Tanzanian experience, it is clear that the performance of the public sector to date has been below expectation. Most analysts have been inclined to explain this by reference to managerial inefficiencies or bourgeois class interests blocking the socialist transformation effort. While it would be wrong to dismiss the validity of these explanations altogether, they hardly get to the root of the problem. The main blockage to socialist transformation in Tanzania is to be found in the pre-capitalist structures still kept alive by an active peasant mode of production. Our analysis of the public sector has demonstrated that pre-capitalist formations also stand in the way of socialism in what officially constitutes the modern sector. This is confirmed by an Eastern European economist who shows that between 1966 and 1977 there was a serious deterioration in effectiveness of use of the labour factor (19·2 per cent) implying grave losses in industrial production.[40] Therefore it has been difficult for Tanzania's socialist leadership to make really significant gains with the new policies without engaging in policies that heighten the conflict between socialist managers and workers. It has been necessary to break the hold of the economy of affection and encourage the articulation of class conflicts. These measures are not necessarily contrary to the future development of socialist relations of production in Tanzania, as many political economists have been inclined to conclude. On the contrary, in the context of Tanzania's pre-capitalist structures, they are a prerequisite for a transformation of society in a socialist direction. They form part of the effort to enlarge the material base for socialist development. They also contribute to reducing the opportunities of workers and peasants to ignore the demands of the ruling petty-bourgeoisie and thus force them to fight antagonistic class interests within the context of a modern mode of production.

So far neither the capitalist nor the socialist mode has attained a real hold on the producers in Tanzania. The building of a socialist society in Tanzania, therefore, is still at an incipient stage. At this stage, the task implies more than anything else the creation of the preconditions for a socialist development. In this perspective, it is not surprising that President Nyerere in his review of the first ten years after the Arusha Declaration declared:

> But I am a very poor prophet. In 1956 I was asked how long it would take Tanganyika to become independent. I thought 10 to 12 years. We became independent 6 years later! In 1967 a group of the youth who were marching in support of the Arusha Declaration asked me how long it would take Tanzania to become socialist. I thought 30 years. I was wrong again: I am now sure it will take us much longer.[41]

It may not be wrong to say that the Tanzanian leadership, in its effort to construct a socialist society, discovered some years after the Arusha Declaration that the capitalist sector was only the top of an iceberg. The real blockages to socialist transformation were hidden under the surface: in the peasant mode of production and the pre-capitalist formations it had given rise to. The lesson learned from the first ten years after the Arusha Declaration was that Tanzania's development premises were not only pre-capitalist; they were at the same time pre-socialist. Building socialism in a pre-capitalist setting was no easier than building capitalism! Given that many other African states are characterized by similar conditions, and engaged in building some form of socialist society, this lesson is bound to have wider implications. This will be the subject matter of the next two chapters.

References and notes

1. For a positive evaluation of Tanzanian nationalizations, see Johannes A Masare, 'Socialist ideology and practice in Tanzania: TANU Governmen efforts to control the national economy 1967–1976', unpublished Ph.D dissertation, Department of Political Science, University of Californie Berkeley, 1978. For a more critical analysis, see, for instance, Issa Shivj Class Struggles in Tanzania, (Heinemann Educational Books, 1976) Uchumi Editorial Board, Towards Socialist Planning (Dar es Salaam Tanzania Publishing House, 1974) and the special issue of Maji Maji n 17 (August 1974), organ of the TANU Youth League branch at th University of Dar es Salaam which is devoted to the 'workers' revolution in Tanzania'.

2. National Development Corporation, Third and Fourth Annual Reports an Accounts (Dar es Salaam 1967 and 1968).

3. Philip C. Packard, 'Management and control of parastatal organizations' in Uchumi Editorial Board, op. cit., p. 87.

4. The Standard (Dar es Salaam), 29 June 1971.

5. The Nationalist (Dar es Salaam), 18 June 1969.

6. 'The Establishment of Workers' Councils, Executive Boards and Board of Directors', Presidential Circular, No. 1 (1970).

7. Mwongozo – The Party Guidelines (Dar es Salaam: Printpak, 1971) paragraph 28.

8. Michaela von Freyhold, 'The Workers, the Nizers and the Peasants' mimeo., Department of Sociology, University of Dar es Salaam, n.d.

9. Peter Marris, 'African city life', Nkanga (Kampala) vol. 1, no. 1 (1968), p 10.

10. See, for instance, Peter C. W. Gutkind, The Emergent African Urban Proletariat, Occasional Paper Series No. 8, Centre for Developing-Are Studies, McGill University, Montreal, 1974.

11. Otto Neuloh, et al., Der Ostafrikanische Industriearbeiter zwische Schamba und Maschine (München: Weltforum Verlag, 1966), p. 254.

12. Hans Rogger and Eugen Weber (eds), The European Right (Berkeley University of California Press, 1966), p. 504.

13. A. N. Nderingo, 'Which way workers?', The Standard, 11 November 1971

14. Hadji Konde, 'The price of workers' awakening', *The Standard*, 5 March 1972.
15. Guido Magomc, 'Who should discipline whom?', *Daily News*, 19 March 1973.
16. 'We need to tighten our parastatals', by a special correspondent, *Daily News*, 16 May 1972.
17. Robert Rweyemamu, 'Can we afford labour unrest?', *Sunday News*, 24 February 1974.
18. See Shivji, op. cit., and *Maji Maji*, op. cit.
19. Richard E. Stren, *Urban Inequality and Housing Policy in Tanzania*, Research Series No. 24, Institute of International Studies, University of California, Berkeley, 1975.
20. This led to a major investigation of the affairs of the National Housing Corporation in 1976, leading in turn to a major shake-up within that parastatal.
21. Ralph Dahrendorff, *Class and Class Conflict in Industrial Society* (Stanford: Stanford University Press, 1959).
22. Nderingo, op. cit.
23. 'We need to tighten our parastatals', op. cit.
24. Peter Ekeh, 'Colonialism and the two publics in Africa: a theoretical statement', *Comparative Studies in Society and History*, vol. 17, no. 1 (1975), pp. 91–112.
25. *Daily News*, 2 May 1974.
26. ibid., 20 September 1974.
27. ibid., 5 August 1975.
28. ibid., 24 September 1974.
29. ibid., 23 September 1974.
30. ibid., 6 November 1974.
31. ibid., 22 May 1975.
32. Joel Samoff, 'The bureaucracy and the bourgeoisie: decentralization and class structure in Tanzania', paper delivered at the Annual Meeting of the African Studies Association, Boston, November 1976, p. 14.
33. James R. Finucane, *Rural Development and Bureaucracy in Tanzania: The Case of Mwanza Region* (Uppsala: Scandinavian Institute of African Studies, 1974), p. 188.
34. Ministry of Agriculture, *Price Policy Recommendations for the 1977/78 Agricultural Price Review*, Vol. II, Dar es Salaam (July 1976), pp. 1–6.
35. ibid., p. 4.
36. These figures are available in the Economic Surveys published by the Ministry of Economic Affairs and Development of Planning, and also in Annual Reports of the Bank of Tanzania for the period covered.
37. *Daily News*, 30 November 1976.
38. ibid., 20 August 1976.
39. I have examined the policy-making system in Tanzania more closely in 'Administration and public policy-making in Kenya and Tanzania', in Joel D. Barkan and John J. Okumu (eds), *Politics and Public Policy in Kenya and Tanzania* (Praeger, 1979).
40. Jerzy Jedruzek, 'Economic Efficiency and the Process of Development', public lecture, University of Dar es Salaam, 26 October 1978, p. 8.
41. Julius K. Nyerere, *The Arusha Declaration Ten Years After* (Dar es Salaam: Government Printer, 1977), p. 1.

CHAPTER 7

The pervasiveness of small:
peasants and petty-bourgeois rulers in Africa

This analysis has acknowledged the existence of social classes in Africa but it has carefully avoided elevating them to the status of being the singularly most important units of social action, as is the case in conventional Marxist class analysis. The reason is that two of its premises appear doubtful in the African context. It presupposes the existence of a social system in which people are irreversibly caught in contradictory relations and to which there is no solution but confrontation. This analysis of Tanzania has shown the inadequacy of that assumption. People have the option or remaining indifferent to demands by the ruling classes, thus avoiding confrontation in favour of the socially more convenient withdrawal. The second fallacy in the prevailing class analysis is the assumption that capitalism is the main determinant of social behaviour; that the market society has replaced the status society. I have tried to show that communal action still encapsules class action. In the process of social change the economy of affection offers alternative solutions to those provided by the presumably rational bourgeois state.

To deal with the problems caused by the structural anomaly of rural Africa I have not abandoned the political economy approach, only transcended its conventional boundaries. In adopting the notion of a bimodal situation in African societies I am not bringing back the 'dual economy' through the back-door.[1] I am emphasizing the existence of two contending modes of production, neither of which can be said really to prevail. Thus, the state, while originally created as the extended arm of international capital, is held at bay by forces originating in the precapitalist, peasant mode of production. The social class situation in Africa cannot be understood in the context of one single mode of production. While an increasing number of people in Africa may accept the premises of either modern capitalism or modern socialism, the vast majority of the producers remain locked up in pre-capitalist or, as suggested in the last chapter, pre-socialist relations. The economic structures of this mode have their own rationale and limit the accessibility of the producers to the demands imposed on them by modern capitalism or modern socialism. The challenge is the same for both: how to penetrate the pre-capitalist mode in such a way as to increase productivity and make producers more attuned to modern development? In short, both face the problems of modernization.

Intellectual escapism

There is a common tendency among political economists studying Africa to avoid tackling the issue of ethnicity or tribalism. Although they seem aware of the problems caused by the forces of tribalism, they either refuse to acknowledge the issue, or they blame it on capitalism (as if tribalism is impossible under socialism). They reduce it to a matter of 'mystification' or 'false consciousness', without acknowledging its structural roots. This is an unfortunate form of intellectual escapism. By taking a short cut in analysing the social realities in Africa, that is, doing it through a ready-made model, the analysts become insensitive to how structures are really articulated through social praxis. This is a major shortcoming, given the structural complexity of the situation where two modes of production contest with each other.

A certain ambivalence towards tribalism is noticeable also in Colin Leys' perceptive analysis of Kenya's predicament. While insisting that the Kenyan situation is best understood through the use of class analysis, he still occasionally admits the significance of communal action, that is, the practice of tribalism, as for instance in the statement that in Kenya in 1970: 'the rich and powerful people in the cities were not yet seen as a race apart; their own rural origins were mostly recent, and while the link between them and the poorest peasants was becoming artificial and mystified, it was still quite active and personal.'[2] The general point to be made here is that articulation of the peasant mode will continue to be important in Africa, certainly as long as its structural roots are active. Communal forms of action have economic origins although they may not be modern capitalist or socialist. They have to be studied as part of a political economy approach.

The treatment of Africa by many Marxists resembles the dilemma facing the French rationalists in the eighteenth century who, according to Znaniecki, were aware of the problems of irrationality in cultural life but would not study them lest the ideal of a perfectly rational new social order be thereby endangered.[3] Socialism, in the Marxist perspective, can only be understood as a product of capitalism; hence, everything has to be blamed on capitalist forces, by analytically subordinated or even consciously ignored, in order to make the new socialist order comprehensible. Curiously enough, contemporary French Marxists have been more imaginative than their Anglo-Saxon colleagues. Anthropologists like Godelier, Meillassoux and Terray, mentioned in the first chapter, have tried to understand the social structure of Africa's pre-colonial societies through the use of Marxist methodology. It is unfortunate that they have been unwilling to acknowledge the relevance of their findings to the contemporary problems of production and reproduction in rural Africa, where pre-capitalist structures still prevail. Mahmood Mamdani is probably the one Marxist who comes closest to recognizing the significance of these structures. In his analysis of Ugandan politics, he traces the rationale of traditionalist political ideologies to a social structure with origins in a pre-capitalist mode of production.[4]

The political economy approach will fail to be relevant to Africa's problems of underdevelopment as long as it fails to recognize that capitalism alone does not set the parameters of social action. Capitalism is being constantly diluted by pre-capitalist forces, because those who articulate the interests of capitalism do not have any effective hold on the majority of Africa's producers. The agents of international capital may have influence on Africa's petty-bourgeois rulers, but they, even when supported by foreign capital, often find the peasantry unresponsive to their demands. If the peasants go along with them at all, they often do so on their own terms. In studying rural development in Africa we have reason to question, as Robert Bates does, the notion that peasants are merely 'passive victims' of the process of change.[5]

It is not only in Tanzania that small has remained powerful. Pre-capitalist forces, through the economy of affection and the ability to withdraw, have held back capitalist development in other areas. In highlighting the constraints on capitalism this chapter will also discuss why socialism is likely to be a much more attractive development alternative to African leaders but why, at the same time, such a task requires a serious rethinking of the role of socialism in the development of African societies.

The parameters of agricultural modernization

It has already been noted that African agriculture is still highly dependent on the forces of nature, notably the tropical climate in which rainfall rather than temperature determines the seasons. Great variations in rainfall may occur from year to year and even within the same year. As Kamarck notes rainfall in the tropical parts of Africa is usually too much or too little.[6] Average annual rainfall means little when one year there is three times as much rain as the next, or when it does not rain evenly throughout a given season of the year but falls in torrents for brief periods. In these circumstances, the ideal conditions for agricultural development occur very rarely. The peasant farmer has to adjust himself to the changing weather conditions, and an ability to read and anticipate these changes is one of the most important aspects of agricultural production in Africa. As one perceptive newspaper reporter once noted:

More than 85 per cent of Africa's 300 million people eke out their
livings as peasant farmers, and a failure of the rains to come can
be a devastating economic disaster. If the question, 'How do
Africans live?' means how do most of them spend the majority of
their time, the answer probably is 'Thinking about rain'. Life
tends to be organized around it, in the way that consumer goods
are the centrepiece of Western societies.[7]

RAIN

Continuous heat and the absence of frost means that the process of
reproduction continues the whole year. Growth of plants as well as the
growth of other kinds of life: weeds, insects, birds, parasitic fungi,
microbes, viruses and parasites on man, his crops and his animals takes
place unconstrained. Life in tropical Africa, therefore, takes on many
forms, but fierce competition results. Reproduction on the farm is an
exercise requiring constant attention to environmental forces. For
instance, the soil has to be protected against the burning sun and against
torrential rainstorms that may wash away its organic matter.
Otherwise, the productive periods falling between droughts and floods
will yield little. All over Africa peasants have developed farming
systems that take these weather factors into consideration, as far as is
humanly possible.

The second factor of basic importance in African agriculture are soils.
Laterite soils predominate and have often forced the producers into
systems of shifting cultivation. Restoration of fertility has only been
possible by leaving the land fallow. This has guaranteed survival in
many parts of Africa, but at a high cost. Above all, it has prevented the
growth of settled communities, an advantage associated with agriculture in most other parts of the world. Successful peasant agriculture in
Africa has often been pursued on lands where soils are either alluvial or
volcanic. The former are found in river valleys and along lakes, while
the latter can be found on mountain slopes, notably in central and
eastern Africa. Particularly in altitudes where the soil is protected from
great heat, it may be fertile and rich in humus.

SOIL

How little outsiders know of the African soil conditions was no better
illustrated than in the case of the Groundnut Scheme, referred to in
Chapter 2. It is no exaggeration to say that peasants often still
intuitively achieve better soil management than many of the
government-planned agricultural development schemes. Yet these
indigenous management systems are inefficient; they cannot sustain an
increasing population. They need to be developed and improved. With
better soil management systems it is estimated that another 550 million
hectares of uncultivated but potentially arable land in Africa can be
made available for agricultural production.[8]

Peasants in Africa also have to cope with a wide range of enemies that
limit their achievements. These include tryponosomiasis,[9] transmitted
through the actual bite of an infected tsetse fly which, in sucking the

blood, introduces the parasite into the blood. Locusts are enduring enemies of agriculture in large parts of eastern Africa, although in recent years they have been controlled through the International Red Locust Control Service. The desert locust in West Africa is a greater problem and still causes severe damage in that part of the continent. Weaverbirds pose yet another danger to African agriculture. Wild pigs and other vermin may also cause considerable damage to crops and their presence requires constant vigil. Finally, weeds are difficult to control and when left in the ground they consume nutrients and water that would otherwise go to domestic crops.

African agriculture is still overwhelmingly dependent on the natural resource endowment, on human labour and on relatively simple hand tools. The task of production, and of reproduction, on the peasant farm is both time-consuming and complicated. To ignore this fact is to disregard some of the most important determinants of the existence rationality of the peasant. In the case of most of them, willingness and capacity to respond to outside initiatives are determined by how far reproductive needs monopolize peasant thinking.

Where peasant agriculture has been modernized or in other respects developed, ecological factors have played a major part. Policy-makers have simply been able to take advantage of favourable circumstances: good soils, reasonably predictable weather conditions or concentration of human settlements sufficient to scare away vermin. Here peasants have been able to accommodate innovations, even the use of modern production techniques, as the case of Kilimanjaro in Tanzania suggested. Outside of these ecologically favourable areas, however, government achievements have been much more modest. In the light of what we have said about African agriculture above, it is not at all surprising. Not only do governments have to overcome an intrinsic suspicion of state intervention but, even if that structural hurdle is overcome, the management task itself is so enormous that it would be unfair to expect major breakthroughs. For instance, the great heterogeneity of the physical environment complicates the task of evolving new and more productive technologies. The variation in the production of food crops within single countries makes the development of better crops expensive and a socially sensitive matter. The peasants have remained absorbed in their own reproductive cycles and thus been able to support increased public demands on them only to a limited extent. There have been different conceptions of priorities between peasants and the authorities. One case in point is crop specialization, a favourite policy goal of African governments concerned with raising agricultural productivity. Here peasant rationality has demanded crop diversification and in most cases this has prevailed in spite of official pressure in the opposite direction.

The problems of agricultural development in Africa have been intensified by rapid population growth and accelerated development goals after independence. African countries have found it increasingly difficult to keep pace with their own ambitions. This is indicated by the fact that while the increase in food production in African countries between 1961 and 1970 was 2·6 per cent per annum, the figure declined to 1·5 per cent for the period 1970 to 1976.[10] To be sure, the severe drought in 1973/74 is partly responsible for this decline. The most important factor, however, is the resilience of the peasant mode. Modern production methods, whether introduced in the name of capitalism or socialism, have failed to make an impact on agricultural productivity. Kenya is usually quoted as virtually the only exception to this trend.

Agricultural modernization in Kenya

The experience of Kenya's peasant agriculture immediately before and after independence is such that it is used to illustrate the potentials of smallholder production in Africa. Furthermore, it is cited as an example of how far ordinary peasants are willing to respond to incentives provided through the market or by government institutions. The questions which we need to ask ourselves in the context of this book are: 'How far is the Kenyan achievement unique?'; 'To what extent are the conditions of peasant agriculture in that country exceptional?'

It was noted earlier that colonization in Kenya meant the establishment of large-scale agriculture practised by immigrant European settler farmers. Large parts of the most fertile areas in the Kenya highlands were alienated to these Europeans. Their demands also implied a colonial policy that virtually precluded all cash-crop farming in those areas from which labourers for the settler farms were recruited. The adverse effects of the settler presence are usually emphasized in the literature on Kenya and there is no reason to deny those. Africans were denied opportunities to develop and they were humiliated. The accumulated effect of this social alienation, however, was to spark off an intensified development effort once the Mau Mau uprising and the subsequent changes in colonial policy allowed them the opportunity to develop their own farm land. Furthermore, the settler presence had exposed Africans to modern farming and the European farmers had proved that much could be done on the land. It is wrong to overlook the educational effects of working on the settler farms. Large numbers of Africans learnt new ways of harnessing natural resources in the course of being employed on these farms. The European settlers started from scratch, often with a number of African farm-workers. They were not using sophisticated machines to achieve their ends. They did it the hard way. Having been through this kind of learning process, many Africans had internalized the techniques as much as their European boss had. They could never have picked up these techniques and become as effective in their agricultural practices had this been done in the context of a farmers' training centre.

Another important effect of the settler agriculture on the African farm labourers was to make them look at agriculture as a job, not a way of life. In other words, by being uprooted from their traditional peasant environments and forced to till the land on capitalist premises, many African labourers returned to farming on their own land with a very different approach from that of the ordinary peasant. Many of these former farm labourers have been in the forefront of developing Kenya's peasant agriculture. Among the ordinary peasants, however, the colonial administration in Kenya faced the same resistance as in Tanzania. Both Moris[11] and Alila[12] have shown how efforts by colonial agricultural officers to encourage African peasants to adopt better crop varieties and attempts to introduce destocking met with resistance or indifference. The same structural dilemma was at play in Kenya where peasants insisted that state intervention complicated the task of managing their farms. Even when the colonial officials used demonstration plots they failed to achieve their objectives. There is evidence to suggest that for most African peasants, learning from work on the European settler farms was more effective. The settlers were able to demonstrate with their own resources that it was possible to achieve agricultural advancement. To the peasant this was a far more persuasive factor than the advice and the education offered by the extension service. Peasants are always inclined to learn from the most successful practitioners of their occupation. The European settler farmers, while having denied their African workers a lot, did expose them to a range of new values and techniques. When eventually the Africans were given a chance on their own, many proved that they could, on their small farms, do as well or even better than the Europeans had on their large-scale farms.

There are other reasons, which again are rather peculiar to the Kenyan situation, which explain the relative success of the modernization of peasant agriculture to date. Land registration and land consolidation, to facilitate the commercialization of peasant agriculture, were carried out in the central highlands during the political emergency imposed in the wake of the Mau Mau uprising. Those who remained loyal to the British were able to take advantage of this policy measure to increase their holding as well as security of tenure. The consolidation policy had the effect of removing some people from the land altogether. This was mainly possible because these people were fighting in the forests. When the same policies were applied later on to other parts of Kenya where such emergency conditions did not exist, land consolidation efforts were dropped and land registration was achieved only through laborious negotiations with clan elders whose approval had to be obtained. Today, the vast majority of land occupied by peasant producers in Kenya has been registered.

Kenyan peasants have been quite ready to adopt new crops and diversify their farming. Many have adopted tea cultivation, often in combination with dairy farming. The reasons for more intensified land usage are many. One obvious factor is pressure on land. In order to sustain the peasant population it has become necessary to adopt a more intensive agriculture. As a result, peasant farmers have had to turn to outside agencies for help. New inputs have become necessary and output has grown. To that extent peasants have given up much of their autonomy. They are more closely incorporated into the capitalist economy than peasants elsewhere in Africa. This relatively high degree of incorporation, however, is mainly sustained by a good infrastructure and a well-functioning service sector. The economic and physical infrastructural investments were originally made in response to settler demands, but after independence there has been a deliberate effort to provide these in response to smallholder needs. Particularly important have been the 'tea-roads', built in conjunction with the spread of tea cultivation among smallholder peasants in central and western Kenya. The Kenya Tea Development Authority is one of many public institutions in Kenya which has been effective in sustaining peasant interest in good cash-crop farming. The work of KTDA and Kenya Co-operative Creameries, to mention two of the most important institutions catering for Kenya's peasant farmers, shows how important the reliable services of outside agencies are to these farmers.[13]

This experience stands in sharp contrast with the developments in Uganda, once a country with a highly successful commercial peasant agriculture. By removing some of the institutions serving the peasants and severely hampering the work of others, the Amin regime effectively crippled the country's cash-crop farming. Cotton, which at one time was the most important export crop, has been virtually wiped out since 1973. Coffee production still continues, mainly because it is a perennial crop. Amin, more by default than by design, achieved the ruin of Uganda's capitalist economy. Peasants have withdrawn from their previously active role in the economy. By virtue of their ability to sustain a livelihood independent of the state they managed to escape the worst effects of the whims of Amin. His regime proved that previous achievements of capitalism can easily be reversed and pre-capitalist structures invited to replace modern economic institutions. Between 1972 and 1975 virtually everybody who had been responsible in some way or other for sustaining modern capitalist institutions was forced to leave the country or was killed. The door was opened for petty-capitalist elements with little or no experience of managing large, modern organizations.

Pre-capitalist forces are by no means dead in Kenya. Despite the extensive integration of peasants into the market economy, these forces have survived. In the outlying pastoral areas, people have continued to exercise their exit option. To date, the Kenya Government, despite efforts, has failed to develop policies that make it possible for the pastoralists to transcend the boundaries of their pre-capitalist mode of production.[14] In the agricultural areas, peasants have invariably moved into the capitalist economy carrying their pre-capitalist baggage along with them.

It would be wrong to assume that capitalist and peasant values are always irreconcilable. Sometimes they are complementary. Such seems to be the case, at least with reference to some core values, in a situation like that of Kenya, where capitalism is capable of modernizing peasant agriculture. What is derived from capitalism and what from the peasant mode is difficult to identify. Colin Leys has stressed exactly this point:

> The new bourgeoisie also accelerates (by precept and example) the diffusion of commercial and acquisitive values throughout peasant society from which it is derived (and to which it remains linked by kinship and landownership); it is the normal function of the elite to fulfil this role for the peasantry. In the case of Kenya, I am inclined to think that the sight and sound of this process in full operation may lead some observers to mistake it for the creation of a capitalist economy and society, whereas it is really contributing to the development of a peasant one. The values of acquisitiveness, individualism, thrift, etc., are as intrinsic to one as it is to the other.[15]

This complementarity of capitalism to the peasant mode should make us extra careful before drawing conclusions about cause and effect in African development situations. Even where capitalism appears to triumph, peasant values and structures thrive. For instance, peasants rarely give up such basic characteristics as their subsistence orientation. That became apparent when African squatters were settled on former settler farms as part of a co-operative resettlement effort. Although government officials expected commercial production on these farms to continue, the inclination of the African peasants was to use the land to support their subsistence needs. One survey shows that in one settlement, nine out of ten farm plots accommodated people outside the settler's nuclear family. Most of these extended family members had no cash wage and supported themselves by working for the settler in return for the right to farm small plots for their own crops.[16] The pre-capitalist barriers to capitalist expansion manifested themselves here in the same way as they prevented the growth of socialist production on the former capitalist farms in Ismani, Tanzania (cf. Chapter 4).

Peasants are more inclined to improve what they have than to replace existing factors of production with new ones. They are also likely to be more interested in raising their production if they have something worthwhile to spend their money on. These peasant orientations have been effectively sustained by the capitalist economy in Kenya. The efficiency of wholesale and retail distribution in the rural areas has exposed the peasants to a great variety of goods in demand by them. These include better clothing material, bicycles and radios, corrugated iron for roofing, to mention only a few of the more popular items. The official policy has clearly been to allow peasants to modernize their economic outlook as much as possible by participating in the capitalist economy.

President Kenyatta and other leaders have set an example in this direction and Kenyatta even went as far as blaming those leaders who have not proved their ability to take advantage of the capitalist economy. There have been no brakes applied on acquisitiveness from the top. Having witnessed it from their *ujamaa* premises, it is no surprise that Tanzanians have referred to Kenya as a 'man-eats-man' society.[17] This kind of personal involvement by leaders of the state in efforts to achieve an economic modernization along capitalist lines is by no means unique. It has characterized virtually all societies in transition from a pre-capitalist to a capitalist mode of production. Sombart has the following quotation about Gustavus Vassa, who in the years of the Reformation tried to set Sweden on the path towards capitalism:

> He was the chief undertaker of his nation. Not only did he know how to discover and utilize for the crown the mineral wealth of Sweden, but by commercial treaties and protective duties, and last but not least, by engaging himself in foreign trade on a large scale, he acted as an example to his merchants. Everything was due to his initiative.[18]

The point here is that in all societies in which capitalism is being internalized, ruling kings and presidents, including their state officials, have been in the forefront in keeping alive the spirit of capitalist undertaking. They have often been the earliest representatives of the modern economic outlook, forcing other people to follow in their footsteps.

While Kenya appears much more nakedly capitalist than Tanzania, because capitalism is relatively more dominant, Kenya has an active economy of affection. In fact the latter has been used to obtain goods and services which are difficult to get by using the official channels of the capitalist economy. The principles of familial and village organization have been applied to trade and politics. Frank Holmquist,[19] Mbithi and Rasmusson[20] are among the many who have studied the application of these principles to rural development. Groups and associations, based on primordial loyalties, are set up to exercise pressures on the policy-making structures. The competitive nature of the Kenyan society tends to reinforce such loyalties. Resort to the economy of affection often becomes the safest way of obtaining desired goods and services.

The tribal organizations have also flowed over into the modern economy where they have contributed to raising local capital for investment. Particularly important has been the Gikuyu, Embu and Meru Association (GEMA), embracing members of the three tribes occupying the central highlands. GEMA has its own holding company which, in addition to sponsoring local capitalists in need of funds, also more recently has engaged in buying up the property of multi-national corporations.[21]

The most important effect of the economy of affection, however, is not at the political but at the social level. It performs an important welfare function in that, within the social networks, based on the principles of that economy, a significant, unofficial redistribution of wealth takes place. Payments to poor relatives, financial support for the education of youngsters, and provision of employment are some of the more common means by which the resources are circulated within the economy of affection. From the viewpoint of the individual the prevalence of this kind of unofficial economy protects him from the most negative effects of the capitalist economy. It helps him keep afloat and obtain resources which he otherwise would not get. But it is an economy that increases the cost to capitalism and limits its ability to transform relations of production. Furthermore, it is an economy that dampens the revolutionary potential of the peasants and the workers. Because they have alternative means to satisfy their needs, their willingness to rise against the capitalist system, even if they remain poor, is definitely lowered.

The interests of the peasant mode and those of capitalism, however, are only complementary up to a certain point. Beyond that, antagonism is inevitable. In order to satisfy its own needs, capitalism must sweep away the remnants of pre-capitalist formations; yet, in doing so, it sets off social reactions that may lead to its own downfall. The revolutionary potential of the proletariat in Kenya will depend on how far the prevailing pre-capitalist forces are broken down.

With a growing population and thus difficulties in securing a livelihood on the land in Kenya, the social forces that hold back the development of a class society are likely to prevail, at least in the short run. Communal action will continue to encapsule the process of class formation, thereby weakening the social forces set in motion by capitalism. The economy will remain embedded in pre-capitalist social formations to such an extent that the alienating effects of capitalism are mitigated. To expect that the Kenyan leaders would wish to solve these conflicts through a rational state intervention along social democratic lines, as for instance was suggested by the ILO Mission to Kenya in 1972, reveals a lack of understanding of how the African economies operate.[22] However, the reason for government reluctance to adopt the ILO proposals is not, as Colin Leys implies, merely because their class interests forbid.[23] Although Kenyan leaders may be bourgeois in many of their orientations they still retain personal links with the poorer sections of the population through the economy of affection. Many have a direct welfare concern that Western observers lack. Welfare to most of the latter is reduced to a policy equation and a problem of the state. Also the social links that originate in the economy of affection provide alternative political solutions which to the African leaders imply greater gains than those suggested by observers who look at Kenya through the lenses of modern capitalism alone.

Capitalism has helped to modernize the peasant mode of production to such an extent that in Kenya pre-capitalist and capitalist forces are closely intertwined. Capitalism has offered new opportunities for large numbers of small peasants, and those who have become victims of capitalist penetration have usually been rescued by pre-capitalist forces. This process has been most apparent in the central highlands of Kenya, where capitalism has had its strongest impact. After independence, it was extended to other parts of the country. For instance, new hybrid maize varieties have been adopted in western Kenya at a rate, which according to one observer is 'somewhat more rapid than hybrid corn was adopted by American farmers thirty years earlier.[24] This has not only improved the subsistence base of many small farms. This innovation, brought about by capitalist-funded research efforts, has also increased farm income and raised the commercial value of land.

It is true, however, that so far agricultural modernization brought about with the support of capitalism has been confined to the 'high potential' areas of Kenya. Population in lower altitude areas, for instance near Lake Victoria, have not benefited to the same extent from the process. Nor have people in the semi-arid areas of eastern Kenya – Embu, Machakos and Kitui Districts. The reason for this is mainly that agricultural research has failed to develop profitable and feasible innovations adapted to the ecology of these areas. This does not mean that research efforts in this direction have been lacking. They have developed the drought-resistant Katumani maize, which has appreciable yield advantages over local varieties of the same crop. No feasible farming system, however, has yet been developed for these semi-arid areas and the prospects of an effective agriculture in these places appear slim in the absence of major innovations. While the Katumani variety offers advantages under normal weather conditions, the spread of it may have the effect of accentuating famine problems, because it contributes to the substitution of maize for sorghum and millet, drought-resistant cereals which are better suited to the marginal moisture conditions prevailing under conditions of below-normal rainfall.[25] The greater vulnerability of millet and sorghum to bird damage has reinforced peasant willingness to adopt the Katumani maize variety.

The development of more productive farming systems for the semi-arid parts of Kenya – and the rest of Africa, for that matter – remains unsolved. It requires attention to a number of difficult issues: moisture-

and soil-conserving practices, suitable equipment, and improved tillage. This is likely to be a time-consuming and costly exercise, if for no other reason than that local conditions, even within semi-arid zones, may vary significantly enough to render an innovation in one area unsuitable in another without major modifications.

The limits of capitalism

This raises the question of how far capitalism can serve as a modernizing force in Africa. Conditions in Kenya are rather unusual. Other African countries have not experienced the same influences of settler agriculture. Climatic and soil conditions are not as favourable. Therefore it is wrong to assume that because innovations have been successful in Kenya they can be easily replicated elsewhere in Africa. Kenyan peasants are responsive to market and other outside influences to an extent which is not true of peasants elsewhere. This is no doubt the result of capitalist penetration, not merely incorporation into the market economy. Kenyan peasants have taken one step out of a purely resource-based agriculture. They have proved that modernization of peasant agriculture is possible. In that respect the Kenyan experience is important, but equally significant is the fact that the Kenyan peasants are ahead of other African peasants as far as modernization of their farming is concerned for two reasons unique to Kenya: favourable climatic and ecological circumstances, and unusually strong capitalist penetration.

Thus it is wrong to conceive of Kenya as necessarily presenting a pattern of development that will be followed elsewhere on the continent.[26] The main reason is that in most of Africa capitalism has had only a marginal impact. It has not laid a sufficiently strong base for its own reproduction. Virtually, all over the continent, peasant farmers producing export crops continue to grow most of the food they consume. A large part of the items that they buy are also necessities of life: meat, fish, bread, clothes, etc. In this situation it is wrong to speak of capitalist domination. It is more correct to talk of capitalism having entered into a 'marriage of convenience' with pre-capitalism. That way it has secured a niche in the African economies, but it is far from being dominant. Pre-capitalist relations have continued to retard productivity growth, particularly in the production of the means of subsistence. In the periphery of the peasant world economy there are structural constraints that limit the modernizing influence of capitalism to such an extent that the agents of capitalism are in fact held hostages. They have invested money, but no returns are in sight.

Even in those instances when it has 'sharpened its claws' and initiated drives for productivity increases in peasant agriculture, it has encountered constraints. Any successful capitalist penetration presupposes a social mobilization that increases its accessibility to producers and wage earners. In most such instances, pre-capitalist forces have reasserted themselves, thereby again reducing the effectiveness of capitalist action. For instance, in Senegal where production of groundnuts has been pushed at the expense of the prevailing subsistence crop – paddy – and thus the import of rice has become necessary, peasant reaction has been to avoid the most difficult demands of government policies either by withdrawing into subsistence production or by intensifying the search for alternative solutions through the economy of affection.[27] The same has been true of cocoa farmers in Western Nigeria. Faced in this case with the additional problem of low prices, peasant farmers have sold to smugglers or even confronted the authorities directly by rebelling.[28] Because the dependence on the market tends to be more pronounced in the coastal belt of West Africa, peasant control over economic assets and opportunities is more limited. This does not mean, however, that peasants have been passive victims. They have often acquired alternative means to control the market or to get access to it. This has been done through a variety of strategies including the experimentation with new crops or occupations (in addition to farming) and the use of political channels provided by the social networks that form part of the pre-capitalist social formation. Diversification of assets as well as affiliations has been an essential part of peasant strategies aimed at coping with the effects of incorporation into the market economy. This way they have been able to dilute original policy objectives and maintain their own income and status. They have also supported traditional kinship and community organizations. Sara Berry has summarized the predicament of peasants and workers in West Africa in the following words:

> Class interests exist and are perceived, but individuals' particular class interests vary over time, and people seek to advance them through a variety of organizational mechanisms, some of which may cut across or dilute the emergence of class solidarity, both ideologically and organizationally. Thus, collective protest against economic exploitation or discrimination is often organized through community structures. Neither a specific pattern of class consciousness nor a single set of class-based institutions have emerged as *the* major determinants of either the perception of collective interests or the organization of collective action in West Africa. Class antagonism and conflict have certainly occurred and will continue to do so, but the overthrow of state capitalism led by the proletariat, the peasantry or a West African *smychka* seems at present a remote possibility.[29]

Her conclusion is very similar to the observation by Peel, derived from a study of social conflict in a western Nigerian town, where communal action often took precedence over class action.[30] The latter is only likely to be an effective weapon and be preferred by the workers or the peasants in a situation where the communal systems of action have been exhausted or eliminated. In an economy where the majority of the producers are independent peasants, albeit small, or petty-bourgeois, the economic structures do not easily produce class action. They reinforce social attitudes that go contrary to the demands of the modern economy.

The limits of capitalism as a modernizing agent have also been dramatically manifested in Zaire, where peasant agriculture has declined as a result of arbitrary government action. The main reason for this seems to be the weak economic and political infrastructure of that country. Not only are there big difficulties in moving physically from one place to another in Zaire. The economic system is highly fragmented and the ruling classes do not have effective control over the means of production. In spite of nationalization of the mining industry and the promotion of more effective participation by local petty-bourgeois traders in wholesale and retail business, the control exercised by the ruling classes over the economy is very limited.

The only way in which the Zairean regimes have been able to sustain themselves in power has been by investing heavily in building up bonds of solidarity based on personal loyalty to the President. It has been necessary to use the economy to support politics. Money and material resources have been the principal means by which these bonds have been sustained. Mobutu's chief claim to leadership has been his ability to get money for distribution to his followers. In recent years when copper prices have been down, a lot of money has been taken out of state funds. Control of the state apparatus has been vital for the survival of the Mobutu regime. As David Gould notes in his study of corruption in Zaire:

> General Mobutu's continuous giving top administrators access to corruption is thus vital to his success and chances of survival. Theft on a massive scale then must take place at all levels of the political/administrative hierarchy .... theft from the State, from each other and from the public. The President said as much in an important public meeting on May 1, 1976: *ibana mayele* (in Lingala: steal cleverly).[31]

Mobutu's problems are not unique. Everywhere in Africa economic resources are used to boost political power in a way that does not take the national economy forward. That orientation, as noted earlier (Chapter 1), is structurally induced and a sign of lack of real power. The petty-bourgeois excesses in Zaire are induced by the need to buy political support in a situation where state power is still fragile. The great diversity and the poor infrastructure of that country are, no doubt, factors that reinforce this phenomenon. Political maintenance in Africa is a costly affair, as the agencies of international capital have experienced in their dealings with the Mobutu regime in Zaire. Without an effective power structure that can secure a reasonable return on capital, the latter cannot thrive. To argue as if capitalism prevails in Zaire is far off the point. In fact, it can convincingly be argued that socialist regimes, provided their leadership is morally honest, provide a better environment for capital investment in Africa than the weaker regimes with a capitalist orientation. The socialist morality, if it can be maintained, is more supportive of capitalist aspirations in Africa than the petty-bourgeois orientation that prevails where state power is weak. Thus an effective socialist regime (there are still few of them in Africa) has more in common with capitalism than the petty-bourgeois regimes which pretend to be capitalist but which are obliged to use capital only to maintain themselves. The example of Zaire certainly suggests that capital is not safe even if the regime professes its support of a capitalist development strategy.

The ineffectiveness of the Zairean state is also manifest at the local level, where petty-bourgeois officials are allowed to help themselves to booty from the peasant population. Michael Schatzberg has witnessed how tax collection is carried out in a local community in the Kwilu Province:

> When tax collectors, police, and other local officials appear, they [the villagers] leave for either the deep forest or the islands in the river. They know the purposes of these visits and are aware that no benefit will be forthcoming from them. They know, too, of the way the local court system operates. As one respondent put it, 'If you are before the prosecutor and you have a bit of money, it suffices to spend some of it and your business will be forgotten.'[32]

It would of course be wrong to deduce from this and other similar examples that capitalism is the dominant mode of production. It cannot be as its reproduction is not achieved through such means. Nor can these raids be taken as evidence of state power. Such naked applications of power, on the contrary, often have a boomerang effect. Certainly, as long as the peasants can use their exit option, or can evade state action by using alternative channels, there is little room for 'development administration'. The pre-capitalist forces do not allow themselves to be captured for 'rational' bourgeois demands. State action is effectively diluted and the opportunities for a development approach based on local resources seriously hampered. Capitalism is unable, outside of the plantation sector, to penetrate the relations of production on the land. Zaire is a good example of where the agents of capitalism are held hostage. To argue as if capitalism dominates reveals a total lack of understanding of the economic realities of that country.

Like Tanzania, other African countries have tried to achieve modernization of their agriculture by resettling peasants on new land. As Gavin Williams notes, all these settlement schemes have assumed that production could be transformed by removing peasants from their 'traditional, conservative environment' to places where they would be more amenable to the advice of expert supervisors.[33] By concentrating farmers in villages, they would be better organized for governments to supply them the investments and technical and social services necessary for rural modernization. However, virtually all studies of settlement schemes demonstrate their limitations as instruments of modernization.[34] Initial investments and continuing overhead costs have been high. Settlers have often come to regard themselves as labourers working on government farms for low pay. Production has rarely been high enough to pay off the costs of running these schemes. In short, the planned targets of these settlements have been seriously diluted as settler needs have taken precedence over the demands of the official 'social engineers'. The following quotation of what happened in a co-operative settlement scheme in Benin (Dahomey) is by no means untypical:

> The proposals suggesting the abolition of mixed cropping (*cultures associées*) were resisted until a formula was found which provided for special plots where mixed cropping could be continued alongside plots where improved crop rotation techniques were being used. More serious was another difficulty raised by farmers' critical assessment of the value of some crops recommended to them. This refers in particular to cotton, which was recommended as a quick return cash crop and above all as a much needed foreign exchange earner. Co-operative members found that the crop was too demanding in labour and inputs (expensive fertilizers and pesticides, great quantities of scarce water) for a rather insignificant profit. Here is an illustration of clashes between national (macro-economic) targets and individual (micro-economic) objectives. Needless to say, the producers have the last word. Good as this may be, such a situation can disturb the overall economics of the co-operative unit, for example, by overemphasizing crops for internal consumption to the detriment of commodities which could be sold in national and international markets and compensate for the eventual loss due to low productivity of the oil-palm plantations.[35]

In some instances, governments have selected urban unemployed people to become members of new rural settlements. These have been overwhelmingly young, and often educated individuals. This was the case with many of the farm settlements in western Nigeria, where the hope was that young and educated settlers would quickly turn into progressive farmers. Although armed with modern techniques and machinery, productivity on the settlements remained low. Instead of becoming monuments to the government's modernizing capability, the farm settlements became, as Frances Hill concludes,[36] costly examples of its ineptitude. Five years after the inception of the programme, there were only twenty settlements with as few as 1200 settlers. To produce this result, the Western Region Government had spent 40 per cent of its whole agricultural budget and 7·5 per cent of its total capital programme.[37] By that time, the settlers had come to see themselves more as government employees than as independent farmers. Government officials were closely controlling the daily activities of the settlements. The settlers had become highly dependent on government, but in this case, it was still worthwhile. Despite their dependence, they were a privileged minority in the public sector. They received a more lucrative package of wages and benefits than did the field staff in the Ministry of Agriculture. The farm settlements continued for a few more years, in Hill's view, primarily because the government did not know how to terminate them without accepting some role in their failure.[38] It required the civil war to provide a legitimate excuse for withdrawing support for these schemes.

There are a few examples of successful rural capitalism. The most notable are the cocoa farmers in Ghana, who on land alienated by the local chiefs were able to establish farms that were run successfully on essentially capitalist lines.[39] These are exceptional, however, and developed under conditions which do not easily apply to other places. The general conclusion to be drawn from capitalist involvement in African agriculture is that it has failed to replace pre-capitalist relations of production. In fact, capitalism has often reinforced them and thereby created barriers to its own expansion. It has failed to transform agriculture to meet modern development demands. In a situation where labour rather than land is the critical variable it has been difficult for capitalism to penetrate peasant production. It is no coincidence that capitalism has been most successful in those parts of Africa where land is becoming increasingly scarce. Even there, however, capitalism faces barriers to its own expansion as the economy of affection continues to operate as an alternative economy.

Thus one can say that capitalism has hardly achieved its expanded reproduction on the basis of its own force. Demographic circumstances have often facilitated the process. So have ecological factors in those areas where they have aggravated reproduction within the confines of the peasant mode. Floods and droughts have worked in the interest of capitalism in that these natural calamities have made local peasant know-how inoperative. The social classes that serve as carriers of the capitalist faith have no reason to take much credit for capitalist penetration in Africa. Certainly, in the rural areas, such penetration is as much a product of circumstances as it is of purposive class action.

In the light of this experience, it is no surprise that an increasing number of governments in Africa have turned away from capitalism and instead chosen socialist policy measures to achieve their ends. They have abandoned capitalism not so much because of its exploitative nature, but because of a growing awareness that it is insufficient for their development ambitions.

The reasons for socialism

Most African governments have adopted a socialist development approach quite unprepared. There has been no revolutionary struggle, or other such emergency condition, generating the premises on which socialism has been successfully built in other parts of the world. In Africa socialism has been quite arbitrarily introduced by petty-bourgeois rulers to cope with the intrinsic instability of modernization under capitalism. The latter sets in motion a competition that tends to divide members of the petty-bourgeoisie along ethnic or tribal lines. Socialism has often been introduced to pre-empt the negative consequences of this process. It offers the rulers a greater opportunity to control the market forces and gives them a chance to influence the process in a more direct fashion. By concentrating power, it facilitates the creation of a unified superstructure, the logical measure to deal with the fragmented nature of African economies. The socialist ideology is the natural base for justifying this move. It fills the gap between the existing conditions and the future society they look forward to. Socialism inserts between the two a real and active movement. It establishes a seat of authority which is expected to give unquestioned guidance to any doubter within society.

The capitalist market offers the policy-makers a range of subtle tools that are necessary for the modernization of the productive forces. With the introduction of socialism, these have often been sacrificed in favour of tools that deal more effectively with the problems generated at the superstructural level. The dilemma consequently facing African socialists is that since capitalism failed really to revolutionize the means of production, their transition to socialism is not supported by dynamic forces generated under capitalism, for example, an articulate class consciousness, adherence to the principles of modern organization, technical know-how and a general sense of control of the forces of nature. The bourgeois mentality has simply failed to have an impact in most parts of Africa. This means that the principal function of socialism will be to achieve exactly those things that capitalism has failed to attain. The conditions under which socialism has to be built in Africa, therefore, are bound to be very different from what has been experienced elsewhere. The uncritical application of the Marxist paradigm is of little help in coping with Africa's problems of underdevelopment. The first African leader to learn this was Nkrumah who, after having failed to obtain the support of Ghana's independent smallholder producers, went out of his way to create a new group of producers who would be more dependent upon the government. In 1960, Nkrumah decided that state farms should become the first priority in agriculture. Although alternative approaches, for example, co-operative farms, were conceivable, the regime opted for state farms on the grounds that it would help to establish a class system along Marxist lines. That approach would generate a public sector agricultural proletariat and thereby widen the political base of the regime.[40]

Ghanaian planners asserted that these socialist means of production would modernize agriculture and increase agricultural production. The link between mechanization and increased production was contended on the basis of a general faith in socialism as a tool of modernization. Of course, neither the proposition itself, nor its applicability to specific conditions had been tested. The Ghanaian Government moved headlong into state farm investments without any desire to invest the time necessary to plan them. Over a period of five years, $30 million were spent on state farms with only meagre results in return. Neither food production nor the production of export crops increased. Instead, the country had to import food to feed its own population.

The experience of state farms in Ghana revealed the same kind of shortcomings experienced in settlements schemes set up on capitalist premises. The workers on the state farms had little experience in agriculture and were unable to use properly and maintain the complex machinery used. They took little interest in the farm operations. For instance, the workers' committees dealt almost exclusively with the rights of the workers rather than with the organization of production. Managers were in many cases both dedicated and capable but they had little leverage over the workers who were paid a flat rate for their labour, leaving them with little incentive to work productively.

Most African governments have been careful not to place all their eggs in the state farm basket. Yet where socialist governments have come to power, state farms have at least been attempted. We noted Tanzania's wish to start state farms in the wake of failing to mobilize its independent smallholders to meet socialist development demands. The revolutionary regime in Ethiopia has also established such farms to supplement the production of the peasants, who immediately after the downfall of the imperial regime were organized into peasants' associations with the ultimate aim of using these as the basis for the development of collectively owned means of production.[41] It is too early to comment on the outcome of the socialist policies of the Ethiopian regime. The political turmoil which has characterized that country since 1975 contains too many unknown variables to allow for any assessment at this stage of how its socialist agriculture has fared.

Liberation struggle and the peasants

Nowhere else in Africa has the irrelevance of the state to the peasant

mode of production been better manifested than in the former
Portuguese colonies where factions of the small, indigenous petty-
bourgeoisie revolted against the colonial authority and began waging a
liberation struggle. While there is no reason to degrade the importance
of their organizational efforts, one of the secrets of their success, which
has not been mentioned in the literature on these liberation struggles
was the relative ease with which alternative means for peasant repro
duction could be established in these colonies where the majority of the
rural producers had been little affected by capitalism. Rudebeck, for
instance, in his study of Guinea-Bissau, does not really identify the
structural factors in such an economy that give support to efforts to
replace the colonial state with alternative modes of organizing life and
work.[42] Bienen notes that in Guinea-Bissau, unlike Angola, there were
no plantations and agricultural companies, and no expropriation of
land, which remained basically the co-operative property of the
village.[43] In this situation, Cabral himself argued that exploitation
could not be direct, only indirect. The main task was not to reverse
prevailing relations of production, but to mobilize people around
detailed and concrete demands. As he directed his comrades in Guinea-
Bissau in the days of the struggle:

> Always bear in mind that the people are not fighting for ideas, for
> the things in anyone's head. They are fighting to win material
> benefits, to live better, and in peace, to see their lives go forward
> to guarantee the future of their children.[44]

This means that the peasants will not be behind in giving support for
a struggle aimed at liberating them from the oppression of the colonial
state. For them the sacrifice is minimal and since the peasant mode does
not presuppose the existence of social classes, a liberation movement
that promises the abolition of such classes, once it has removed fear
among people, has no difficulty in gaining the support of the peasants.
It was the strength of Amilcar Cabral to be able to interpret the pre
capitalist foundations of the liberation struggle in his country. The
peasants were effectively liberated by the Partido Africano da Indepen
dencia da Guiné e Cabo Verde (PAIGC), thanks to its application of
the right tools.

It is clear, however, that it has been a major task to keep the peasant
supporting the demands of the new PAIGC government after inde
pendence. The peasants were struggling for their cause, which prior to
independence was similar to that of the liberation movement. After
1975, the government was forced to place demands on the peasantry in
the same way as any other modern government. It has been necessary to
encroach on peasant autonomy in order to obtain enough resources to
support the development demands. The new socialist government has
been compelled to perform the painful task of modernizing agriculture
and thereby finding itself in the position of reviving the structural

ontradiction inherent in the peasant mode itself, between peasants and hose controlling the state. Because Guinea-Bissau is a small country nd it has been able to attract foreign aid to supplement its own esources, this contradiction has not been too apparent. Yet it is there nd has to be tackled, particularly if Guinea-Bissau is going to realize a reater national self-reliance. Given the problems of transforming the easant mode of production, the co-operation between the regime in Juinea-Bissau and the agencies of international capital is quite nderstandable. As Aaby notes:

> The alternative to this strategy could easily be that the state would have to obtain more loans or increase the appropriation of the surplus product from the peasantry just to survive. The last course would probably create an antagonism between the peasantry and the state apparatus and therefore further impede the necessary structural transformation.[45]

The point is, of course, that an enhanced contradiction between the easantry and those who control the state, contrary to what Aaby sug-ests, is a precondition for development in Africa, capitalist or socialist. he unproductive relations between the petty-bourgeoisie and the easantry within the economy of affection, must give way to the ocial dynamics of contradictions generated by the modern modes of roduction, both capitalist and socialist. Even countries with a revolu-onary ambition, like Mozambique, cannot escape this dilemma, articularly as long as the national economy suffers from poor manage-ient as a result of shortage of manpower and indiscipline among orkers.[46] The majority of the producers are still small peasants with ttle stake in the market economy. Whether they produce individually r collectively, they are difficult to get at. While they were quick to ipport Frelimo in its efforts to liberate Mozambique from colonial ile, they are like all peasants, reluctant to subordinate themselves to emands that increase their dependence on other social classes, what-ver their development orientation.

It would be wrong to assume that those who operate from a position f strength in post-independence Mozambique are the Frelimo cadres. he peasants are still independent enough as producers to ignore the emands placed on them by the new regime. The latter tries to minimize ie friction by insisting that 'the struggle still continues' (al lutta ntinua), hoping that the peasants and the workers will fail to sense the ontradictions between the country's socialist and pre-socialist econ-mic structures. To overcome some of these limitations, the new regime as also tried to take advantage of situations where peasants have been pset by the forces of nature. One case in point is the resettlement of ousands of peasants in communal villages as a result of the flooding of ie Limpopo River in 1976.

The regimes now in power in the former Portuguese colonies have a

better start for their ambition to develop socialist societies in that the
have all grown out of prolonged liberation struggles. However, the
have been forced to take over economies in which pre-socialist relation
are even more deeply embedded than in many other African countrie
Their task will inevitably be to capture the peasants for the needs of
modern socialist society. They will have to engage in the difficult tas
of removing the many pre-socialist barriers to the realization of soc
alism, a policy that will be at the expense of the peasantry. The preser
regime may be better equipped to deal with this problem than its coloni
predecessors, but it will encounter the same structural conflicts as the
did. Moreover, it will be compelled to do what capitalism unde
Portuguese rule failed to do: develop the productive forces sufficient t
support increasing public demands for capital.

The assertion, often made by outside observers, that the forme
Portuguese colonies are socialist because of the Marxist appearance c
their post-independence regimes is highly misleading. Although thes
regimes may have got a flying start in their effort to build socialism, the
begin from pre-socialist premises. These have to be transcended an
transformed before a modern socialist mode of production will b
effectively established. That is a task which will inevitably require th
modernization of individual viewpoints, the creation of new forms c
discipline and the development of new production techniques, particu
larly in the rural areas. As long as the peasant mode remains, th
objective must be achieved by a 'push from above'. Because th
peasantry does not presuppose the existence of other classes for its ow
reproduction, it carries no revolutionary potential, only an anti-coloni
or an anti-state one. Peasants are quick to support measures aimed a
mitigating the burden imposed on them by other social classes. They ar
reluctant, obviously, to support measures in the opposite direction. Y
this is what both the capitalist and the socialist development strategie
mean to the peasants. Therefore, there is no reason to believe that th
socialist development task will be any easier than the capitalist one.

Conclusions

After making a tour of African capitals in 1963 Chou en-Lai declare
that the revolutionary situation in Africa was excellent. As Gera
Chaliand observed a few years later, nothing could be further from th
truth.[47] The social realities in Africa had quickly begun to appear i
their true light. While a change of regime was a simple matte
development proved a much harder task. Soviet Marxists have bee
quicker to grasp these realities than analysts in Western countries wh
insist on applying their preconceived models to Africa. The form
acknowledge that Africa is neither capitalist nor socialist, and prefer t
speak of these countries as 'non-capitalist'.[48] They do not rule out th
possibility of building socialism by skipping the capitalist stage, b

they insist that the main task is not nationalization of the means of
production, but modernization of the productive forces.

The inward-orientation of villagers in Asia and Latin America that
writers like Migdal[49] and Scott[50] relegate to historical artefacts in the
contemporary situation, still prevails in many parts of Africa. Much of
the productive efforts are still carried out by individual households
quite independently of the work in other such production units. It is as if
everybody is paddling his own canoe rather than accepting the implications of working on a larger sailing vessel, where roles are assigned
according to functional needs. This situation has to be changed, because
socialist strategies as much as capitalist ones require subordination of
peasant resources to public demands. As Gavin Williams notes:

> Peasant households control and manage their means of pro-
> duction, thus allowing them a measure of autonomy vis-à-vis
> other classes. This autonomy must be broken down if peasant
> production is to be applied to the requirements of urban, in-
> dustrial capital formation and state development planning.
> Peasants must be made dependent on external markets and power
> holders for access to the resources which come to be necessary to
> their way of life, or they must be coerced into organizing
> production to meet external requirements.[51]

The point which I have tried to make in this chapter is that capitalism
has, by and large, failed to provide sufficient means to capture the
peasants. Thus there has been a gradual shift in post-independence
years towards strategies that borrow policy tools from modern socialism. State control of the African economies has increased mainly as
a result of capitalism's own inadequacies as a modernizing force. With
more and more governments in Africa using a socialist, or at least a
quasi-socialist approach to develop their countries there is bound to
arise a great discrepancy between development ambition and orientation, on the one hand, and the potential of the material base, on the
other. It is this dilemma that the next chapter looks at.

References and notes

1. J. H. Boeke, *Economics and Economic Policy of Dual Societies* (New York:
   Institute of Pacific Relations, 1935), in his analysis of the economic
   structures of Indonesia, was the first to use this concept.
2. Colin Leys, *Underdevelopment in Kenya* (Berkeley: University of California
   Press, 1975), p. 190.
3. Florian Znaniecki, *The Social Role of the Man of Knowledge* (New York:
   Octagon Press, 1975), p. 181.
4. Mahmood Mamdani, *Politics and Class Formation in Uganda* (New York:
   Monthly Review Press, 1976).

5. Robert H. Bates, 'People in villages: micro-level studies in political economy', *World Politics* (forthcoming 1979).
6. Andrew M. Kamarck, *The Tropics and Economic Development* (Baltimore: Johns Hopkins University Press, 1976), p. 15.
7. Jim Hoagland, 'Africa: fragments in the mind', *Washington Post*, 18 February 1973.
8. P. Buringh, H. D. J. van Heemst and G. J. Staring, *Computation of the Absolute Maximum Food Production of the World* (Wageningen: Department of Tropical Soil Sciences, Agricultural University, 1975), p. 68.
9. Trypanosomes, a protozoan flagellate, is a parasite transmitted through the actual bite of an infected tsetse fly.
10. Food and Agricultural Organization of the United Nations, *Monthly Bulletin of Agricultural Economics and Statistics*, vol. 26 (1977), pp. 20–9
11. Jon R. Moris, 'Managerial structures and plan implementation in colonia and modern agricultural extension', in David K. Leonard, *Rural Administration in Kenya* (Nairobi: East African Literature Bureau, 1973) especially pp. 107–109.
12. Patrick O. Alila, 'Kenyan agricultural policy: the colonial roots of African smallholder agricultural policy and services', Institute for Development Studies, Working Paper No. 327, University of Nairobi, 1977.
13. The KTDA is given special attention as a successful example of rural development administration in Uma Lele's authoritative review, *The Design of Rural Development: Lessons from Africa* (Baltimore: Johns Hopkins University Press, 1975).
14. This is well documented and analysed by Michael Halderman 'Pastoralism and development in Eastern Africa', unpublished MA thesis, Department of Political Science, University of California, Berkeley, 1978.
15. Colin Leys, 'Politics in Kenya: the development of peasant society' Institute for Development Studies Discussion Paper No. 102, University of Nairobi, 1970, pp. 16–17.
16. W. Nguyo, 'Some socio-economic aspects of land settlement in Kenya' University of East Africa Social Science Conference, Makerere University Kampala, December 1966.
17. Kenyans have retorted that Tanzania is a 'man-eats-nothing' society alluding to the problems that country has faced in organizing the distribution of its essential commodities.
18. Werner Sombart, *The Quintessence of Capitalism* (New York: Howard Fertig, 1967), p. 84.
19. Frank Holmquist, 'Class structure and rural self-help in Kenya and Tanzania', in Joel D. Barkan and John J. Okumu (eds) *Politics and Public Policy in Kenya and Tanzania* (New York: Praeger, 1979).
20. Philip Mbithi and Rasmus Rasmusson, 'The structure of grassroots Harambee within the context of national planning', mimeo., Department of Sociology, University of Nairobi, December 1974.
21. Nicola Swainson, 'The rise of a national bourgeoisie in Kenya', mimeo. Department of Political Science, University of Dar es Salaam, 1976.
22. International Labor Organization of the United Nations, *Employment Incomes and Equality* (Geneva: ILO, 1972).
23. Leys, op. cit., pp. 260–2.
24. John Gerhart, *The Diffusion of Hybrid Maize in Western Kenya* (Mexico

City: Centro Internacional de Mejoramiento de Maize y Trigo, 1975), p. 47.

25. These are observations for which I am grateful to Professor Bruce Johnston, Food Research Institute, Stanford University.

26. The country that may come closest to replicating the Kenyan pattern is Zimbabwe, although this very much depends on the outcome of the current struggle of power between forces inside and outside that country. Michael Bratton, in his article, 'Structural transformation in Zimbabwe: comparative notes from the neo-colonization of Kenya', *Journal of Modern African Studies,* vol. 15, no. 4 (1977), pp. 591–611 stresses the importance of the structural similarities between the two countries.

27. D. B. Cruise O'Brien, *Saints and Politicians: Essays on the Organization of a Senegalese Peasant Society* (Cambridge University Press, 1974).

28. Gavin Williams, 'Taking the part of peasants: rural development in Nigeria and Tanzania', in Peter C. W. Gutkind and Immanuel Wallerstein (eds), *The Political Economy of Contemporary Africa* (Beverly Hills: Sage Publications, 1976), p. 133.

29. Sara Berry, 'Risk aversion and rural class formation in West Africa', paper presented to the Graduate Seminar on African Agriculture at the University of California, Los Angeles, spring quarter, 1978, pp. 19–20.

30. J. D. Y. Peel, 'Inequality and action: the forms of Ijesha social conflict', Conference on 'Inequality in Africa' of the Social Science Research Council at Mount Kisco, New York, September 1976.

31. David J. Gould, 'Disorganization theory and underdevelopment administration: local "organization" in the framework of Zairean national development , paper presented to the Joint Meeting of the African Studies and Latin American Studies Associations, Houston, November 1977, p. 5.

32. Michael G. Schatzberg, 'Bureaucracy, business and beer: the political dynamics of class formation in Lisala, Zaire', unpublished Ph.D. dissertation, Department of Political Science, University of Wisconsin, Madison, 1977, p. 429.

33. Williams, op. cit., p. 135.

34. Robert Chambers, *Settlement Schemes in Tropical Africa* (Routledge & Kegan Paul, 1969) provides the most extensive overview and analysis of settlement schemes in Africa.

35. Moise C. Mensah, 'An experience of group farming in Dahomey: the rural development cooperatives', in Peter Dorner (ed.) *Cooperative and Commune: Group Farming in the Economic Development of Agriculture* (Madison: University of Wisconsin Press, 1977), p. 284.

36. Frances Hill, 'Experiments with a public sector peasantry: agricultural schemes and class formation in Africa', paper presented to the African Studies Association Conference, Boston, November 1976.

37. These figures are offered by Werner Roider, *Farm Settlements for Socio-Economic Development: The Western Nigerian Case* (München: Weltforum Verlag, 1971), p. 80.

38. Hill, op. cit., p. 15.

39. Polly Hill, *Studies in Rural Capitalism in West Africa* (Cambridge University Press, 1970) offers the best account of that experience.

40. F. Hill, op. cit., p. 16.

41. John M. Cohen, Arthur A. Goldsmith and John W. Mellor, 'Revolution and land reform in Ethiopia: peasant associations, local government and

208 THE PERVASIVENESS OF SMALL

Comittee, Center for International Studies, Cornell University, 1976.
42. Lars Rudebeck, 'Political mobilization for development in Guinea-Bissau'
Journal of Modern African Studies, vol. 10, no. 1 (1972), pp. 1–18.
43. Henry Bienen, 'State and revolution: the work of Amilcar Cabral', *Journa*
of Modern African Studies, vol. 15, no. 4 (1977), p. 561.
44. Amilcar Cabral, *Revolution in Guinea* (Love & Malcolmson, 1969), p. 70
45. Peter Aaby, 'The state of Guinea-Bissau: African socialism or socialism i
Africa?', Research Report No. 45, Scandinavian Institute of Africar
Studies, Uppsala, 1978, p. 24.
46. President Samora Machel has issued several warnings to lazy and in
disciplined workers. See, for instance, report in *Sunday News* (Dar e
Salaam), 26 July 1976.
47. Gerard Chaliand, *Armed Struggle in Africa* (New York: Monthly Review
Press, 1969), p. 109.
48. For an account of Soviet Views on the political economy of Africa, see Y
Popov, *Marxist Political Economy as Applied to the African Scene*
(Moscow: Novosti Press, 1973).
49. Joel S. Migdal, *Peasants, Politics and Revolution: Pressures towar*
Political and Social Change in the Third World (Princeton: Princeto
University Press, 1974), p. 129.
50. James C. Scott, *The Moral Economy of the Peasant: Rebellion an*
Subsistence in Southeast Asia (New Haven: Yale University Press, 1976)
51. Williams, op. cit., p. 148.

CHAPTER 8

Is small really beautiful?
The dilemma of socialist development

It is no coincidence that African governments have adopted the same attitude towards the peasants as the colonial authorities used to have. There is in many countries a despair similar to that of the colonial days: the same feeling that peasants are lazy, unwilling to make a contribution to the national economy, etc. The problem may be couched in different language today, but it reflects the fact that capitalism in Africa has failed to subordinate the pre-capitalist forces of peasant society to its demands. The post-independence governments have been forced to start from more or less the same premises as their colonial predecessors. The dilemma of how to make the peasant more responsive to official policies still remains because the economic structures of the peasant mode have not been transformed in most African countries. We have seen how in the case of Tanzania and elsewhere on the continent small is powerful by being able to withdraw from government demands and by being able to undermine official policies through alternative channels of need satisfaction provided by the economy of affection.

'State power' is a hollow concept in the African context where those who presumably control the state do not control the country's economy. The hard fact of the African political economy is that it is easier to control foreign capital than it is to control the majority of the country's domestic producers – the peasants. Those who control the state have very limited accessibility to the peasant producers because the relations of production do not allow the same kinds of control as the modern capitalist and socialist modes do. In these, producers have no choice but to offer their labour in return for access to the necessities of life (and hopefully a little more). In the pre-capitalist, peasant mode of Africa such antagonistic relations do not exist. In the majority of these countries, governments have great scope in initiating rural development policies, mainly because the state is not functionally integrated into the rural production systems. That is why, of course, most rural development policies are desk products. To the extent that there is a common foundation on which policies can be formulated jointly, it is so narrow that in most cases government officials and peasants end up talking past each other.

The paradox of this situation is that vis-à-via each other, both government and peasants have a considerable degree of autonomy, bu because they are not functionally integrated in a productive sense, the powers that stem from this autonomy cancel each other out. Wha government proudly initiates can easily be undone by the peasants in conjunction with the implementation of these policies.

Thus the political situation in Africa is not quite as favourable for th task of modernizing peasant society, as for instance Guy Hunte suggests when he writes:

> As to political will, the situation in most of Tropical Africa is no really difficult. Without an established landlord and merchan domination of the rural community, there is no obstructive powe which needs to be broken. The old chiefly power has bee undermined; the last obstacle, and that weakening year by year may be some still solid tribal culture, often among pastoral group such as the Masai or Samburu of Kenya, which is impervious t modernization. This is increasingly a marginal problem, an probably solved by administrative and technical policies rathe than by politics.[1]

It is true that, unlike Asia and Latin America where the local powe structure stands in the way of progress, Africa has fewer such politica obstacles. This does not mean, however, that peasant producers ar more easily reached with government policies. On the contrary experience has shown that they are more difficult to reach in thos societies where the capitalist economy has not given rise to a socia structure in which the rulers effectively control the submerged classes In this situation, government policies will inevitably fail to create a adequate response among the perceived target groups. In the absence c effective social control by other social classes, peasants will continue t preoccupy themselves with the natural priority of their own repro duction. In a situation where agricultural production is not ye modernized, it is no surprise that peasants will find little time left t worry about government priorities. Their reproductive needs are ofte so overwhelming that even government policies aimed at facilitating th task, for example, improvement in public health, only have a limite impact on the overall problem of increasing peasant responsiveness t modern development demands.

The 'trained incapacity' of the Westerner

Westerners who go to work in Africa are generally ill-equipped to serv as consultants or advisers to government. They have no person experience of pre-capitalist economies. They cannot conceive the operating principles. They cannot experience the structural constrain mposed on the actors by these economies. Their own theories are exclusively deductive, derived from modern economic systems, capialist or socialist. They presuppose a *nature artificielle*, an environment hat can be manipulated to suit modern development objectives. These heories do not ask what the local actors are like; they presuppose a certain type of behaviour. Consequently we create images of the African peasantry that suit our models. For instance, international aid agencies promote images of the peasants as willing collaborators with government. On such an assumption they are usually able to sell their agricultural development policies to those who provide the finance. Western socialists often engage in a similar approach. In the context of their theory, the peasants are revolutionary and the bourgeoisie the main stumbling-block to a more far-reaching transformation of society. Most of this is wishful thinking, if not outright ignorance.

Nobody has more eloquently alerted us to the limitations of our deductive approach to understanding the peasantry than James Scott. In his study of the fate of the peasantry in Southeast Asia, he stresses that the world unfolds itself to the peasant in a very different fashion from the way outsiders conceive the situation. The peasant has 'his own durable moral economy which continues to define the situation for him.'[2] In Southeast Asia, the economic structures that gave rise to his outlook have long since been effectively undermined. To that extent, his economy is purely moral, it is only a superstructural expression lacking support from the prevailing economic structures. It has been reduced to the status of historical artefact. It survives but it has no influence on the course of events. In Africa, however, as noted earlier, peasant rationality does have structural roots. The peasant mode of production provides an economic base for the primacy of the subsistence rights and other such views associated with peasant rationality. African peasants are still in the process of entering the historical arena and no other social class has yet managed effectively to subordinate them to its demands. Therefore it would be wrong to dismiss peasant articulations as unimportant. Peasant rationality cannot be written off as merely 'false consciousness'. While this may be a valid argument in societies where peasants have been totally submerged, it is invalid in Africa where the peasant mode still forms an active part of the political economy. In Africa we have a unique opportunity to study the peasantry as a social class which still enjoys a considerable degree of autonomy vis-à-vis other social classes. Yet we continue to treat them as if they were already subdued with no alternative but to meet the demands that are placed on them by the social classes controlling the state. Unfortunately, this is where our deductive theories inevitably take us. It is part of our own socialization and education in societies where that is the only option. Therefore, when most Western observers extend their analysis to Africa, they miss the essentials of the political economy of those countries. Conditions are different, but they find it impossible to

conceive the world in terms other than those which their home politica
ideology or professional discipline dictates. To that extent we suffe
from 'trained incapacity', as Thorstein Veblen once labelled it.

A few examples of this intellectual ailment may be necessary
Common among Western policy advisers and analysts in Africa is tc
start, explicitly or implicitly, from the assumption that social realitie
are reduced to a systems analogy in which parts are interdependent anc
therefore change in one system variable inevitably triggers off response
elsewhere in the system. This is how I myself a priori conceived the
African situation in my first study.[3] I was even able to prove that at the
political level, there existed an official system that transcended the
discontinuities caused by a lack of a developed physical and economic
infrastructure. What I have learned from living in East Africa more
than from reading books is that this system is of limited significance tc
development efforts, because it is not rooted in the economic structures
It is a superstructural expression that exists in isolation of much of the
productive efforts going on in society. The peasants may be very much
part of the system by showing overt loyalty to the new nation and it
political regime, but they can still ignore it at the economic level
Government penetration efforts evaporate as they reach out toward
the independent smallholder peasants, who are by no means locked up
in systems relations as we create them in our own models.

The systems analogy is particularly inappropriate in the context o
rural development analysis. Still Western analysts insist on using it in
that field as indiscriminately as elsewhere. While it may make in
tellectual sense to the African government officials with whom the
expatriates presumably interact, the premises of such a policy analysi
are hopelessly false. The creation of integrated rural developmen
programmes and various management systems applicable to rura
development are largely misguided efforts.[4] Still they are insisted upon
often as a prerequisite for the initiation of rural development pro
grammes, by international aid donor agencies. They all start from the
questionable assumption that the official is an important person in the
context of rural development. They also wrongly assume that the
administrators and peasant producers are locked up in structures in
which the former have leverage over the latter for the purpose o
bringing about development. The official may have some leverage ove
the peasant; they may even be part of the same social system, but it is a
system that exists in isolation of the demands for policy output; fo
results that are meaningful in the context of the management system o
government. Nobody has better illustrated this problem than Jon
Moris, who argues that what in Western eyes appears as a highly
inefficient administrative system still persists because it is able to
perform certain social functions which in the context of the local actor
appear relevant.[5] What Moris does not stress is the fact that these
management systems are not functionally integrated into the local

economies. In the views of the local peasants they form an artifical superstructural creation. Thus there should be no surprise that to the extent that these administrative structures become at all part of the local economies, their original principles of operation are diluted.

The main reason for the many failures and shortcomings in the field of rural development is structural. That explains what one observer has referred to as the 'low rate of natural reproduction' of rural development projects.[6] What we have is mere replication of projects by governments, usually with diminishing returns. The peasant mode of production does not open the door to government intervention very easily. Certainly producers and government administrators are not interdependent parts of the same economic system in such a way that officials operate from a position of strength. The sooner governments in Africa and international aid agencies acknowledge this structural anomaly, the quicker a more relevant perspective on the rural development task can be developed. Spending large sums on streamlining management structures for rural development, particularly for the purpose of the integrated variety, is a waste. If rural development programmes fail it is not primarily because of the inadequacy of management structures or because government officials deliberately bungle the policies. It is time we realized that in most African countries the structural opportunities for effective management of rural development are so limited that when engaging in that task we are often asking for the impossible. Should government officials appear not to do what is expected of them, reasons for such behaviour can often be traced to the persistence of pre-capitalist formations in which they feel far more at home than in the modern organizational forms supplied by government (often the creation of colonial officials or, after independence, of Western management consultants).

Another example of our 'trained incapacity' emerges out of our use of the concept of 'efficiency' in public choice. Particularly those who, like the representatives of the 'Chicago School' of economics, accept the premises of what de Gregori calls 'methodological individualism', there is a great danger of evolving irrelevant policy advice.[7] This approach tries to explain collective decision-making as primarily the summation of different, individual decisions made separately. To be rational in that model implies the ability to see every relevant experience as a problem which can be broken down into parts, reassembled, manipulated in practical ways and measured in its effects. Man is 'economic man' in the sense that he allows himself to be guided by priorities and tastes as expressed in the market. In his efficiency calculus, he comes to treat essentially economic variables; the tangible and quantifiable factors in society. The rest are reduced to the status of 'externalities'.

It is inevitable that important social values are excluded in this form of calculus. It simply would be impossible otherwise. The shortcomings of this approach may be less apparent and less serious in a society where the market force is predominant. In a pre-capitalist society, however, methodological individualism is a very misleading approach. Our 'obsolete market mentality' really takes us wide of the mark. What we are led to treat as 'externalities' are often part of the calculus in pre-capitalist societies. As Goulet stresses:

> In fact, most non-Western societies continue to make a calculus of efficiency which internalizes religious, kinship, aesthetic, and recreational values in the performance of 'economic' activities like agricultural work, and hunting and fishing expeditions.[8]

Neither our systems approach nor our conception of how individuals behave in decision-making situations is helpful in African policy analysis. Both take us off in directions that estrange us from the policy-making realities. The same is true of class analysis. Here modern rationality is simply projected to collective units of action called social classes. The assumptions of what enter into the decision-making calculus are the same as in methodological individualism. Their main intellectual preoccupation is to compromise the pluralist conception of power.[9] This is evident also in the study of peasant societies where they contrast their view of horizontal cleavages with the pluralist view of 'factions' and 'patron–client relationships', which all essentially imply that the most important social cleavages are vertical. Alavi, for instance, insists that the latter only offer a post facto rationalization of existing political alignments. It does not probe into the reasons for what it superficially observes.[10] In his view, patron–client relationships are nothing but incidents of class domination. While this criticism is valid in a situation where the patrons are members of a class that have full control over the social classes from which clients are recruited, it carries little if any validity in a society where that situation has not yet emerged. Alavi clearly writes with the Asian situation in mind: 'The core of the factional alignment consists of the peasants, sharecroppers and landless labourers, who are directly dependent on the landlord who decides to set himself up in business as a political leader.'[11] Thus although it would be wrong to accuse Alavi of a Western bias, his view that factions and patron-client relationships are mere instances of the articulation of class power is misleading. It misses the point that in a society where the majority of the producers remain independent smallholder peasants, class structures are not singularly important. The structural con-tradiction in the peasant mode arises from the fact that state approp-riation of the peasant surplus is not necessary for peasant reproduction. This is a non-productive contradiction. The peasant mode also gives rise to vertical cleavages by virtue of the fact that local units of production are not interdependent. In this situation, communal action based on affinity with a local community is often used to mitigate, or even resist, class action. Such action in the African context cannot be written off as merely manifesting false consciousness. Communal action has an objective base in the peasant mode of production and is dictated by the conflict with capitalism. Communal action is a normal articulation of the conflict between the pre-capitalist and the capitalist modes of production. It is part of our 'trained incapacity' not to be able to acknowledge this and instead continue to portray these societies in terms derived from other historical experiences.

Yet another example of this incapacity is our focus on formal organizations in the discussion of development. In recent years, for instance, there has been considerable discussion about the need for popular participation in local development efforts. Policies and strategies have been devised which try to offer institutional channels for local participation in decision-making. The assumption underlying this approach is the absence of such participation among poorer people in the rural areas. While this contention may be correct in many instances, it is by no means valid to assume that in rural Africa there is no participation. In the earlier discussion of Tanzania it was shown that in one part of that country, there were as many as twelve different single-purpose associations in operation in the same village. The situation may not be as diverse as that in other parts of Tanzania or of Africa, but it is clear that the peasants have their own institutional networks which keep them preoccupied. Although these in most instances are unregistered and thus do not exist on the list of formal organizations, they are important to the peasants because they are integral parts of the prevailing pre-capitalist formations. Their existence means, of course, that peasants do participate in local affairs. The issue is how far the peasants are willing to participate in the formal structures that link them with the wider policy-making system. Most peasants do not consider that such participation is as important as their involvement in local, informal structures. First of all, the wider system is not important in the context of their production system. Thus peasants in Africa usually leave participation in political structures outside the rural communities to those petty-capitalist farmers who may benefit from it. These farmers are also better equipped to protect the peasants against controversial state intervention in their affairs. In the eyes of the peasants such protection is a manifestation of power, although what they do not always realize is that for the petty-capitalist farmer such a measure is often in his own interest. When he can contribute to the dilution of government policies aimed, for instance, at modernization of peasant agriculture, he can retain his competitive edge over the other members of his rural community. Among other things, he increases his own chances of obtaining access to the inputs supplied by outside agencies.

This is not to suggest that peasants are totally uninterested in participating in political structures that link them with the state. In addition to proving their political loyalty by attending meetings in full force whenever a senior politician visits their community, they also involve themselves whenever there is a chance of obtaining resources or benefits from government which are seen to facilitate their life or work. In such situations, peasants are willing to act as pressure groups. The best example of this, referred to above, is self-help work in fields where the government has committed itself to assist local efforts.

Our 'trained incapacity' has also been manifest in recent efforts to evolve alternative forms of development; those forms which are not as costly in resource utilization and social stratification as the modern capitalist (and increasingly the modern socialist) mode. While many interesting new ideas have been introduced (but few have been put into practice), they have all reflected the values of modern society. New packages and programmes have generally been conceived in the context of modern organizational forms. To be fair, there are exceptions to this orientation, but the most successful advocates of 'alternative development' have themselves become part of the international circuit in which the development issues are decided.[12] By becoming part of this establishment, it is increasingly difficult to retain originality and sensitivity to new issues.

The Dag Hammarskjöld Foundation has probably done more than other international institutions to foster thinking about alternative forms of development.[13] Even in this forum, however, participants have not really acknowledged the major limitation of the debate about alternative development: that it is only an alternative within the premises of an inorganic environment. This, for instance, is true of the contribution of four Asian intellectuals in which their alternative is a strategy of 'collective creativity'.[14] Their approach carries all the dominant emotions of modern development thinking but shows little understanding of the structures that dictate social action at the local level.

Many advocates of alternative development have to learn the limits of their own paradigms and discover through personal experience the vulnerability of their own models in the context of a pre-capitalist society. They need to discover that emotions which are real for those who experience them are not real for those who merely observe them. Above all, modern man needs to learn that to peasants who still labour under pre-capitalist formations, the problem of underdevelopment is more like a mystery. The peasants are not approaching it like modern man does: as a difficulty one encounters along the way. They cannot step back from it, measure it, devise solutions, and perhaps overcome it, as modern rationality allows decision-makers to do. They cannot situate themselves outside the dilemma. A problematic element is present, but the viewer himself is part of the problem. This is also true of the official who pretends he has solutions to the problems encountered in peasant society. In the eyes of the peasants, the official is part of the problem. The epistemological differences between modern and pre-modern knowledge create structural barriers which are not easily overcome by sticking to conventional approaches to problem-solving. As Denis Goulet has noted:

> Therefore, if he [modern decision-maker] chooses to treat the matter as a mere problem extrinsic to himself, he is condemned to misunderstand it and not solve it. He needs to be shocked into discovering the falsity of the certitudes he brought with him into the 'problem arena'. He must make the dramatic discovery that there exists an inherent structural paternalism in the very relationship between him as helper and the other as helpee, between him as 'developed' and the other as 'underdeveloped'.[15]

Paulo Freire has devoted special attention to this structural contradiction. He advocates that rather than engaging in technical problem-solving, the main task in a situation of underdevelopment is to be able to 'problematize'.[16] By this he means the engagement of the entire population of a given community in the task of codifying its total reality into symbols capable of generating critical consciousness and empowering them to alter their relations with nature and the social forces determining their existence. This approach is aimed at increasing the collective capacity of groups or local communities to transform an oppressive reality in which they have been placed by the forces of history.

The conditions which give rise to a successful application of this 'problematization' approach, however, are not found everywhere. In a situation, for instance, like that of rural Africa, where the process of marginalization has not yet begun to take a significant human toll and where the pre-capitalist economy is regarded as more human and socially acceptable than its modern alternative, the task of problematizing is bound to be a long and often frustrating experience. The rationale for transforming social reality does not appear particularly immediate in such a situation. People are more likely to seek improvements within existing structures.

In the intensified efforts in recent years to explain underdevelopment with reference to the adverse impact of global forces, technology has increasingly come to occupy a key position. Modern, capital-intensive operations, requiring a large-scale format, have become the special target of criticism. Nobody has more effectively pursued this criticism that the late E. F. Schumacher. In his book, *Small is Beautiful,* he castigates modern economics and modern technology for producing solutions which waste our natural resources and prevent the development of human creativity.[17] Based on his experience of India, he argues against both orthodox capitalism and orthodox socialism, in which the inevitable trend has been to supplant the 'pygmy property of the many' with the 'giant property of the few'. Schumacher elevates scale of organization to the status of key variable in the development equation.

He sees in the small-scale unit of operation freedom, efficiency and creativity.

While there certainly is a reason for modern society to take Schumacher seriously – and there is evidence that some highly-placed officials, such as Governor Jerry Brown of California, are doing so – the question is how far he really offers an alternative development approach for Third World countries. As far as Africa goes, I have tried to show that small has not yet been overpowered by big. The majority of that continent's producers are small but, most importantly, they are not marginalized by other social classes in a manner that characterizes large parts of Asia and South America. Does this mean that Africa is particularly suitable for the Schumacher approach?

My answer to that question is that Africa does indeed provide a unique opportunity for the application of the idea that 'small is beautiful'. However, because small is already powerful it is not very likely that these opportunities will be seized. In other words, because the smallholder peasantry and the petty-bourgeois producers do have a social autonomy that gives rise to a highly fragile social base in African societies, there will be strong pressures within governments to replace the countless number of small units of production with large ones. This has nothing to do with a fascination with 'modern' or 'big', as many Western observers believe when despairing over this orientation in African countries. It is politically dictated, as for instance the case of Nkrumah's Ghana (discussed in Chapter 7), so candidly demonstrates. The small cannot very easily be made to respond to modern development needs in societies where they are not irreversibly controlled by other social classes. Small will not be beautiful in the eyes of African governments until their negative power to subvert official policies has been erased. Thus, in addition to achieving this, governments will be strongly inclined to invest resources in alternative forms of production, notably large-scale ones. They may even go as far as starving the peasant sector of additional resources, although that is a shortsighted approach since it is likely to increase peasant willingness to use their exit option.

There is still another reason why small may be abandoned by African governments: the costly and time-consuming task of overcoming the shortcomings of existing technology in rural Africa. It would be wrong to romanticize the status of indigenous technologies in Africa. The reasons for Africa's underdevelopment cannot be blamed on modern technology alone. It is true that a lot of mistakes have been committed by private and public agencies responsible for the transfer of capital and technology to Africa. These mistakes, however, do not mean that the indigenous technologies offer ready alternatives. It is fair to say that the indigenous tools and techniques in rural Africa are as responsible for the predicament in which those countries find themselves as is modern technology. There is plenty of evidence given here to show that the rationality underlying the indigenous technology helps to preserve the peasant mode of production. Because the peasant mode is not productive enough to support government demands, particularly in socialist countries seeking an acceleration of that process or a transformation of its main parameters, officials in African countries will be more anxious to replace these outmoded techniques and tools rather than waiting for research to provide modifications that prove more efficient.

Tanzania has invested a lot of money and intellectual resources in the development of intermediate technologies that are suitable for peasant agriculture. Despite achievements at the various research stations, there have been problems in disseminating innovations in the rural areas. Some problems may be purely administrative, but they have roots deeper than that. Indigenous technology has one overwhelming advantage over competing technologies, even those which we call intermediate. It is adapted to specific environmental and social factors prevailing in that area. It is emotionally acceptable because it is part and parcel of the complex array of institutional practices and cultural traditions.[18] Particularly in a situation where 'mechanical' forms of solidarity prevail, the indigenous technology may be very difficult to modify or replace, because it is an integral part of this form of social organization.

Research used to develop indigenous technology is bound to be a highly expensive affair, given the localized nature of such technologies, their close integration into social forms of organization, and the reluctance on the part of governments to maintain such forms of social organization. Most African governments would wish to see more 'organic' forms of solidarity, those which are functionally determined by the material development needs of society. To that extent the African governments have little choice but to accept the 'modern' organization, even if it means that behind its curtains, articulations of mechanical solidarity may continue to exist. As seen in Chapter 6, the super-structural values derived from the peasant mode spill over into the modern economy and play havoc with efforts to increase productivity. The reason for this conflict is not difficult to trace as the mode of operation of capitalism or socialism and the economy of affection are fundamentally different. Larger political and economic units of organization cannot easily be combined with the organizational mode of the economy of affection.

Having their hands full with the problem of making the many small producers in the rural areas more productive, African officials are not very likely to support the notion that 'small is beautiful'. Their experience is that small is powerful and as such constitutes an obstacle to development.

The socialist challenge

The peasant mode, in which smallness prevails, is a very unstable and unreliable base for modern political institutions. The fact that capitalism has failed to transform the pre-capitalist formations of the peasant mode means that African governments have been forced to spend considerable resources on political maintenance. Plenty of examples have already been given of how economics is used to feed politics – domestic capital is used to buy political support and to maintain modern political institutions. In addition, there is a growing inclination on the part of African governments to rely on foreign troops, yet another indication of the internal instability of political regimes established on pre-capitalist social formations.

Capitalism changes the context in which these formations are allowed to operate and tends to undermine the cultural superstructure that has previously held these formations together in a stable fashion, before it has any significant impact on the relations of production. In Africa, capitalism has achieved enough social subversion to encourage vertical conflicts, but it has not yet penetrated the economy sufficiently to achieve a modernization of the productive forces and consequently a transformation of the relations of production. Africa knows only the bad side of capitalism and it is no coincidence that Africans by and large see it as the main source of evil.

In the light of this colonial and neo-colonial experience, it is only natural that African leaders have been inclined to reduce their dependence on the market in favour of the political market-place, in which the pre-capitalist formations can be restored. The impersonal forces of the capitalist market are replaced by more direct and personal interventions by political leaders. These may be called bureaucratic measures, but they are not the impersonal, regulatory interventions of the modern type of bureaucracy. It is an approach in which the political ends of the regime are employed by the leaders to justify the use of the state machinery regardless of what the formal rules and regulations prescribe.

As noted earlier, the replacement of the capitalist market as the principal determinant of the process of change in society implies that the African governments also abandon the policy tools that the market automatically offers. The relative diversity of policy tools available under modern capitalism are giving way to a more concentrated use of a few policy measures that are expected to deal more effectively with the constraints imposed by pre-capitalist forces. These forces, as noted earlier, are at the same time pre-socialist; they do not automatically lend support to modern socialist objectives. Given capitalism's inability to overcome the pre-capitalist barriers, many African governments, however, are likely to turn to the socialist policy measures to achieve modernization. Rather than accepting the predicament in which world capitalism has placed them, they will turn to socialism out of impatience and despair.

This poses a great challenge to socialism and those who are committed to its realization. Nowhere in the world has socialism been brought about as a result of the maturation of capitalism. Socialist revolutions have materialized under conditions where the main impact of capitalism has been to destroy or deform pre-capitalist formations, but where the latter have not been fully replaced by capitalist relations of production. In other words, socialist *revolutions* have generally been successful only in conditions of incipient capitalism; where the latter has had a socially mobilizing and politically consciousness-raising effect. There is no doubt that capitalism has had such an effect also in Africa. In that respect, therefore, the situation in Africa resembles that of those countries where socialist revolutions have brought about new social formations. This, however, is also where the similarity ends. In those countries in the Third World where socialism has triumphed, by revolution, the vast majority of the producers have experienced exploitation by feudal landlords or capitalist owners of the means of production. They have been forced by these social classes to devote most of their time and energy to produce a surplus over which they have no control. There have been social contradictions which the socialist paradigm explains in a convincing manner. These countries have had a social class base on which socialism could be effectively built.

In the vast majority of African countries social conditions differ in significant respects. The working-class is very small and still closely linked to the pre-socialist formations. Peasants form part of a mode of production of their own which still largely awaits to be modernized. The petty-bourgeoisie, which has committed itself to socialism, has not come to power through a protracted struggle, the only exceptions to this being the former Portuguese colonies. Furthermore, this petty-bourgeoisie often possesses general skills in politics, administration and commerce, but is much less well equipped in the professional and technical fields.

Thus the first challenge to socialism in Africa is modernization. Socialists in Africa start from a situation in which peasants, and to a large extent also workers, labour under traditional conceptions of production and exchange. The impact of capitalism has not removed these orientations, and progressive leaders in Africa will have to destroy what must appear to them as the pre-socialist 'metaphysics' of production. As Aaby shows in his study of Guinea-Bissau, the peasants prefer to invest in social reproduction rather than technological innovations.[19] As long as the rural producers are absorbed by the social logic of the peasant mode, there is little room for modern socialism. Polygamy, gerontocracy, funeral feasts and other institutions supported by the economy of affection, are not reconcilable with the socialist mode of production. Socialists will have to accept the responsibility of modernizing, rationalizing economic life in a way that facilitates a more productive use of human resources. This task, which can also be described as the removal of the pre-modern barriers to economic development, has in many other societies been performed wholly or in part by capitalism. Its importance has been stressed by both Weber and Marx. Marx noted that the transition to modern capitalism is only completed when direct force is employed as a matter of exception, and a new set of attitudes to replace old traditions and habits has developed among the workers:

> It is not enough that the conditions of labour are concentrated in a mass, in the shape of capital, at the one pole of society, while at the other are grouped masses of men who have nothing to sell but their labour power. Neither is it enough that they are compelled to sell it voluntarily. The advance of capitalist production develops a working class, which by education, tradition, habit, looks upon the conditions of that mode of production as self-evident laws of nature.[20]

Also Weber stressed the importance to capitalism of work being treated as an end in itself by the workers:

> Labour must ... be performed as if it were an absolute end in itself, a calling. But such an attitude is by no means a product of nature. It cannot be evoked by low wages or high ones alone, but can only be the product of a long and arduous process of education. Today, capitalism once in the saddle, can recruit its labouring force in all industrial countries with comparative ease. In the past this was in every case an extremely difficult problem.[21]

Work is not an end in itself to workers in Africa and it is no coincidence that political leaders continuously stress the importance and virtue of work. This kind of political education is not going to be enough to achieve a modernization of the outlook of the work-force in African countries. This will be most effectively carried out at the work-places by managers and supervisors to whom work is a calling. The problem which has been repeatedly demonstrated in African countries is that even these people have not always internalized the modern work ethic. They are unable to set personal examples to the workers, because their own attitude towards work has not been transformed. The review of the situation in the public sector in Tanzania revealed that the task of modernization requires a change of outlook not only at the level of the workers but also in the management cadre. One of the gravest problems facing the African countries is the shortage of 'those men of action', which Reinhard Bendix says, have the inevitable but unenviable task of subordinating other people to the demands of modern economic enterprise; to impose authority and discipline but at the same time find an ideological justification for their exercise of power.[22]

Socialist managers will have to demand the same kind of subordination to authority as their capitalist colleagues. But socialists have usually come to power by portraying capitalist management techniques as evil. Workers, therefore, will not respond more favourably to socialist management demands for discipline and subordination, as for instance the Tanzanian case suggests. To expect self-discipline – the internalization of a modern work ethic – to develop more quickly under socialist forms of production is illusory in a society where pre-socialist forces still predominate. Therefore, it is inevitable that the task of socialist modernization will imply the use of force in the same way as capitalist modernization did. It will be the painful task of socialist leaders to find the ideological justification for this in a situation where social expectations go in a contrary direction.

The problems of cadre work

Many socialists would take issue with this point on the grounds that politically educated cadres can bring about a change in attitude more effectively than modern management. While I agree that the cadre approach *may* be more effective, there are structural constraints in the African situation that are likely to impede the effectiveness of this work. Cadres have easy access to the exploited and oppressed in societies where these people can be convinced that their predicament is clearly due to exploitation by other social classes. Where workers and peasants are irreversibly caught in relations of production that give them no option but to fight the existing system, cadres can be very effective in raising political consciousness. They can with relative ease be convinced that a socialist transformation will give them more freedom. In societies where the peasants have been submerged, they would welcome socialism because it promises them more time for meeting their own reproductive needs. The problem that faces countries which transform relations of production in a socialist direction is that these peasants are inclined to give such strong priority to their own needs that the socialist government finds it difficult to incorporate them effectively into the modern development process. This is what happened when the capitalist farms were given to peasants in Ismani in Tanzania. The same problem has been reported from Peru.[23]

In the majority of cases in Africa cadres find themselves up against the structural constraints of the peasant mode. An independent peasant who has enough autonomy to withdraw from government demands is not an easy target for socialist cadre penetration. He is no more easily convinced to become a socialist than a capitalist. The structures which support his livelihood limit his interest in the socialist message. Even where the direct exit option is denied the peasant, and instead he has taken refuge in the economy of affection, modern socialism has a limited appeal. It presupposes an environment in which the peasants can be manipulated from outside and it implies increased production for the use of other social classes. In this perspective, the economy of affection appears far more attractive. The cadre has little to offer which the peasant cannot be more reliably assured of in the context of his own economy.

Another reason why the socialist cadres are likely to run into difficulties in their task of socialist transformation in Africa is that it is essentially one of modernization. Removing the barriers of pre-modern society is as important to the socialist as it is to the capitalist. Achieving that objective through cadre work requires people equipped with patience and the ability to help the local population problematize their own predicament. Without such qualities cadres will have little impact. Sending them to the rural areas of Africa will be like sending soldiers behind the enemy lines supplied with blank ammunition.

The cadre approach is an important part of socialist modernization but the danger of the cadre remaining an outsider to the peasants is reinforced, in the African context, by the fact that the know-how required in production is highly localized. It is non-universal and difficult to replicate. In this respect Africa differs from Asia, where in societies practising irrigated agriculture a body of knowledge has developed over generations that is applicable not only in a small part of the country but all over. In the situation prevailing in East Asian countries, the cadre has no difficulty in communicating with the peasants in a language that is comprehensible in the context of local production. The cadre has no problem of legitimizing himself provided he approaches the peasant producers with respect. In Africa, by contrast, the peasant can hardly fail to see the cadre as a complicating factor, unless there is a situation of national liberation or one where the logic of the peasant mode has ceased to be dominant. It is almost inevitable that the socialist modernizer will have to depend on such means as intimidation and coercion. His access to the peasantry is so limited that, whether it is a question of peasant production on private plots or in communal villages, there is not much room for anything but a zero-sum game, in which one emerges as the total winner, the other as a total loser. The experiment in trying to create an alternative class base by establishing state farms has already proved itself inadequate.

In those countries where the petty-bourgeoisie has come to power as a result of a liberation struggle, socialist achievements have been attained by virtue of the fact that the situation has forced the peasantry to alter their mode of existence in some important respects. Although coercion and intimidation are part of such a liberation struggle they are not felt in the same way as in situations of non-struggle. To that extent, such a struggle may serve as the midwife of socialist modernization. The peasantry may emerge out of such an experience with greater accessibility to alternative forms of social organization and production. The problem, however, once the struggle is over and the petty-bourgeois leaders have established themselves in power, is to keep the socialist baby alive. Rural Africa is not particularly hospitable to the development of socialist forms of production, and they have to be kept alive by constant vigil and support. This is likely to imply the use of coercion in conditions other than that of struggle. The effects of such measures would then be different. Much of the dynamics that leaders got used to in the struggle situation no longer manifests itself, because in the normal situation the peasant mode does not allow any revolutionizing of the means of production.

The colonial officials were strongly criticized by African nationalists for using coercion to achieve their ends. In those days, African leaders accepted the peasant perspective on development. The experience of governing these countries after independence has taught them that to obtain adequate response from the peasants is virtually impossible without coercive measures that alter the premises of their behaviour. The colonial authorities used the market – and to that extent felt free to take advantage of the policy tools it supplies – but even so they were able to reach effectively only a limited number of peasants, essentially those who were really capable of responding to the modernization lures of the capitalist market. African governments, anxious to avoid the costs associated with the capitalist approach, find themselves in the dilemma of being virtually locked out of access to the peasants unless they apply coercive measures to change the premises of peasant action.

The similarity between colonial and post-colonial approaches to the peasantry in Africa stems from the structural barriers of the peasant mode of production. Turning the peasant producer into a modern farmer is not a unilinear process that can be achieved by education, training, and government services alone, as many Western liberals believe.[24] It is likely to be a process full of discontinuities and conflicts. Those who believe that it can be achieved without coercion are well-advised to look back into the history of their own country. As Barrington Moore demonstrates, nowhere has the peasantry been spared coercive measures. The latter are a necessary evil of modernization, capitalist or socialist.[25]

It is fashionable among liberals (and also Marxists who assume that the individual liberties can be combined with socialism) to criticize African governments for being too coercive and authoritarian, leaving little or no room for civil liberties. Such criticism fails to take into consideration the conditions of those societies. The critics forget that the structural conditions of those economies are such that very often the only approach available implies authoritarianism. If governments were to depend on participatory and grass-roots approaches alone, there would be no modernization, no development. That predicament applies to socialist governments as much as those which follow a more capitalist approach. In many cases, Westerners should praise African governments for not using more coercion than they do. For instance, in the case of Tanzania, serious attempts have been made to implant democratic procedures in an environment where the process of development invites more coercion. Political freedom, as conceived by Westerners is not the key variable that promotes development in African societies. Such are the historical circumstances under which these countries are becoming part of the modern development process. This is not to say that indiscriminate tyrants like Amin should be condoned. His regime was just an example of what excesses the structures of African countries may allow. In the light of such opportunities of abuse, the genuine efforts in countries like Kenya and Tanzania to maintain some form of democratic rule must be praised, even if political practice is sometimes allowed to deviate from the ideal.

The role of bureaucracy

The most critical test of government capacity is not in relation to democratic freedoms but in conjunction with its expected role as supplier of necessary inputs for modernization. Colonial governments are rightly criticized for having given attention to their own priorities, making the involvement of African producers only incidental to their own ends. However, the colonial administration did ensure that those who accepted the premises of its development were properly supported in their productive efforts. An efficient administration was a key objective of colonial rule.

Operational efficiency has not been a priority to the same extent after independence. This is not to say that African governments are less concerned with efficiency. The parameters of assessing efficiency, however, have changed. The macro-efficiency of the political system has often been considered supreme and thus, as in the case of Tanzania, allowed to interfere with the micro-efficiency concerns of individual public institutions. Moreover, African governments after independence have generally expanded their development programmes to include sectors that were not given the same priority during the colonial period. Thus government capacity in relation to set objectives has been small. Consequently, both organizational efficiency and effectiveness have been low.

In relation to official political objectives, most African governments have operated with a chronic under-capacity which has often frustrated development efforts. By biting off more than they can chew, they have not always been able to give peasant farmers reliable support. In a situation where peasant farmers might otherwise have shown some interest in government modernization programmes, they have turned their back on the officials. Tanzania is by no means unique in having experienced this problem.

In Kenya, as Leonard stresses, the scarcity of resources available for development purposes has frequently produced internal power struggles that have stood in the way of a more effective use of government organizations:

> Most Kenya Africans see economic development as deriving from access to scarce resources and not from their productive use. When the development process is understood in this way and social conflict groups are organized on ethnic lines, most political and administrative energies are burned up in competition for resources and too little attention is given to the technological and organizational innovations that are actually essential to successful agricultural development on a national basis.[26]

Public institutions, therefore, often become the arena of factional struggles that place severe limits on how far these organizations can serve as development-oriented agencies. Frank Holmquist has demonstrated how they become captured by outside interests and are unable to pursue original policy objectives effectively.[27] This may not always be a bad thing, but if it becomes the rule, effective government action is precluded. Leonard perceives room for improvement and even goes as far as to argue that bureaucracy can be development oriented. In other words, he takes issue with the orthodox argument in the development administration literature that bureaucratic organizations are intrinsically ill-equipped to promote development because they stress routine and replication rather than flexibility and innovation.[28]

While it is true that in any situation there is likely to be room for organizational improvement, the impact of organizational reforms is likely to vary from case to case. In some situations the critical bottleneck may be organizational or managerial but only too often the key factors are extra-organizational. It seems true of the African countries where the state is not yet a major factor in rural production that government organizations are likely to be exposed to pressures other than those which facilitate their internal operations. To be able to function according to the rules of modern organization they will have to cut themselves off from their social environment. Participation by outside groups in policy and plan formulation leads to a dilution of overall government objectives and conflicts which cannot be resolved without wasting a lot of human energy, as Leonard indicates. Rule by the bureaucracy and mass participation are fundamentally inconsistent, as Samoff notes,[29] but the reason for this inconsistency is not that bureaucrats have already established themselves in power and guard their privileges. The situation is more complex than that. What most analysts have failed to realize is that the African rulers, irrespective of development orientation, must provide room for the development of class structures. The latter obviously exist but their articulation is so weak that it is highly misleading to reduce the discussion of social formations in Africa to social classes alone. The problem in contemporary Africa is that through the economy of affection other modes of social organization are kept alive. These prevent the articulation of class conflict and hold back the development of a social dynamic necessary for development, capitalist and socialist alike. Thus there is no reason to lament the development of the African bourgeoisie. The bureaucratic variation of this social class (of which so much has been written, particularly in relation to Tanzania[30]) is an inevitable outcome of the efforts to create a socialist state. There is no escape from such a trend anywhere in Africa, be it Tanzania, Mozambique, Ethiopia or Guinea-Bissau. The socialist governments need to protect themselves against the small, because in the same way it let capitalism down, it will subvert socialism if not subdued to its demands.

The notion that the African petty-bourgeoisie should be capable of committing 'class suicide', as Amilcar Cabral once put it, is hardly compatible with the development realities of contemporary Africa. While it is easy to understand the origin of this notion in the liberation struggle, it is more correct to say that after coming to power, the petty-bourgeoisie in Africa is forced to commit 'adultery' against the peasantry.

When writers such as Shivji[31], Meillassoux[32] and Salum[33] blame certain economic control measures on the state bureaucratic leadership, they overlook the fact that a revolutionary leadership would be interested in undertaking the same type of measures. For instance, all these leaders would have to undertake measures that bring the smallholder producers, in a private or communal capacity, into exchange relationships involving the 'cash nexus', as Lipton also stresses.[34] The blame that is usually placed on the bureaucratic bourgeoisie in Africa may appear reasonable because it is made post facto – only at a time when the socialist transformation is blocked. It is time it was recognized that the features used to identify the petty-bourgeois leadership in Africa, for example, social background, appropriation, distinct consumption pattern and political repression, also apply to a revolutionary leadership and its policy. Aaby notes the same phenomenon when he writes that 'the cause of success or failure is thus not to be found in the class character of the leadership but rather in the adequacy of its policy in relation to the maintenance of a transformative dynamic, which creates both economic growth and popular support.'[35] 'Petty-bourgeois' and 'revolutionary' are simply qualitative determinations of the same form of leadership and not indications of different class positions. Both are faced with the tasks of modernization, and an authoritative statement about the nature of the regime can only be made in the light of how effectively the barriers to socialist transformation can be removed. In a society where the peasant mode still prevails, it is inevitable that socialist transformation and modernization must refer to essentially the same problematic.

The limits of socialist planning

There is no Third World country which does not pride itself on having a plan for its development. In proportion to its popularity and the amount of money invested in it, no other policy tool has been as ineffective as planning.[36] Analysts have often blamed the failure of planning on the nature of the Third World economies, notably their dependence on the unpredictable world market. While this is obviously a factor of importance, the problems of planning, at least in Africa, go far beyond such a single-factor explanation.

One main constraint on development planning in Africa is the irrelevance of such efforts to the vast majority of the producers. They are not in a position where they are willing to, let alone capable of, responding to government targets or policy measures that presuppose their integration into the wider social economy. The peasant units of production are essentially independent of each other and there are few if any functional interdependencies that promote any understanding of collective action beyond what the local economy of affection may call for in case of emergency. In this situation, planning simply makes no sense. It is ineffectual as both a co-ordinating and mobilizing instrument. As Eugen Pusic has noted, conflict resolution can only be achieved by creating a hierarchical organization that uses power as its principal instrument:

> In its beginnings, power serves the all-important purpose of cheaply and simply reducing the almost unbearable uncertainty stemming from man's social environment. It is difficult to see how the basic integration of small groups into larger societies, indispensable for progress of any kind, could otherwise have been achieved.[37]

Wherever the productive forces are at a low level of development, there is no other way to resolve social conflicts developing within larger social aggregates than to resort to power. This is why in the political market-place in Africa, governments are bound to approach the peasants in the context of a zero-sum game. In addition, the organic environment of peasant society does not easily lend itself to planning. It is not malleable in a manner that development planning presupposes. Furthermore, peasants are not anxious to express their view because by doing so they get drawn into a political process in which they will have difficulty in defending their autonomy. Participation in government policy-making is rarely seen by the peasants as an advantage. Efforts to involve peasants in development planning are likely to produce very limited results. It serves symbolic rather than substantive purposes. Virtually the only place in which development plans are taken seriously is in the international aid arena. Donors still insist, for their own managerial purposes, that recipient governments produce plans which can be used to justify specific aid allocations.

This is not to imply that the planning exercise is unimportant. To the extent that planning is used to manipulate and time future prospects to secure needed present behaviour, it is part of the art of government. Where political leaders cannot resort to the notion that 'the struggle continues', and present sacrifices are seen in exchange for future gains, development planning is called upon to perform that function. This is so particularly in countries committed to a socialist form of development. Planning goals, therefore, are used more as incentives or carrots rather than as realistic predictions. As part of the art of government in Third World countries, the use of planning goals, rather than the method of planning, is important. The use of prospects of the future as inducement or balm in securing present obedience, co-operation or sacrifice is the most effective way of reducing the most adverse effects of the political zero-sum game. It is no coincidence that planning goals have been given much more prominence than planning methods in Africa. Operating in pre-modern social environments, the political use of planning by government leaders has mainly been to hold out the prospect of a future terminal date for the present wretchedness.[38]

To expect planning to be an important *economic* development tool in the context of the African economies is illusory. African leaders are quite rational in not taking it too seriously. Experience has shown that where development planning is taken seriously, it creates new barriers to development. Plans do not create development, as Colin Leys has stressed in his analysis of planning.[39] Nor can development be stage-managed, as an African with long inside experience notes:

> In short, development cannot be planned. One can provide the incentives but many of the activities of men who are at the centre of development elude rational planning. At least, it is necessary to accept that planning is not the answer to everything. Many of the plans emerging from the Third World seem to give the opposite impression. True development is not rationalist in character. It occurs through consistent efforts of individuals and peoples trying, modifying, testing, discarding and replacing. The development process occurs in the midst of waste and inefficiency but the trend is always upward and always finding new levels after each change has worked itself out.[40]

If creativity is an essential part of development, socialist governments in Africa are well advised not to pursue an approach which assumes that by planning they can achieve greater control of the process of change. The fragmented nature of the pre-socialist economies in Africa inevitably turns planning into a fictional exercise. Solutions to most of Africa's problems of underdevelopment do not lie where there is already light, in the modern economy which lends itself to some degree of manipulation, but in the peasant mode of production, where a plunge into darkness is the only available option. Development, at least in the African context, is as much a matter of breaking new ground as it is handling already known resources in an optimal manner.

Peasants and development

This chapter has essentially pointed to the difficulties of getting at the African peasantry. The purpose of this discussion has been to place the development debate in a better perspective. Our conception of development has been derived from an inorganic environment in which it is possible to manipulate variables in a cause-and-effect manner in order to achieve developmental results. Much of this discussion has taken place outside the premises of the organic environment of the peasant mode. The social logic that characterizes the latter has been ignored or simply impossible to incorporate into our policy discussions. It is time it was recognized that there is a fundamental contradiction between the modern development logic, and the social logic of the peasant mode. Problems of rural development go much deeper than simply poor implementation or lack of incentives.

It may be necessary to restate that the problem, in my view, is not that peasants are uninterested in development. The problem is that (*a*) they are interested only in those aspects of development that cost money – that is, policies aimed at facilitating social reproduction – and much less so in policies that change the parameters of the peasant mode; and (*b*) the pace at which they are prepared to transform their means of production is too slow in relation to the macro-development needs of the economy at large. The point of this study is that the peasants still have an influence on the terms of development. In analysing development in Africa this factor cannot be ignored. The rulers and the peasants talk past each other, and they operate with totally different time perspectives. In this situation, it is understandable if the development equation is often reduced to a zero-sum game. As this study has shown, the winners of these games are by no means always the rulers. The African peasant is hardly a hero in the light of current development thinking, but by using his deceptive skills he has often defeated the authorities.

The development challenge of the African regimes is heavier than anywhere else in the world, particularly because of the limitations in the agricultural sector. In this light it seems impossible to conceive of development of these economies without rapid diversification and dependence on imported capital and technical expertise. The degree of this dependence will stand in inverted relationship to the degree of agricultural development that can be achieved. In other words, development in a direction towards greater national self-reliance is improbable without a successful subordination of the peasantry to the demands of the ruling classes, whether they are identified as 'petty-bourgeois' or 'revolutionary'. The latter can only reduce their dependence on the metropolitan bourgeoisie by forcing the peasants into more effective relations of dependence. Such is the development logic in contemporary Africa. Nobody ought to be surprised if the peasants object to the logic of this process.

Both the metropolitan bourgeoisie, and more recently the African petty-bourgeoisie, have worked hard to subdue the peasantry. Their policy instruments have had difficulties in penetrating the peasant mode. While it has been relatively easy to introduce new crops as long as they do not interfere with the existing farming systems in a fundamental manner, and while it has been possible to increase agricultural production through new acreages, it has been considerably more difficult to improve techniques and encourage a modern form of agriculture using inputs from other sectors. Thus much control over the variables that determine agricultural output has remained within the mode of peasant production.

There are many real constraints in African agricultural development. The conventional policy instruments, such as price incentives, will work, but only within the confines imposed by the peasant mode. Only those who are freed from the constraints of the peasant mode will be the real beneficiaries of the pricing policies. As long as the peasants remain outside effective control of the authorities, their only means of attracting peasant interest in issues related to the development of the means of production are twofold. The first is the provision of reliable services by the various organs that are necessary to serve modern agriculture. (That is why the issues discussed in Chapter 6 are important.) The second means is to approach the peasant as a consumer and not only as a producer. The peasant can be indirectly encouraged to increase productivity, at least be pressed to do so of his own volition, if he has a range of consumer and capital goods that appeal to his needs. These two means are in fact preconditions for the successful applications of any other policy instruments available in the economic market.

Conclusions

We still have to wake up to the true realities of development in Africa. The writings on the subject are still characterized by wishful thinking; by images that bear little relationship to the social realities of the African continent. What the socialist writers who claim special expertise in analysing the political economy must face up to is that the roots of Africa's underdevelopment are not found in the international system, but in the rural areas of that continent. The success of the pre-modern social formations in holding capitalism at bay means that the historical forces which in other parts of the world have facilitated the transition to socialism have not yet been set in motion in Africa. The argument of this chapter has been that socialism will increasingly be called upon to substitute capitalism in trying to achieve that objective – that is, to serve as the main agent of modernization.

While obviously changes in the international economic system could be important for the development of Africa, such changes are only secondary. Without a transformation of the peasant mode of production, benefits accruing from structural changes in the world economy will have little impact on the African economies. The peasant mode will continue to serve as an effective barrier to socialist transformation in Africa even if these countries were part of a socialist world economy. Moreover, the international system is a policy variable over which African countries in the foreseeable future are likely to have very little control, even if it is more strongly influenced by socialist countries.

While most African governments do not have much control of the peasantry, the opportunities for an increase of such control are far greater than any policy control that these governments can expect to have over the international economy. The gains are also potentially much greater. This means, however, that African governments, and particularly those which adopt a socialist approach, will have to face up to the unpleasant and controversial issues that transformation of the peasant mode implies. Development is not only a matter of capital accumulation. The latter will not be achieved unless the socialists address themselves to the issues of modernization – the problems of achieving changes in values and role perceptions which in turn may facilitate alternative forms of social action, organization and identity. The socialist cannot dodge the issues of modernization simply because they have earlier been carried by 'bourgeois' thinkers.

Socialists and liberals alike have to accept that development in Africa, let alone the race-conscious southern tip of the continent, is not going to be a matter of smooth and balanced progress along the lines of their favourite models. Development in Africa requires elements which these models do not contain. Above all, it requires creating the conditions for the articulation of class power in a way that the peasant mode now forbids. Regardless of whether analysts subsume this under the concept of socialist transformation or not, it is, in the African context, a precondition for bringing into being a new set of relations of production through revolutionary struggle – the conventional Marxist definition of what constitutes socialism. It is in this important respect that the conventional Marxist paradigm has to be transcended in the study of Africa.

We all have to prepare ourselves for the fact that development, while being pursued in Africa increasingly with socialist rather than capitalist tools, will be a risky venture with contradictions and irrationalities which cannot be analysed with the help of rationally deductive theories. Vulnerability, arbitrariness and domination, as Goulet has noted, will all enter into the development equation.[41] Even the most carefully prepared strategy is bound to be filled with unforeseeable consequences. In the words of the French writer, Jacques Austruy, development is a scandal: a shockingly ambiguous admixture of goods and evils, a truly dialectical process.[42] Most people in the world, and notably those in the industrial countries, have no way of escaping its consequences, anticipated or unanticipated. By comparison, the African peasants are fortunate: they constitute the only social class with power to ignore the modern development process and its insistent demands on man. If they show reluctance towards socialist modernization measures, there is no reason to be surprised. Whether the modernizer is capitalist or socialist his task is to impose his *nature artificielle;* to capture everybody in social relations that negate the values of which the peasant mode is the only guarantor. As long as peasants in Africa are able to enjoy the power of small, it can never become beautiful to its rulers.

References and notes

1. Guy Hunter, *Modernizing Peasant Societies* (Oxford University Press, 1969), p. 231.
2. James C. Scott, *The Moral Economy of the Peasant: Rebellion and Subsistence in Southeast Asia* (New Haven: Yale University Press, 1976), p. 32.
3. Goran Hyden, *Political Development in Rural Tanzania: A West Lake Study* (Nairobi: East African Publishing House, 1969).
4. For a critique of these models, see Vernon Ruttan, 'Integrated rural development programs: a skeptical perspective', *International Development Review,* vol. 17, no. 4 (1975), pp. 392–418.
5. Jon R. Moris, 'The transferability of Western management concepts and programs: an East African perspective', in Joseph E. Black, James S. Coleman and Laurence D. Stifel (eds), *Education and Training for Public Sector Management in Developing Countries* (New York: Rockefeller Foundation, 1977).
6. Paul Devitt, 'Notes of poverty-oriented rural development', mimeo., Overseas Development Institute, London, 1977.
7. Thomas R. de Gregori, 'Caveat emptor: a critique of the emerging paradigm of public choice', *Administration and Society*, vol. 6, no. 2 (August 1974), pp. 205–28.
8. Denis Goulet, *The Uncertain Promise* (New York: IDOC/North America, 1977), p. 18.
9. For instance, see the work of Gordon Tullock and J. M. Buchanan, *The Calculus of Consent: Logical Foundations of Constitutional Democracy* (Ann Arbor: University of Michigan Press, 1962).

10. Hamza Alavi, 'Dependence, autonomy and the articulation of power', Working Paper No. 7, Centre for Developing-Area Studies, McGill University, Montreal, p. 13.
11. ibid., p. 14.
12. So fashionable is the notion of 'alternative development' that an American consultancy firm has made it its trade name: Development Alternatives Inc.
13. See, for instance its report, *What Now: Another Development* (Uppsala: Dag Hammarskjöld Foundation, 1975).
14. Wahidul Haque, Niranjan Mehta, Anisur Rahman and Ponna Wignaraja, 'Towards a theory of rural development', *Development Dialogue*, no. 2 (1977).
15. Denis Goulet, *The Cruel Choice* (New York: Atheneum, 1973), p. 25.
16. Paulo Freire, *The Pedagogy of the Oppressed* (New York: Herder & Herder, 1970).
17. E. F. Schumacher, *Small is Beautiful: Economics as if People Mattered* (New York: Harper & Row, 1973).
18. Thomas R. de Gregori, 'Technology for development: a definition of appropriateness', mimeo., University of Houston, Houston, n.d., p. 9.
19. Peter Aaby, 'The State of Guinea-Bissau: African socialism or socialism in Africa?', Research Report no. 45, Scandinavian Institute of African Studies, Uppsala 1978, p. 21.
20. Karl Marx, *Capital,* Volume 1 (New York: International Publishers, 1967), p. 737.
21. Max Weber, *The Protestant Ethic and the Spirit of Capitalism* (New York: Charles Scribner's Sons, 1958), p. 62.
22. Reinhard Bendix, *Work and Authority in Industry* (New York: Harper & Row, 1963).
23. Norman Long and David Winder, 'From peasant community to production cooperative: an analysis of recent government policy in Peru', *Journal of Development Studies,* vol. 12, no. 1 (1975), pp. 75–94.
24. See for instance, Ranon Weitz, *From Peasant to Farmer: A Revolutionary Strategy for Development* (New York: Columbia University Press, 1971).
25. Barrington Moore Jr., *The Social Origins of Dictatorship and Democracy: Lord and Peasant in the Making of the Modern World* (Boston: Beacon Press, 1966).
26. David K. Leonard, *Reaching the Peasant Farmer* (Chicago: Chicago University Press, 1977), p. 257.
27. Frank Holmquist, 'Implementing rural development', in Goran Hyden, Robert H. Jackson and John J. Okumu (eds) *Development Administration: The Kenya Experience* (Nairobi: Oxford University Press, 1970).
28. For a review of the development administration literature, see Bernard B. Schaffer, 'The deadlock of development administration', in Colin Leys (ed.), *Politics and Change in Developing Countries* (Cambridge University Press, 1969).
29. Joel Samoff, 'Class, class conflict, and the state: notes on the political economy of Africa', paper presented to the Joint Meeting of the African Studies and Latin American Studies Associations, Houston, November 1977, p. 28.
30. This term has been used by, for example, Issa Shivji, *Class Struggles in Tanzania* (Heinemann Educational Books, 1976).

31. ibid.
32. Claude Meillassoux, 'A class analysis of the bureaucratic process in Mali', *The Journal of Development Studies*, vol. 6, no. 2 (1970), pp. 91–110.
33. S. Salum, 'The Tanzanian state: a critique', *Monthly Review*, vol. 28, no. 8 (1977), pp. 51–60.
34. Michael Lipton, *Why Poor People Stay Poor* (Temple Smith, 1977), pp. 107–8.
35. Aaby, op. cit., p. 31.
36. For a critique of planning as applied in the context of development, see Colin Leys, 'The analysis of planning', in Colin Leys, op. cit.
37. Eugen Pusic, 'Power, planning, development', *Development and Change*, vol. 1, no. 1 (1969), p. 27.
38. For a discussion of the use and abuse of planning, see Edwin A. Bock, 'The last colonialism? Governmental problems arising from the use and abuse of the future', Comparative Administrative Group Occasional Paper, Indiana University, Bloomington, 1967.
39. Leys, op cit.
40. C. C. Onyemelukwe, *Economic Underdevelopment: An Inside View* (Longman, 1974), p. 85.
41. Goulet, 'The cruel choice', op. cit., p. 108.
42. Jacques Austruy, *Le Scandale du Développement* (Paris: Marcel Riviere, 1965).

CHAPTER 9

Why small remains unexplored: the inadequacy of prevailing paradigms

This book has been written to show that the roots of underdevelopment in Africa lie in the peasant mode of production. The key to development lies in changes in modes of production rather than in changes in exchange relations. By holding the barricades against capitalist penetration the peasant mode has saved the many small rural producers in Africa from the type of proletarianization that characterizes the peasantry elsewhere in the Third World. At the same time, however, the resistance, and resilience, of the peasant mode means that there is a very limited indigenous base for the development of a modern economy, capitalist or socialist. This is why the international dimension of Africa's development efforts has become important. The petty-bourgeoisie in Africa needs the support of foreign capital and foreign aid as long as the barriers of the peasant mode do not give way. This foreign dependence is not just induced because the ruling classes in Africa are bourgeois, or willing to serve as an 'auxiliary' to the international bourgeoisie. It is the product of a *force majeure*: the ability of the countless number of small peasants to ignore the modern development demands placed on them by those controlling the state. The powers of the small have proved a formidable challenge not only to modernization efforts which follow conventional neo-colonial lines, but also those which have been inspired by a socialist ideology.

There is little room in prevailing development paradigms or models for the notion that small is powerful. The inorganic environment of modern society does not carry such implications, and we have an almost total immunity to that conception. This chapter is meant to show that this immunity prevents us from really understanding and assisting in the effort to overcome underdevelopment in Africa. First it will discuss how we have become captives of certain intellectual paradigms and then take up the issue of what the intellectual in Africa can do in order to live up to his social responsibilities.

The growth of a *nature artificielle*

In order to understand the dilemma which this book deals with it is necessary to take a brief look at our intellectual history: the story of the creation of an inorganic environment – the growth of a *nature artificielle*. This is a world in which science, technology and rationalized economy prevails. Modern man takes this environment for granted. To him it symbolizes development. The *prevalence* of an inorganic environment, however, is a relatively recent phenomenon, and it is not totally dominant, not even in modern society. Magic and religion which used to be employed to explain man's predicament are still with us. None the less, in the industrialized world today, the scientific method, derived from the Western conception of reason, guides our mental schemes, thus building, as one observer notes,[1] 'a cumulative fabric of knowledge whose weft are abstract concepts and whose warp are empirical observations.' The pursuit of science, being the organized, continuous and self-correcting process of knowledge generation, lies behind the progress of both productive and social activities in the contemporary world. It is the main driving force for development. The emergence of scientific and technological capabilities in the West is reflected in the evolution of ideas that led to science, the successive transformation of production techniques, and the merging of these two currents.

The beginnings of Western thought were the efforts by the pre-Socratic philosophers who tried to evolve abstractions of the world surrounding them. These were followed by Plato's contribution towards the conceptualization of ideals and Aristotle's equally important work to formalize logic and scientific methods. By building and relating concepts abstracted from reality the inorganic environment of mankind began to take shape. Very little was added to these initial efforts by Greek philosophers during the time of the Roman Empire and the Middle Ages. Only towards the end of the latter did something important and new happen: the development of schemes for manipulating concepts and symbols, notably algebra. These skills had already been developed in the Arab world and were now borrowed for use in the development of Western science. The new methods encouraged a return to a closer examination of natural phenomena.

Copernicus and Galileo made discoveries about the celestial order that paved the way for the triumph of reason over dogma. Their discoveries, perhaps more than anything else, mark the transition from religion to science as a means of explaining natural phenomena. Their work was followed by Bacon who contributed the idea that man can master and control nature through understanding and Newton who argued that the universe is predictable and obeys certain laws which can be known and tested.

These discoveries, however, might never have been quite so in-

Generative link between science + production

fluential had it not been for the parallel development of techniques used in productive activities. At the time of the Renaissance, a cumulative evolution of the artisan crafts was gradually transformed into manufacturing activities, and less than two hundred years later, to industrial activities proper. The emergence of large-scale industry in the seventeenth and eighteenth century was signalled by a relentless shift from a polytechnic era, characterized by local technological responses to specific environmental conditions, towards a monotechnic era in which the variety of responses is reduced and instead a few specific production technologies begin to prevail in each field of activity.[2]

The industrial revolution that occurred in the eighteenth century in Europe was the product of both currents: the evolution of scientific thinking and the evolution of new technologies. Science and productive techniques began to condition each other. This was a long process that saw craftsmen and manufacturers making a relatively greater contribution in its first stage, for example, by creating new instruments for experimentation. In its second stage during the nineteenth century scientists became relatively more important. Findings related to mechanics, chemistry, optics, thermo-dynamics and other areas of knowledge now became the most important contributions. Particularly important was the emergence of the electric and chemical industries. Since then the contribution of science to production has grown at an accelerated pace. The closer relations between science and production took place at the same time as techniques of lower efficiency were being abandoned, often in accordance with capitalist economic criteria.

This is a very brief sketch of a complex historical process; there is no room to tell the full story here. For the purpose of this study, however, it is important to acknowledge the generative link between science and production. The attempts to create an inorganic environment, in which man and matter could be manipulated to suit 'higher ends', did not remain confined to the cultural superstructure alone. They were linked with the productive activities in society in such a way that the development of science and technology became an end in itself. Generating knowledge in an organized and cumulative manner was no longer just a matter for a few individuals. By contrast, that activity has in the course of this century increasingly become a key determinant of the development of individual societies. Consequently, the pursuit of science is currently undertaken by fully fledged scientific communities granted generous facilities. Scientists have become scarce resources that countries try to retain at often very high prices. Sagasti makes the following observation about the scientific community:

> This community acquired legitimacy not only because of the increasingly coherent explanations it gave to natural and, to a lesser extent, social phenomena, but mainly because it demonstrated its usefulness for the development of production tech-

Supported directed by religion

niques, a usefulness anticipated by Bacon in the early 17th century when he stated that knowledge in itself is the source of power.[3]

The marriage between scientific and productive activities also paved the way for a more general diffusion through society of the values and modes of thinking associated with the scientific technological revolution. The notion that it is possible to understand, predict and control the phenomena surrounding us, and that men are able to overcome the limitations imposed on them by nature and by other men, has greatly influenced the development of modern society. This stands in contrast to the situation in pre-modern societies, where man is still responding to the challenges of an organic environment without access to a scientific body of knowledge.

The inorganic environment is so much part of the industrialized world that we take it for granted. We are all absorbed by it; born into it, so to speak. Our models and paradigms of development all reflect this mode of thinking. Our social and economic environment can be planned, managed and transformed in a rational manner. If we take a policy initiative, a response is inevitable because we are all linked together in relations of production. The functional interdependencies of the system we have created around ourselves leave us no option but to respond to its own demands. As captives of the mode of thinking that characterizes an inorganic environment, we are insensitive to the challenge of the organic environment. In fact many of us are not even prepared to recognize that there is a fundamentally different social logic from that of our modern modes of production. Problems of development can be conceived only in the context of a capitalist or a socialist model. We forget that the structural premises on which many producers act in Third World countries are pre-modern. The manipulative or transformative potential is so limited in many of these countries that both capitalist and socialist theories, as conventionally conceived, have very little to offer towards a better understanding of the problems of underdevelopment in those environments. We presuppose a social reality that, at least in the context of Africa, has yet to be constructed. A closer examination of the bourgeois and Marxist development models may illustrate this better.

The rise of bourgeois positivism

The story of the capitalist or bourgeois development paradigm centres largely on the concept of 'rationality'; how it has been transformed by the scientific-technological revolution in the West. Only one century ago man was still engaged in creating the walls of our inorganic environment. Today he is a captive of that structure. He is only able to achieve incremental improvements.

Descartes who, like Bacon, believed that man could master his environment was an influential forbear of modern rationality, particularly as it applies to decision-making, problem-solving and management.[4] His argument was that man, unlike other species, can think – and think rationally – and thus in a voluntary fashion break out of a 'natural', predetermined order. By using his ability to reason he does not only find explanation of strange phenomena, but he increasingly liberates himself from the bonds that tie him to tradition and to nature. Man has the unique ability of impressing his will on history if, as a decision-maker, he employs and develops his gift to reason.

Three dimensions of the Cartesian concept of decision concern us here. The first is his linear conception of time. The act of deciding begins with the conception of a wish or a project and ends with its satisfactory realization. The decision is taken somewhere halfway between conception and satisfaction. The decision in the Cartesian scheme always originates from man. It is his subjective decision and it represents his will to break away from a predetermined order. As such it is an act of liberation but without a vision of a specific future. According to Descartes, the past is simply a succession of presents and the future does not really exist in any specific shape.

The second is its rational dimension. The notion of a straight line supposes some kind of continuity, an order of succession. In the Cartesian scheme, this order also denotes a chain of causes and effects. Human reason is behind action and thus rationality and causality is one and the same thing. The notion of a rational decision implies that all components from motivation to execution are clearly ordered so that one engenders the other in a logical manner.

The third dimension – the freedom of the actor – is in a way a precondition of the other two. Linearity and rationality in Descartes' view are only possible if man is perceived as capable of freeing himself from constraints. Man acts alone and is solely responsible for his acts, but his freedom is infinite in that his quest for knowledge has no limits. Because man is free, he is also able to conquer the forces of darkness and passion. He alone can break the determinism of external forces.

Homo politicus, in Descartes' sense, is the 'lone modernizer' who charts his way out of the organic environment. By reflecting on the nature of the latter he is able to lay the foundation for an inorganic environment: one in which man is master and captive at one and the same time. When Descartes was writing, it was still the unlimited potential of the application of human reason that was most striking. The 'Prometheus unbound' mentality also survived into this century, albeit in modified forms. It resurfaces, for instance, in the notion of *homo oeconomicus:* the completely informed, infinitely perceptive and rational individual who is able to conceive all possible courses of action and even anticipate their consequences; who can perceive the variations in his environment in such a way as to obtain maximum utility. In the modern planning literature, economic man appears as the guarantor of correct choice.[5]

Another caricature of the same 'hyper-rationalist' model of man is Frederick Taylor's 'scientific manager'. He is free from the constraints that limit the creativity and capacity of other men. He is capable of finding 'the best way', albeit, in Taylor's case, not through deductive logic but through experimentation.[6] By thinking about business rather than just doing business, the manager can develop it according to his own wishes and overcome the hurdles of running complex organizations. Man – or at least manager – is above organization.

The model of planning was the product of deductive logic while scientific management stemmed from the advancement of production techniques. These two approaches show how the symbiosis between science and production influences the mode of thinking also in the social sciences.

The classical conceptions of planning and management, however, have both been overtaken by events. The advancement of man's inorganic environment has reached such a stage that it is too complex to be comprehended, let alone manipulated, through the use of one single model. Most contemporary writers on planning and management start from the assumption that man is subordinated to the system he has created for himself. Rationality is no longer unbound; it has definite limitations. This is particularly evident in the literature on organizations and management. Herbert Simon, for instance, stresses that while man is rational, his rationality is confined by a variety of factors that characterize modern society.[7] The complexity of many variables that go into decision-making in modern organizations is often so great that individual contributions to decision-making can only be incidental or incremental. Modern man has not really learnt the true lessons of the changes that have forced him into a cog-in-machine-like situation. Instead of realizing that he rides on the tide of progress without being able to have any fundamental influence on its course, he continues to insist on identifying rational causes of human action even where they do not apply. Man, however, is no longer in the driver's seat. Individual actors do not really matter. Above all, individual rationalities are submerged in a macro-rationality that requires its own explanation.

This is why the pluralist conception of power, as illustrated for instance in Robert Dahl's work, has definite limitations.[8] Focusing attention only on the articulation of power in the context of conflict over manifest issues, his study, and other similar studies, overlook the fact that the most effective and insidious use of power is to prevent such conflicts from arising in the first place. Human perceptions, cognitions and preferences have already been shaped by the system to such an extent that man does not question them.[9] He does not realize the narrow premises of his choice and credits himself with more power than he really has. In other words, man in modern society labours under great illusions about his freedom and power to influence the course of events.[10] Moreover, people in developed countries have surrendered themselves to the dynamisms and determinisms of the scientific-technological revolution to such an extent that not only are they insensitive to pre-modern values but also to the structures that keep these alive. Their preoccupation is with the inorganic environment in which answers to questions can be sought through scientific investigations, and the effects of solutions to specific problems measured. As David Schuman notes about modern society:

> Rationality is the tinkering with the 'machine' in order to get a greater output from it. Being 'rational' will require as much standardization of parts of the machine as possible, so that functions can become more predictable, so that cause and effect may indeed occur, and so that there can be changes of parts if there is a malfunction.[11]

Our patterns of social interaction, our language and other cultural expressions tend to be subordinated to, and certainly reflect, the hegemonic rationality of the 'machine'. Although man may turn his rationality against modern society and modern organization, as for instance Crozier shows, such cultural 'obstruction' does not prevent the modern 'machine' from having its way.[12] We all remain part of a society in which self-reification of men under categories of purposive-rational action and adaptive behaviour is the predominant exercise, as Habermas, among others, has noted.[13]

The multiple rationalities that we proudly associate with modern, pluralist society are firmly anchored in its economic base. With the institutionalization of scientific-technical progress in modern society, there is virtually no choice but to do business within the system. Human existence is not possible in isolation of the system. Man's freedom and power, like his rationality, are all system derivatives. They are determined for him by forces beyond his control.

Bourgeois positivism has increasingly come under criticism as ethically wrong and politically dangerous. There are those who argue that in a world of shrinking natural resources, it is wrong to pursue relentlessly the expansion of the capitalist economy. It is an economy which consumes large quantities of organic energy. Less and less of it is left for industrializing 'latecomers'. The underdeveloped countries will have no choice but to bank on the ability of the industrialized world to produce inorganic energy and material to support future generations. This implies a permanent dependence. The present world economy, however, is also a fragile creation, as we have witnessed especially in recent years. Its operation is frightfully dependent on oil production. Bourgeois positivism, therefore, if pursued too uncritically, is politically dangerous.

Yet the major weakness of such positivism is its inability to conceive the world outside the system, or rather the possibility that there exists a world that does not lend itself to positivist interventions. It is this shortcoming that reduces the validity of this approach in the context of African development problems. Where agriculture is resource-based and the market economy incapable of creating the conditions for development of the means of production, 'tinkering with the machine' is a far-fetched conception of the problem. There is little room for effective management, for constructive manipulation in the interest of a larger system. The relative autonomy of the many small units of production makes them difficult to get at through the use of a systems approach to development. Thus bourgeois positivism has its definite limitations in the context of African development, not only as an instrument of development but also as a conceptual framework for understanding how these societies operate.

The Marxist 'alternative'

As Shanin has emphasized, the peasantry is the social phenomenon in which the Marxist tradition of class analysis meets the main conceptual dichotomy of non-Marxist sociological thinking like that of Tonnies and Durkheim.[14] There have been few constructive exchanges between these two approaches. One reason may be that in all societies that Marx and Engels were able to study, directly or indirectly, the peasantry had already been subordinated to the demands of other social classes. Such was the situation in Europe, Asia and the Americas. Africa never entered into Marx' writings. It remained an empty spot on his map of knowledge. Had he been able to extend his studies to sub-Saharan Africa, subsequent conceptions of the peasantry by Marxists may well have been different from what it is today. After all, Marx' theories were all deduced from his own experience of the contemporary world. The importance of Marxism does not stem from its presumed possession of historical truths but from Marx' powerful methods of analysis of social realities. It is a great pity, therefore, that the problem of an uncaptured peasantry has been ignored by Marxist writers. Instead they have tried to incorporate the peasantry into their scheme of analysis, even in those cases where it is a priori highly doubtful that the dependence, as opposed to the autonomy of the peasantry, is the most important dimension of its social position. For polemical reasons they' have usually allowed themselves to become captives of their own paradigm to such an extent that they have become insensitive to the existence of historically anomalous cases. Polemics alone, however, does not explain the inability of Marxists to capture the essence of the problem of underdevelopment in Africa. A brief look at the epistemological foundations of Marx' own theories may be necessary in order to understand why the Marxist method has not been used more imaginatively in the study of Africa.

The first thing to remember about Marxism is that it reflects the prevailing conceptions of Western Europe at a time when the foundation of modern society had already been laid. It is no coincidence that Marx, and subsequently Marxist writers in their discussion of socialism and socialist transformation, implicitly accept a model of man that is the product of capitalist relations of production. In fact, the only way by which Marx could effectively argue his case of historical materialism was to assume the capacity of capitalism to complete its historical cause: to erase all traces of pre-modern social formations by achieving an accelerated transformation of the means of production. Marx expected that socialism at least in one respect, would build on the achievements of capitalism: the scientific-technological development that had been accelerated under capitalism was equally essential to socialism.

In spite of the significant differences that exist between capitalism and socialism, they start from a common foundation. Advocates of both operate with a 'universal' model of man which is derived from an inorganic environment. Socialism, according to Marx, is possible because man has been left with no choice but to take history in his own hands. Only by mastering nature and history can man realize his mission of creating a society that is good, not just to the few but to the many. The scientific method is as important to the socialist as it is to the capitalist. It is no coincidence that Marx and Engels wished to label their form of socialism 'scientific'.

Because of polemic and a rather uncritical belief in the significance of 'dialectical materialism', the epistemological similarities between bourgeois and Marxist social science have usually been overlooked. Dialectical materialism is only one variation of the conventional Western reasoning. At least from a non-Western perspective, that method has a lot in common with linear programming and other bourgeois devices for manipulating the human environment. The notion of 'synthesis', for instance, rather than offering a solution to the problems inherent in the unilinear causality that is typical of Western thought, only turns it into a vicious circle of reasoning to which there is no response but mythical irrationalism.

The misleading assumption in the Marxist scheme is that the social alienation of man was exclusively the product of capitalism and not the product of scientific and technological developments. Marx and Engels were both ready to give the bourgeoisie credit as the first social class in world history to have developed a mode of production in which self-sustained growth is institutionalized. This observation is illustrated by the fact that before the seventeenth century, when bourgeois power first began to manifest itself, no major social system had been able to produce annual per capita incomes above a maximum of two hundred US dollars.[15] By their rapid development of the forces of production, the capitalists actively subjected nature to human control and thus forced the institutional framework of society into passive adaptation. In previous modes of production the trend had been the reverse: the institutional framework was the active force, the forces of production the passively adaptable. In the pre-modern, polytechnic era, production techniques never really threatened the institutional framework of society. Technological innovations and organizational improvements could be accommodated within the institutional framework of such societies without calling its legitimacy into question. With capitalism this was dramatically reversed. The industrial system promoted by capitalism is freed from its institutional framework and thus can be connected with institutional mechanisms other than that of the utilization of private capital. On the basis of this observation, Marx argues that a further refinement of the forces of production is possible without leading to the same type of social alienation found under capitalism.

The assumption that the industrial system developed by capitalism can be freed from its institutional framework is essential to the Marxist argument about the possibilities of socialism. It is quite understandable that Marx and Engels, writing as they did at a time when science and technology really began to have a dramatic impact on the living standards of people, were quite optimistic about their potential for human liberation. As Acton points out, both Marx and Engels carried strong positivist inclinations which they usually were able to hide behind polemics.[16]

Their positivism was evident, as indicated above, in their use of dialectical materialism, and more specifically the concept of the 'negation of the negative totality' of capitalism, as Marcuse calls it.[17] This negative totality is the all-embracing system that capitalism builds around itself to legitimize the perpetuation of its exploitation of man. The essence of this totality is the constant reduction of concrete to abstract labour. In capitalism there is no room for the subsistence farmer: the means of subsistence must be developed and production made more efficient. Nor is there room for the appropriation of the labour product in its natural form, as is the case in feudal societies. Under capitalism, through the ingenious use of the market, such appropriation is achieved in disguise by the payment of wages. Thus the distinction between necessary labour and surplus labour – which accrues to the capitalist – is hidden. Concealed too is the fact that one class, the working class, labours under the commands of another, the bourgeoisie.

The point that Marx and Engels make here is that the cultural superstructure is an overlay that clouds the real issues in capitalist society. A precondition for the overhaul of the capitalist structure – for the negation of the negative totality of capitalism – is the articulation of these issues through class struggle. The given state of affairs is negative and can only be rendered positive by liberating the possibilities within it. A new order of things, according to Marx and Engels, is necessary. This new state is the truth of the old – that is, it contains the true achievements of capitalism. That truth, however, does not grow steadily and automatically out of the earlier state of affairs. It can only be set free by autonomous acts on the part of men who understand what to save and what to destroy in the system created by capitalism. The transition from capitalism to socialism, therefore, is not an automatic process. There is no trace of inevitability in Marx' concept of this final process, since it is impossible without the autonomous acts of men. Although Marx states in *Capital* that 'capitalist production begets, with the inexorability of a law of nature, its own negation', these inexorable forces which govern the development of capitalism do not apply to the transformation to socialism.[18] These laws only prescribe certain types of action. Whether these laws will be translated into social action, however, depends on the willingness and ability of men to take history in their own hands.

Building socialism requires people who have already been modernized: whose mental scheme is not religious but scientific; whose social position makes them accessible to alternative forms of social and political action. In its conception of man as rational-purposive and socially adaptable, socialism shares its model with capitalism. It must be pointed out, however, that the task that socialists have set themselves is far more difficult than that of the capitalists. In the capitalist system, the market forces provide a free ride through history, so to speak. Men do not realize the speed with which their system is moving forward. They are captured by its own mechanics and do not realize its limitations until it has a breakdown. In a truly socialist system, by contrast, there is no room for a free ride. To be sure, there is the revolution, but its function is only to serve as a springboard. After the jump-off, socialist men are expected to create, by using science and technology, a new vehicle that ensures a different type of human progress than that of capitalism. Not only is this a very demanding exercise; it is also fraught with the dangers of positivist rationality. As Rigby points out, the bourgeois model postulates that 'positivism' becomes positive social praxis by autonomous human acts within the framework of the existing system, while the Marxist model assumes that similarly autonomous human acts can turn 'negative totality' into a positive one.[19] Both presuppose human ability to change things and extract more out of nature, to mobilize efforts so that greater results are achieved. Historical rationality, the notion that there is a conscious human act, individual or collective, behind every social change, prevails in the mind of all modern men because its elements, as Goulet underlines,[20] are amenable to direct observation and manipulation. Other realms of cognition are ignored because they rest on myths or religion and perpetuate 'false consciousness'. Socialism, like capitalism, presupposes an inorganic environment: one in which man can feel a sense of mastery but where there is at the same time a real danger that he creates a structure in which he becomes his own prisoner. The inclination among socialist policy-makers to prove the superiority of their own system certainly reinforces this danger. The Soviet and East European experience, and more recently the political and economic changes in China, indicate that in their effort to achieve this objective, socialist policy-makers are not unwilling to depend on the market forces to accelerate the growth potential of their own systems. Revolutionary struggle lends itself well to the task of undoing things, but it is more difficult to use as an instrument to build and reinforce existing systems.

The limits of the Marxist paradigm

I have tried to show that the Marxist alternative to the bourgeois model of development is different only in a limited sense of the word. It takes historical progress for granted by assuming that capitalism has performed the task of liberating men from their pre-capitalist bonds. To Marxists, by and large, the peasantry has been theoretically uninteresting. Engels' verdict that 'the peasant has so far largely manifested himself as a factor of political power only by his apathy' has resurfaced in the political economy literature many times since.[21] Unlike Maoists, Marxists have seen the peasantry as reactionary and they have generally expected capitalism to carry out the dirty work of polarizing them and alienating them from their means of production.

This view is also prevalent in the contemporary debate about the peasantry in the Third World. Although Marxist writers may differ in terms of how far they see capitalist relations of production as predominant in underdeveloped economies, there is a general agreement that the main blockages to the development of these 'peripheral' economies lie within the capitalist mode of production. Gunder Frank stresses the appropriation of surplus capital and its transfer to the metropolitan economies as the key variable.[22] Others, like Laclau, quote relative shifts in the rate of productivity increases within the capitalist system as the major blockage to development of Third World economies.[23] Kay laments the impact of merchant capital and the absence of industrial capital in these economies.[24] While many of these points have particular relevance to the study of the Asian and Latin American economies, their significance in the study of the African political economy is by no means self-evident. As a recent survey of Marxist perspectives on the Middle East notes: since Marx and Engels were primarily concerned with the theoretical analysis of the capitalist mode of production in order to understand the capitalist societies of Europe, the relevance of their theoretical work for the analysis of other modes of production cannot be taken for granted.[25] The work of conceptualizing pre-capitalist modes of production other than feudalism and the Asiatic mode has only begun.[26] The limits of the Marxist paradigm when it comes to the study of societies in which pre-capitalist modes of production are still important must be acknowledged and attempts made to conceptualize the problematic of these societies in new terms. As this study has shown, in Africa where land is the predominant means of production but not yet a market commodity and where the means of subsistence are controlled by smallholder peasants rather than by the ruling classes, it is misleading to conceive the problems of underdevelopment as stemming merely from the operations of the capitalist mode. By ignoring the social logic of the peasant mode, its economy of affection and the social formations to which it gives rise, it is not easy to comprehend, led alone change, the social realities in Africa. In the same way as modern man is captured within the walls of the capitalist or socialist mode of production, the rural producer in Africa is a captive of the peasant mode. Its walls usually constitute the limits to what the peasant producers are capable of doing on their own. We must accept that the pre-capitalist social formations in Africa usually have a material base of their own, outside the capitalist mode of production. They are not merely parasitic adjuncts to the latter. Articulation of communal action, for instance, is dictated by the prevalence of the peasant mode. It cannot be disposed of as just 'deadly parochialism'. The structural conditons for the articulation of class conflicts are still to be laid in a large part of Africa. That is why the petty-bourgeoisie in Africa, whether it follows a neo-colonial or revolutionary path, will inevitably find itself in growing antagonism with the peasants. Such a conflict is a precondition for the development of these countries.

In the context of Africa, we are faced with the dilemma that while it is likely that the social realities on the continent will in the long run be bent to suit the idiosyncrasies of either the capitalist or the socialist model of development, the conceptualization of these models is found to be inadequate as a means to grasp the problems imposed by the prevalence of the peasant mode of production. We know our battle strategy on this side of the river but we do not yet know how to get the troops across the river. In Africa, the story of the lord and the peasant is still to be told because they have not as yet been brought together in antagonistic relations. Moore's analysis concerns peasants who have already been captured by other social classes. It focuses on how this conflict has been resolved in different social and historical contexts.[27] In Africa the story is different: it is about how to tackle an uncaptured peasantry; how to bring it more effectively into the confines of a modern mode of production. While East European Marxists are largely correct in labelling this process 'non-capitalist', it must be noted that neither are these historical conditions congenial to a socialist type of development.

In spite of the criticism that can be directed against many advocates of the Marxist scheme of analysis, there is little doubt that its fundamental components can be used in overcoming the gap that now characterizes our knowledge of Africa. The problems of underdevelopment on that continent can only be fully grasped in the context of a structural-processual type of analysis that Marxism offers. At the same time, however, it is clear that the credibility of Marxist analyses of Africa can hardly be retained without an effort to transcend the conventional boundaries of Marxism – those that are premised on the argument that capitalism is effectively predominant in the 'periphery' economies of the present world system. A call in the same direction has been made by Hutton and Cohen who in their critical review of sociological approaches to the study of the peasantry note:

> In the case of the Marxists the pre-capitalist economy has until recently not been an area of great theoretical interest, and concern has been with constructing typologies rather than with the analysis of the sort that Marx gave us for capitalist societies. Economic anthropologists have given pre-capitalist economies very detailed consideration, but their emphasis has tended to be on processes of distribution and exchange, rather than on production and changes in production.[28]

We cannot continue to assimilate new knowledge into conventional paradigms as if these were eternally and universally valid. New conceptualizations are necessary, particularly of the development problems caused by active, pre-capitalist modes of production. Without such a reorientation, we are likely to continue our efforts to change the world without really understanding it. With access only to superficial knowledge it is very easy for people to become cynical when faced with the gap between the defined reality and the actual situation. Such reactions are sometimes directed against specific countries, or incumbent regimes in these countries. The socialist leadership in Tanzania, for instance, has in recent years become the victim of many harsh and cynical comments by people who have been unwilling or unable to transcend the limits of conventional Marxist analysis. Instead of realizing that the Tanzanian regime, like all others in Africa, is faced with a structural dilemma that can only be understood by modifying the Marxist paradigm, they have used the latter to 'prove' that the petty-bourgeoisie in Tanzania has abandoned its effort to achieve a socialist transformation.

Cynical reactions, however, have more recently been directed against the Marxist paradigm itself. The 'New Philosophers' in France is the most important of these manifestations.[29] It is difficult to defend the Marxist scheme of analysis if it fails to produce knowledge that is really decisive in helping the progressive regimes in the Third World to overcome underdevelopment. While the social realities in Asia and Latin America are such that the Marxist paradigm can be used without any major modifications, the same can hardly be said of Africa. The structural anomalies in Africa require a re-examination of some basic assumptions underlying the Marxist model. After all, in that model, like in all other social science paradigms, the subjective biases of the analyst are among its key ingredients. There is no reason to apologize for this. We ought to acknowledge it more openly and degrade the 'objective' image of our work. This is not to say that we should abandon professional and scientific ambitions in our work. It is only to remind ourselves that the historical experience from which our predominant paradigms are derived, is not quite as universal as we are often inclined to believe. While social anthropologists have been in the forefront in pointing out this limitation to other social scientists, the latter have been slow in accepting its implication. This book is not written to 're-habilitate' social anthropology, which is vital enough to do without such a gesture. It is written, however, to show that the 'peasant society' tradition within social anthropology ought not to be a strange animal to political economists, particularly in Africa where the peasantry remains largely uncaptured but is still expected to play a key role in the development of the larger economies of that continent.

I am more than willing to admit that in this study I am bringing my own bias to bear on the analysis. By living and working in African societies for virtually the whole of my professional career I am bound to have been influenced by this social environment. I have registered here my conceptualizations of the social realities in Africa as developed through efforts not merely to empathize with the rationality of individual social actors but to understand the structures and processes that determine their actions. It is as a result of these efforts that I have become painfully aware of the great discrepancy that often exists between social reality as defined by our paradigms and social reality as actually experienced. To label this 'false consciousness' is to shy away from the real problem and the real challenge facing social scientists in Africa. Having decided not to do that, certain implications follow. These merit their own explanations.

Research, praxis and development

The social scientist in Western society works in a rather remote corner of our inorganic environment. Although philosophers once played an important role in the creation of this type of human environment, today's social scientists find themselves to be quite marginal to its further advancement. With the institutionalization of science, tech-nology and a rationalized economy, modern society has created its own engines. The problematization of our environment is no longer domin-ted by social scientists. We have been forced into a remote corner of our world, from which we have great difficulty in influencing the process of change. Our research is not easy to relate to problems actually experienced in society. Thus much of our work in Western societies has ended in a blind alley. The debate among social scientists has a scholastic orientation. It is characterized by a polemic that is subjective in the sense of not being related to the actual problems facing our society. This structural predicament affects scholars irrespective of ideological or theoretical orientation. The intellectual efforts to change this situation that followed in the wake of the 1968 student revolts met with great difficulties. These problems only serve to demonstrate how far removed from the social realities most social scientists are in the pursuit of their professional work. There is little room to combine theory and practice into a meaningful social or political praxis. Development goes on in Western societies largely irrespective of what social science researchers do. Such is, somewhat simplified, the predicament of social scientists in modern society.

One consequence of this situation has been that research is being evaluated almost exclusively on the basis of criteria internal to the academic community itself. Ability to handle research methods has been a more important criterion than, say, the extent to which research findings contribute to problem-solving. Conformity with the original logic of a given conceptual model has similarly been considered a manifestation of scholarly competence. While there is no need to question the importance of criteria like these, the problem is that they have been exclusively important, at the cost of the external criteria that can be applied in judging the value of social science research.

Against this background it is no surprise that in recent years much social science research has been initiated outside the walls of academic institutions. In the industrialized countries, there are many private institutions that conduct research on commission from government or private companies. This type of applied research is often linked up with consultancy and not seen as a contribution to academic discussions about theories and concepts. In fact, many of those who engage in commissioned research often scorn the 'theoretical' orientation of their academic colleagues. There is a gulf emerging between pure and applied forms of research.

This division is also evident in research on development and under-development problems in the Third World. Academic research on development is dominated by theoretical concerns. Although some of this debate may spill over into the general thinking about development, the distance is often very far to those who are engaged in executing development programmes. Hence, it is only understandable that many of them have begun to commission research which meets more closely their criteria of validity. In recent years, such research has been labelled 'action research', implying its close links with policy implementation.

The concerns of both pure and applied research are equally valid. It is unfortunate, however, that there is a tendency among their respective advocates to pull apart rather than to work together. Theoretical and practical concerns must be married to each other, particularly in the field of development research. In Africa, for instance, the position of the researcher is very different from that occupied by researchers in Western societies. The inorganic environment in Africa is still undeveloped. The organic environment is in need of exploration and transformation so as to allow a self-sustained development process. Development in Africa will remain an externally induced process as long as the domestic base has not been transformed in the direction towards greater flexibility. A precondition for a self-sustained development process is the generation of an endogenous body of knowledge derived from the local experience. In that respect, research is an important development tool. The researcher has a special social responsibility in this situation. He cannot escape judgement on the issue of how far his work contributes to the task of initiating a self-sustained process of development. In performing this task he must be in a position to combine theory and practice into a meaningful social and political praxis. Although efforts have been made to grapple with this issue, the social science community in Africa still has a long way to go in igniting the sparks that generate an endogenous body of knowledge and thus indirectly promote a self-sustained development process.

The government of Tanzania, in collaboration with the academic community in that country, has been concerned about this issue of how to combine theory and practice. After long discussions it has now been agreed that, in addition to students being required to serve a minimum of two years in practical work prior to gaining entry to the university, all students are to be assessed on practical work that they are required to pursue as part of their academic studies.[30] This is an important step towards making people more sensitive to the relevance and validity of academic concepts and theories to local development problems. If properly pursued this scheme can serve as an important step towards the generation of an endogenous body of knowledge. It is only a first step, however – one that requires complementary measures.

The first of these is the promotion of a critical reflection on the confrontation between theory and practice. Social scientists have a special responsibility in taking a critical look at how practical tasks can be improved in the light of theoretical insights, and theories modified and developed in the light of practical applications. Two decades after gaining political independence most African countries have acquired an impressive experience of tackling development problems. The intellectual insights of this experience, however, still remain to be tapped. While African regimes have been right in looking forward and away from the colonial experience, they stand increasingly to gain from looking back on their own experience. They must draw lessons from it, irrespective of whether the experience has been positive or negative. An important dimension of development is the ability to incorporate the lessons of the past in such a way as to increase the ability to stand on one's own feet. The intellectual has a special duty in promoting this type of feedback: to dig up the essence of previous development efforts and turn it into useful information for future work of a similar kind.

Without the generation of such insights, it is difficult to see how the African regimes can mitigate neo-colonial dependencies. This task is both difficult and sensitive since it often implies digging up information that may be interpreted by the incumbent political leaders as inconvenient. Yet a meaningful strategy towards combining theory with practice must involve not only the promotion of manual skills among a group of intellectuals but also the generation of more useful conceptual skills among the population at large. Dirty hands are not a substitute for critical minds. The social and political praxis that the social science intellectuals can contribute to making must include a wish and ability to reflect critically on experience.

It is not an exaggeration to say that social science research in Africa so far has made only a small contribution in that direction. One obvious reason for this is that such research has been dominated by expatriates who generally lack the opportunity to become part of the circles in which development strategies and policies are discussed and hammered out. Many foreign researchers, however, have not even considered this issue and have confined their work to the academic community.

The same applies to the research which in recent years has been conducted under the auspices of international aid organizations. Both multilateral and bilateral agencies have commissioned research to find out the feasibility of potential development projects or to evaluate such projects. These research projects may have influenced individual policy decisions in one direction or another but they have contributed little, if at all, towards generating an endogenous body of knowledge, and thus towards a self-sustained development process. The point to be made here is that 'action research' or 'applied research', if conceived in narrow terms of policy relevance fails to be developmental. 'Development research' must be relevant also to the wider task of creating an intellectual environment in which individual policies, programmes and projects can be meaningfully assessed. More specifically, it must create a 'critical mass', a body of knowledge that is derived from an indigenous experience and designed further to promote national development efforts.

Social science research in Africa must not be reduced to the role of a measuring tool. It must also help to explore new ground and problematize new issues. The second complementary measure that is necessary to support the development of a closer relationship between theory and practise is the encouragement of participatory research in the rural areas. It would be wrong to have very high expectations as to what such research might be able to achieve. Yet, if properly pursued, it might help to facilitate the transformation of the organic environment of rural Africa and enable the peasants to take at least a few steps towards transcending it. Such research would also bring the researchers into direct touch with the actual structural constraints of development. Our critique of the African regimes that run into difficulties in promoting rural development or in attempting a socialist transformation of society will ring hollow as long as we talk of a reality defined in the light of a given abstract model rather than the actual articulations of social relations. It is only when we ourselves have experienced the problems of the development and transformation of the rural areas that our criticism may gain credibility.

The point is, of course, that in the organic environment of rural Africa there is no room for the objective laws of historical materialism. To operate, these laws require an inorganic environment; one in which it is possible for man to feel a mastery of both nature and history. In previous chapters I have argued that it is very likely that the African petty-bourgeoisie, alone or in collaboration with external agencies, will force the peasantry into an inorganic environment where they can be more effectively manipulated. While capturing the peasants is essential for realizing the favourite objective of the petty-bourgeoisie, namely national self-reliance, it is likely to be attained at the expense of the current self-reliance of the peasant class.

Definition of what constitutes a progressive policy in this situation becomes a controversial issue. On the one hand, capturing the peasants is a necessity even for the most revolutionary-inclined leadership in Africa. On the other, it is clear that safeguarding peasant autonomy and power in order to promote a type of development that takes this structural anomaly into consideration may be equally progressive. After all, the peasants are likely to become more and more marginalized, if measures are not taken to allow them to develop on their own terms. This study assumes that although our prevailing social science paradigms are inadequate for the purpose of conceptualizing the development problematic in societies where the peasant mode is still active, political efforts to bend social reality to fit the logic of our existing development paradigms will prevail. Although the potential for alternative and unique forms of development exist in Africa to an extent unknown elsewhere, there is very little to suggest that these opportunities will really be utilized. Non-African observers have little reason to moralize about such a trend of development. Looking back into the history of our own societies, it is the way they have all developed. In this respect there is no difference between east and west, between socialism and capitalism. In the end, other social classes have always prevailed over the peasantry.

This is not to suggest that the intellectual ought to yield to this historical process without trying to influence it. In particular, the social scientist may still be able to make a contribution by trying to help the peasants to become better equipped to move out of their organic environment. This, however, requires an approach to research which differs from that usually adopted. The new approach calls for a closer link between research and the implementation of development projects. To the extent that research has been used in development in Africa, it has been essentially to identify problems. A piece of good research has been able to serve as a source of advice to policy-makers about the feasibility of a proposed project or the outcome of a project already in operation. There have been few efforts, however, to go beyond these types of contribution.

What is proposed here is the need for using research also to identify problem-solving measures by linking the research activity to participation by local people. Research could be used as an instrument to make the local people, say a group of peasants concerned about how to raise their income, able to problematize the issues and internalize the answers to the questions these raise. Policy-makers who deal with the peasants rarely have the time or the patience to engage in this kind of dialogue, but a researcher who takes his task seriously should be able to do it. The research activity, while being an outside intervention, could serve as a catalyst for making something new which the local actors, as a result of the research intervention, would also have come to comprehend. If pursued properly such a research project might serve to increase local commitment to implementation as people understood what the necessary measures to realize their objective were. This new type of 'development research' is particularly appropriate in the context of local self-help projects, but it could also be used on a selective basis in government-sponsored development efforts, if for no other reason than to help bridge the gap between local actors and government officials. Where circumstances permit, it would be quite possible to use this approach also to raise peasant consciousness against unilateral government action, to highlight the contradiction between the peasantry, on the one hand, and the ruling classes, on the other. This is a difficult and time-consuming task but it might carry higher returns than, say, the use of single-minded political cadres.

This type of development research also calls for more imaginative research methods. We must be able to go beyond the situation where the researcher performs merely as an exotic stranger and where the people under study may supply information only because they pity him (or her) for having come such a long way to visit them. Research must also be made an understandable activity in the context of rural Africa. We must accept the limitations of our standard methods of research in a situation where we may be moving on unknown grounds. Hugh Stretton makes the following observation in relation to this point:

> If the native investigator of his own society can use many formal, quantitative methods, and talk confidently of causes, this is often because the meanings of action in this society are so familiar to him that he sees no need to begin by 'understanding' them. The initial tasks of understanding language and social rules and the meanings of actions become more obviously necessary the less familiar the society to be studied. Thus, the study of deviance at

home may look very statistical, while the study of deviance in primitive societies may consist largely in learning to understand those societies' expectations of conformity.[31]

In the writings on Africa social scientists have been only too quick to claim understanding by using deductive theories that offer insights into social action and lend themselves to measurement. In addition to realizing the limitations inherent in that approach, we must also acknowledge the problems inherent in our professional means of communication. Our social science language is a context-free medium of communications, consisting of certain rules and canons which we accept as a result of our professional up-bringing. This medium is not easily accessible for instance, to the peasants whose language, by contrast, is context-specific and follows a different logic.[32] These two languages reflect two different systems of knowledge: one universal, the other particular. Because we are only trained in the former, and it is the only one that lends itself to generalizations, we simply tend to ignore the latter. Our reference point for verification, for example, tends automatically to be the community of fellow social scientists.

With the only possible exception of social anthropologists, social scientists have not allowed their analysis to be judged by the responses of the people under study. Still it ought to be a more general practice, since more than anything else it provides a chance to test the relationship between 'defined' reality and the way it is actually articulated. This method does not have to be confined to registering subjective images of individual actors; it can also be used to trace structural articulations which do not a priori form part of our concept of reality. In this study, for instance, I have, as much as possible, tried to check my interpretations with people who are themselves operating within the structures described. Patterns, processes and structures which I have only been able to presume have, as a result of these checks, become clearer and alive as historical realities.

A genuine development research, involving the people of a given project, would have to aim farther. The researcher would not be allowed to satisfy himself with checking his own interpretations. He must also be in a position to give something in return. He must, above all, help to widen the intellectual horizons of these people. Doing this without becoming presumptuous is a difficult task, but nevertheless essential if research is going to be used as a catalyst of development of the poor. As Peter Rigby very perceptively notes:

> The social scientist's full participation both intellectually and emotionally in the day-to-day activities of any community, within the context of its language and culture, is indispensable to any *critical* understanding of the structures and processes he is trying to elucidate, and *ipso facto* the foundation of any practice which may derive from such knowledge. Other techniques of data

collection, however sophisticated and 'scientific' they may sound, merely complement this; without it they may bear no relation to the reality of the community concerned, and would thus have no reality for knowledge or interest in the social sciences.[33]

As researchers in Africa we must cease merely objectively scrutinizing what is happening (as the behaviourists are inclined to do) or merely scrutinizing what is objectively happening (as most Marxists do). We must explore the types of situational logic to which the competition between the capitalist and peasant modes of production gives rise. This bi-modal situation leaves the social and political actors in the African context with a different range of options from those accessible to actors in a society where the capitalist mode is truly dominant. These options need to be explored if we are going to gain a better understanding of the limits and potential of development in African countries. For instance, much research can still be done on how peasants may be able to use their relative autonomy to tap centrally controlled resources for their own benefit. In such and other development research, however, we are not likely to stumble on new secrets. What is called for is a systematic examination of the methodological implications of engaging in such research work.

It is clear that not only this type of development research but all social science research in Africa is faced with great problems. Generally, local African researchers are likely to be in a better position to carry out research that has a bearing on the tasks of creating an endogenous body of knowledge and facilitating the participation by local people in development-cum-research projects. The expatriate, particularly the one who is able to stay only for a short period of time in Africa, starts from much more difficult premises.

This is not to suggest that the African social scientist can approach this task as if the table were already laid. There are likely to be political hindrances: many politicians and administrators see the researcher as an inconvenient trouble-shooter. It would be unfortunate if African social scientists fell prey to such factors. The kind of research discussed above will not always be in the interest of individual politicians but this must not scare researchers away from their duty to say controversial things. If Africa is going to get out of its neo-colonial hold, critical research, based on a genuine commitment to understand the African social realities, is essential.

There are also factors internal to the African universities that operate against the generation of exciting development research. The academic career is not particularly attractive in comparison with other jobs. It is common to find good academics leave for political or managerial jobs. Status can be achieved without engaging in social science research. In fact, experience has shown that being controversial in African societies rarely enhances status. On the contrary, it often lowers it. Even in the case of those who remain loyal to the university, their opportunity to do meaningful research is limited. The local African teachers are usually called upon to serve in administrative positions such as deans, chairmen, etc. If their teaching burden is added to this, it is only understandable if a large number of African academics rarely go beyond the research that led to their doctoral dissertation.

Even if Africa's more enlightened leaders have realized the importance of research in the context of development, it has been difficult to promote such research. Consequently, it is true that most research in Africa is still carried out by expatriates, often in conjunction with development projects sponsored by international aid agencies. This trend cannot be allowed to prevail if Africa is serious about becoming more self-reliant. The generation of an endogenous body of knowledge, after all, is the responsibility of local African researchers.

Conclusions

Because the development problematic is unique in Africa it offers challenges to social science conceptualizations. Although a lot of interesting books on Africa have already been produced, it is not unfair to say that we still have a long way to go in meeting this challenge. This chapter has tried to show that our conventional paradigms do not take us in the direction of exploring the real structural constraints in the African economies. In these conceptual models of ours there is no room for the notion that small may be powerful, even less so that there is a pre-capitalist, peasant mode that permits such a structural articulation.

The current theoretical debates about development are, at least as far as Africa is concerned, not very helpful. By focusing almost exclusively on the nature of international economic relations as the *cause* of underdevelopment, it puts the cart before the horse. It overdramatizes factors which at least in the present situation are not decisive. In fact, the dependence that stems from unequal exchanges with the richer countries can only be rectified by strengthening the domestic base. The successful resolution of the problems discussed here is a precondition for the development of greater self-reliance in the context of the present world economy.

Social scientists, therefore, must be willing to re-examine their conceptual models and also take a fresh look at their research methods. The historical uniqueness of Africa poses both epistemological and methodological challenges. We cannot presume a 'defined' reality a priori as guide for our understanding of the African development problems because our models are built on different historical experiences. Although other societies at one point in time were faced with the same problem of capturing the smallholder peasants, this problematic has not become part of our conceptual models. Prevailing social

science paradigms have virtually nothing to say about them. This phase
of the making of modern society still remains to be fully conceptualized
and analysed. The social element in which pre-capitalist social relations
are realized needs, as Terray emphasizes,[34] to be more clearly defined.
We have reason to initiate an inductive search that will fill the empty
spots in our knowledge of development and thereby enrich our models.
To try to deduce the social realities in Africa through the inner logic of a
given paradigm would be a step backwards. The development problematic in Africa calls for an inventive approach, a willingness to
challenge conventional truths. Such an orientation, however, must not
lead to *hubris*. We are all well-advised to adopt a little of that humility
of which the peasants have such a plenty. We must start from the premise
that change and development are processes about which we still have
only a very limited knowledge. Above all, we must accept that socialist
transformation is no easier or faster than marginalist changes in a
situation where pre-modern structures still prevail. In passing our
judgements, we must make a clearer distinction between 'failure', which
is difficult to discern clearly, and 'time to succeed' – the fact that
development takes time and that it is a process which is characterized by
as many unanticipated as anticipated consequences.

References and notes

1. Francisco R. Sagasti, 'Endogenization of the scientific revolution', *Human Futures* (New Delhi), vol. 1, no. 2 (Summer 1978), p. 89.
2. For a discussion of this process, see Lewis Mumford, *The Myth of the Machine* (New York: Harcourt Brace, 1972), especially Chapter 6.
3. Sagasti, op. cit., p. 91.
4. For a critical examination of the Cartesian tradition in the literature on decision-making, see Lucien Sfez, *Critique de la décision* (Paris: Armand Colin, 1973).
5. A prominent defendant of this view has been Jan Tinbergen; see, for instance, *The Design of Development* (Baltimore: Johns Hopkins University Press, 1958).
6. The origins of Taylorism are well traced in Reinhard Bendix, *Work and Authority in Industry* (Berkeley: University of California Press, 1956), pp. 274–99.
7. See, for example Herbert Simon, *Administrative Behavior* (New York: New Republic, Inc., 1961).
8. See, in particular, Robert A. Dahl, *Who Governs? Democracy and Power in an American City* (New Haven: Yale University Press, 1961).
9. This is the point made, for example, by Steven Lukes, *Power: A Radical View* (Macmillan, 1974).
10. The illusions of human choices in the context of modern organizations are particularly well analysed by David Schuman, *Bureaucracies, Organizations and Administration: A Political Primer* (New York: Macmillan, 1976).

11. ibid., p. 49.
12. See particularly Michel Crozier's second major book on bureaucracy in France, *La Sociéte Bloquée* (Paris: Editions du Seuil, 1969).
13. Jürgen Habermas, *Toward a Rational Society: Student Protest, Science and Politics* (Boston: Beacon Press, 1970), pp. 105–6.
14. Teodor Shanin, 'The peasantry as a political factor', *The Sociological Review*, vol. 14, no. 1 (March 1966), p. 17.
15. Habermas, op. cit., p. 95.
16. H. B. Acton, *The Illusions of the Epoch* (Cohen & West, 1955), especially pp. 51–104.
17. Herbert Marcuse, *Reason and Revolution* (Routledge & Kegan Paul, 1941), pp. 312–13.
18. Karl Marx, *Capital,* Volume 1 (New York: International Publishers, 1971), p. 837.
19. Peter Rigby, 'The sociologist in decision-making: the logic of false dichotomies', paper presented to the tenth East African Universities Social Science Conference, Makerere University, Kampala, December 1974.
20. Denis Goulet, *The Uncertain Promise* (New York: IDOC/North America, 1977), p. 17.
21. Friedrich Engels,' The peasant question in France and Germany', in Karl Marx and F. Engels, *Selected Works*, Volume II (Moscow: Foreign Languages Publishing House, 1951), p. 381.
22. André Gunder Frank, *Capitalism and Underdevelopment in Latin America* (Harmondsworth: Penguin Books, 1969).
23. Ernesto Laclau, 'Feudalism and capitalism in Latin America', *New Left Review*, no. 67 (May/June 1971), pp. 19–38.
24. Geoffrey Kay, *Development and Underdevelopment: A Marxist Analysis* (Macmillan, 1975).
25. Bryan S. Turner, *Marx and the End of Orientalism* (Allen & Unwin, 1978), p. 2.
26. An important contribution towards such a conceptualization has been made by Barry Hindess and Paul C. Hirst, *Pre-Capitalist Modes of Production* (Routledge & Kegan Paul, 1975).
27. Barrington Moore Jr., *The Social Origins of Dictatorship and Democracy: Lord and Peasant in the Making of the Modern World* (Boston: Beacon Press, 1966).
28. Caroline Hutton and Robin Cohen, 'African peasants and resistance to change', in Ivar Oxaal, Tony Barnett and David Booth (eds), *Beyond the Sociology of Development: Economy and Society in Latin America and Africa* (Routledge & Kegan Paul, 1975), p. 121.
29. See, for instance, the recent works of André Glucksmann, one of the leaders of the student activist movement in France in 1968, *La cuisinière et le mangeur d'hommes* (Paris: Editions du Seuil, 1975).
30. In the Tanzanian scheme, all undergraduate students are required to spend the major part of their long vacation on assignment in a public institution, performing a practical task. In most instances, this work is of a white-collar nature. At the end of the assignment, they are assessed jointly by supervisors from the institution and from the university. The results a student obtains in these practical assignments contribute to his final mark at the university.

31. Hugh Stretton, *The Political Sciences* (Routledge & Kegan Paul, 1969), p. 184.
32. This issue is discussed by Trent Schroyer, 'Toward a critical theory for advanced industrial society', in H. P. Dreitzel (ed.), *Recent Sociology No. 2: Patterns of Communicative Behaviour* (Collier-Macmillan, 1970), pp. 209–34.
33. Peter Rigby, 'Critical participation, mere observation or alienation: notes on research among the Baraguyu Maasai', mimeo., Department of Sociology, University of Dar es Salaam, 1976, p. 24.
34. Emmanuel Terray, *Marxism and 'Primitive' Societies* (New York: Monthly Review Press, 1972), pp. 146–56.

Index

Frank, André Gunder, 20, 35, 248, 261
Freire, Paulo, 217, 235

Geertz, Clifford, 34
Gerhart, John D., 193, 206–7
Ghana, 199, 200, 201, 218
Glucksmann, André, 261
Godelier, Maurice, 183
Goldsmith, Arthur, 207
Gottlieb, Manuel, 80, 93–4
Gould, David, 196, 207
Goulet, Denis, 214, 127, 234, 235, 236, 247
Groundnut Scheme, 63, 64, 185
Guinea, 158
Guinea-Bissau, 202–3, 221–2, 228
Gutkind, Peter, 35, 36, 162, 180, 207

Habermas, Jürgen, 243, 261
Halderman, Michael, x, 206
Hanang District, 151
Handeni District, 60–1
Haque, Wahidul, 235
Hill, Frances 25, 36, 198–9, 207
Hill, Polly, 207
Hindess, Barry, 16, 35, 261
Hirst, Paul C., 16, 35, 261
Hoagland, Jim, 206
Holmquist, Frank, 28, 36, 112, 127, 191, 206, 227, 235
Hunter, Guy, 209, 234
Hutton, Caroline, 250, 261
Hyden, Håkan, x

Ibbot, Ralph, 125
Igongole village, 115
Iliffe, John, 47, 55, 66, 67, 68
Imperialism 20–3, 248–9
Individualism, methodological, 213–14
Ingle, Clyde, 69, 92, 94, 126

Iringa District (Ismani), 63, 80, 102, 110–11, 121, 190, 223

Jackson, Robert H., 37, 235
Jedruzek, Jerzy, 181
Jervis, T. S., 67
Johnston, Bruce, x, 207
Jowitt, Kenneth, x, 35, 90, 95
Joy, Leonard, x

Kabuku village, 72–3, 74, 101, 106, 139
Kagasheki, Suedi, 68
Kamarck, Andrew, 35, 184, 206
Karagwe, 40, 87
Kasumba, 167
Kates, R. W., 93
Katoke, Israel, 66
Kawawa, Rashidi 74, 93, 158
Kay, Geoffrey, 22, 36, 248, 261
Kenya, 41, 42, 44, 63, 89, 122, 156, 162, 183, 187–94, 209, 226, 227
Ker, A. D. R., 35
Kigoma, 41, 110, 152
Kilimanjaro Native Co-operative Union, 54–5
Kilimanjaro Native Planters Association, 54
Kilosa District, 110, 126
Kirilo, Japhet, 68, 69
Kjekshus, Helge, 39, 66, 68, 148–9, 155
Kollman, V., 66
Konde, Hadji, 180
Konter, J. H., 78, 93
Kriesel, Herbert, 94
Kung'atuka, 137–8
Kyela District, 132

Laclau, Ernesto, 22, 36, 248, 261
Lebensaufgabe, 44, 130
Lele, Uma, 206